Beyond Reality

GW00730028

By the same author:
LIFE AFTER DEATH
MIND OVER MATTER
PSYCHIC BREAKTHROUGHS TODAY
THE INFINITE BOUNDARY
THE POLTERGEIST EXPERIENCE
THE RETURN FROM SILENCE

Beyond Reality

The role unseen dimensions play in our lives

D. Scott Rogo

THE AQUARIAN PRESS

First published 1990

British Library Cataloguing in Publication Data

Rogo, D. Scott
Beyond reality: the role unseen dimensions play in our
lives.
1. Psychic phenomena
I. Title
133.8

ISBN 0-85030-886-0

*The Aquarian Press is part of the Thorsons Publishing Group,
Wellingborough, Northamptonshire, NN8 2RQ, England*

Typeset by Harper Phototypesetters Limited, Northampton, England
Printed in Great Britain by Mackays of Chatham, Kent

1 3 5 7 9 10 8 6 4 2

To Jerome Clark,
with thanks for his years of
friendship, support, and information

Contents

Acknowledgements   9
Preface   11

Part I   *Paranormal Realities*
          1   Spontaneous Dematerialization   17
          2   Psychokinesis: East and West   37
          3   Living Ghosts   56
          4   Scientific Evidence for Psychic Self-Defence 69

Part II   *Realities beyond Death*
          5   Children and the Afterlife   83
          6   The Harmonies of Heaven   95
          7   Reincarnation Comes to the West   106

Part III *Extradimensional Realities*
          8   Janice Leslie's UFO Odyssey   123
          9   The Secret Language of UFO Abductions   135
          10   Birth Traumas from Outer Space?   149
          11   A UFO Abduction in Suburbia   162

Part IV   *Miraculous Realities*
          12   Psychic Phenomena and the Communion   187
          13   Medjugorje   198
          14   Recent Cures at Lourdes   217

Epilogue   226
References   230
Index   237

Acknowledgements

I would like to thank several people who helped while I prepared this book.

Rhea White (of the Psi Center in New York) and George Hansen (of the Psychophysical Research Laboratories in New Jersey) helped me locate source material or provided references. Acknowledgement is also extended to Hilary Evans, who tracked down a book for me in England while I worked comfortably back in my California home. Mary Rose Barrington was especially gracious in providing me with information regarding her research into disappearing objects, which I have drawn upon in Chapter 1. Sara Shaw, the late Jan Whitley, Janice Leslie, and Sammy Desmond were perennially open and informative while I probed both their UFO experiences and their minds.

I am grateful, too, to the many people who have written to me concerning their psychic encounters, which I have sometimes used in my writings. This is especially true with regard to the present book.

Sections of this book originally appeared in *Fate* magazine, but have been extensively revised, updated, and expanded. Chapters 8 and 9 are likewise completely revised adaptations of material that was published in the *International UFO Reporter*. Thanks are extended to the editors of both these publications for permission to use this material in my book.

Preface

Parapsychologists in the United States and elsewhere have demonstrated the existence of extrasensory perception and psychokinesis.

More and more evidence is being collected that the Earth is being 'visited' by UFOs and their sometimes strange occupants.

From time immemorial, people have claimed contacts with spiritual realms that transcend the 'plane' on which we live.

These three statements contribute to what is being called the 'New Age', a popular metaphysical world-view gradually overtaking Western culture. It is even making some inroads in Eastern Europe! *Beyond Reality* is primarily designed to survey these three beliefs: both by showing the scientific evidence behind them and by exploring their spiritual implications. The purpose behind this book is to show that the existence of psychic, spiritual, and so-called 'extraterrestrial' forces points to the possibility of multiple realities. Far from being purely independent intrusions into our lives, such phenomena as ghosts, UFOs, and religious miracles reflect the existence of parallel realities probably coexisting in time/space with our everyday reality. Such phenomena probably result when occasional rifts open between our consensus reality and other realms which lie far beyond our sensory capabilities. In fact, I originally wanted to title this book *Intrusions*, but my friend and colleague Hilary Evans—the founder of the Association for the Scientific Study of Anomalous Phenomena in Great Britain—beat me to the punch in 1982.* (Not to mention the fact that the famous British aeronautical engineer J. W. Dunne used it for the title of his autobiography in the 1950s.)

The real thesis central to this book, however, is that these intrusions

---

* Hilary Evans, *Intrusions: Society and the Paranormal* (London, Routledge and Kegan Paul, 1982).

do not occur randomly. It is my contention that under certain circumstances, the subconscious mind produces rifts between our daily reality and these other reality systems, which result in what we call psychic effects, miracles, UFOs, and other strange phenomena. The goal of this volume is to provisionally delineate what these specific circumstances entail.

I couldn't begin to guess the pure number of these multiple realities. So for the purposes of this book, I have decided to concentrate on four of them.

In the first part of the book I show that the mind can produce temporary realities of its own. The existence of psychokinesis ('mind over matter') demonstrates that the psyche can directly interact with physical matter—the very fabric of the Universe. It can cause physical objects to disappear and mysteriously reappear, and even create 'thought-forms' so real that they take on their own lives and characteristics. Many so-called ghosts probably represent such a phenomenon. I know, because I once created such a form, which will be described in considerable detail in Chapter 3.

When the physical body dies, it is unlikely that personal consciousness—whatever its nature—is merely extinguished. So in Part II, I survey considerable evidence that one of these parallel realities becomes the realm of disembodied consciousness when death occurs. The existence of such a realm can explain spontaneous contacts with the dead and other inexplicable psychic phenomena.

It has been my long-held belief that UFOs and their occupants do not represent visitors from other galaxies. They may instead be a phenomenon linked to human consciousness which reposes in some parallel reality just waiting for us to conjure it into our own realm. So in Part III, I focus on close-encounter experiences between ourselves and the UFO occupants, showing that we seem more closely linked to these 'aliens' than people think.

In the concluding section of this book, I hope to show that religious faith possesses a psychic power of its own. This power can create religious miracles, which blossom forth into physical reality from some spiritual realm through our own need to witness and/or believe in them.

The fact that there exist parallel realities to everyday consensus existence is not a novel proposal. Both folklore and traditional occult wisdom have long taught the existence of 'higher worlds' that extend beyond our own. The existence of parallel universes is now even being taken seriously in physics, probably the most practical of all the sciences. In the present book, however, I propose that these realities do not so much parallel consensus reality, but dynamically interface with it in remarkable—but primarily unrecognized—ways.

D. Scott Rogo

PART I
Paranormal Realities

1

Spontaneous Dematerialization

At some time or other, I'm sure that everyone reading this book has confronted the following situation.

You go to a kitchen cupboard or drawer to grab a set of keys—or perhaps a wallet—only to find it mysteriously missing.

Usually we rationalize away these little experiences, and perhaps we're justified in doing so. Drawers tend to get cluttered and people easily mislay their keys and wallets. It is easy simply to believe that we've lost the object, misplaced it, or that somebody in the household has lifted it. But the fact remains that many people constantly 'lose' things which, for some totally inexplicable reason, they never find again. I've encountered these domestic mysteries several times during my life, and they've led me to wonder whether these items were ever really misplaced. Could they have dematerialized into some fourth dimension, the result of some sort of psychic theft? Some of these objects have literally vanished right under my nose, under circumstances too mysterious to be easily dismissed.

Historical research on spontaneous dematerialization

The phenomenon of spontaneous dematerialization is certainly not a subject with which conventional parapsychologists (more skilled and comfortable in the safe confines of the psychology or physics laboratory) have ever been concerned. The subject is, in fact, rarely mentioned in psychic literature.

I know of but a single psychical researcher from the past who ever studied the phenomenon by collecting first-hand reports and publishing them. Dr Hereward Carrington (1880-1958) is best remembered today for his many popular books on psychical research, even though his doctorate was only an honorary degree. Towards the end of 1930, he published a report on the subject in the *Journal of the American Society for Psychical Research* in which he discussed three first-hand cases. Probably his favourite was reported by Fred Keating, who was a famous magician in his day. The incident took place, he reported to Carrington, while he was sitting in his New York residence with his grandmother. The elderly lady was reading to him in order to pass the evening. Keating was lying back comfortably on their living room sofa. The phone rang suddenly and Keating's grandmother immediately rose from her chair, set the book down, and placed her glasses on it. Keating didn't bother to budge but remained in his cosy position, not realizing that a psychic drama was unfolding before him. When his grandmother was through talking on the phone, she came back to her chair only to discover that her glasses had disappeared. Even a complete search of the apartment failed to uncover them, and they were never subsequently found. To use a terrible cliché, it seems that they vanished into thin air.

In order for the reader to get a flavour for the sheer bizarreness of these cases, let me reproduce Carrington's second case:

> Miss K.,—a nurse and a most methodical person, had the habit of invariably placing her bunch of keys on the dining room table the moment she entered her flat. One day she did this as usual (so she declares) and, a short time afterwards, looked for them as she was about to leave the apartment, on another 'case'. Her keys had disappeared. She looked for them everywhere; they were not to be found. She finally had to have other keys made for the front door, etc. Several days later, she wished to get a cork for a medicine bottle, having broken the old one. These corks were kept in a tin box, in the bottom partition of a trunk, standing in the hall. She does not (she says) have occasion to open this drawer more than three or four times a year. There, in the tin box, was her bunch of keys! Miss K. declares most emphatically that she did *not* open this drawer on the day in question, nor subsequently until she looked for the cork. Nevertheless, her keys were there, peacefully reposing in the tin box.

As I said earlier, it is easy to dismiss these little incidents. But as a teenager I witnessed a nearly identical occurrence that I *couldn't* explain normally. It was a summer day and I had been lying on my bed listening to some classical music. I habitually left my car keys on the first shelf of a bookcase set behind the bed. When I decided to leave, I stood up and reached for the keys, but found them missing. I was more annoyed than puzzled and searched the entire room. The keys were simply gone. It was 'obvious' to me that I'd misplaced them elsewhere in the house, so I started to search the bathroom first. But when I returned to my bedroom, there were the keys in plain sight— lying undisturbed on top of the bedcover. Nobody else was in the house when the incident took place, so nobody could have 'planted' them on the bed as a practical joke. Nor could I have overlooked the keys, which seemed to be deliberately positioned for me to find.

I didn't know what to make of this incident in 1965, and I don't think I had yet read Carrington's little article—even though I was fascinated by the paranormal as a teenager and had already done some studying on the subject. I remained simply puzzled by the incident. This was a sentiment I clearly shared with Hereward Carrington, who wrote in 1930: 'I am not contending that these incidents represent anything definitely supernormal, be it understood, merely that they are curious happenings difficult to explain.'

Despite the seasoned researcher's obvious reluctance to endorse cases such as Mrs Keating's dematerialized glasses, similar reports— some even more impressive—have been placed on record from time to time. Probably the best case in the literature was formally recorded in 1972 by Raymond Bayless, a professional landscape artist in Los Angeles. Mr Bayless has devoted many years to investigating the paranormal, and some of his research is chronicled in his *Experiences of a Psychical Researcher*. This entertaining book contains an extremely good example of spontaneous dematerialization. Mr Bayless had previously provided me with a private account of the incident, from which the following description is taken:

> The event occurred in the summer of 1957. I am an artist by profession and was instructing one of my students at the time. The room was bare but for an easel and two four-legged stools. Other than this sparse furniture, *the room was totally stark*. Since the room had a large northern window, it was usually brilliantly lit. The floor was composed of linoleum tiles and was uncarpeted and rug-less.
>
> I was just instructing my student about a fine point of painting. I was holding a long-handled Delta 2 brush. Accidentally the brush slipped from my hand and we both heard a loud 'click' as it struck the floor. I reached down to pick it up . . . but it was gone! It had just vanished into thin air. Now, this is of course impossible. A brush cannot just disappear out of a bare room. But that is what happened. We both looked for it, but it had simply vanished. Remember, the *only* objects in the room were an easel and two stools and ourselves. The brush could not have been lost. Yet it apparently disappeared from the room after obviously striking the floor.

Even the most incredulous sceptic would find this incident difficult to dismiss. So it is a little surprising that the subject of spontaneous dematerialization has never excited the interest of most contemporary parapsychologists.

The tide temporarily changed in the early 1970s, however, when the controversial Israeli psychic Uri Geller took the psychic world by storm. Geller was then a charming, boyish psychic known for bending keys and related metal objects by gently stroking them. His psychokinetic prowess was never documented under completely controlled conditions, and Geller became famous more for his television demonstrations than for his achievements in the laboratory. But many scientists reported witnessing strange dematerializations and rematerializations of objects while working with him. A group of scientists including Dr John B. Hasted (of Birkbeck College, University of London) even claimed that, during one of their experiments together, the psychic dematerialized a portion of a small crystal disc by bringing his hand close to it.

A series of personal experiences

Despite the incidents I witnessed as a teenager, my serious interest in spontaneous dematerialization really dates only from 1972. That was the fateful year that I rented a small and reputedly 'haunted' house in the suburb of Canoga Park, California. I had learned of the house from two previous renters, who both described eerie sights and sounds in the building, which was built in the 1920s. I rented it in February and lived there for two years. Since that time, the house has been torn down to make room for an apartment building—thereby destroying one of California's genuine psychic wonders!

The entire story of my life in that Canoga Park house is given in two previous books, so I won't repeat it in this volume.* Let me merely say that the place was genuinely infested, and I later learned that the original owner had converted the house into a wedding chapel! Somehow the religious services commonly performed in the house 'charged' it and produced the haunting.

Shortly after I moved in, I began to notice that commonly used household items just seemed to disappear mysteriously. I had never encountered such a phenomenon before and I was not particularly prone to misplacing my possessions. (I have a slightly compulsive streak, in fact, and hardly ever place often-used objects—such as my keys or wallet—in the wrong place.) I was especially interested in these seemingly bizarre disappearances since previous residents had complained of similar inconveniences. The disappearances were not initially dramatic, but rather subtle. I would gradually realize, for

---

* See the chapter 'In Search of Haunted Houses' in my In Search of the Unknown (New York, Taplinger, 1976 and 'A Diary of a Haunted House' in my The Haunted House Handbook (New York, Tempo, 1978).

instance, that my stock of steak knives or bed linen was depleted. The disappearance of sheets was probably the most obvious phenomenon. During the time I lived in the Canoga Park house, I developed a standard procedure for changing the sheets. Every week I would change the sheets on my bed until my stock of five or six sets was depleted. I would then take the pile of dirty linen to be laundered. But after several weeks in the house I began to realize that sheets were missing. I was eventually left with only a few and had to purchase more—a serious matter when you're an impoverished ex-college student!

While I was grappling with the 'case of the disappearing sheets', as Sherlock Holmes might have called it, the same phenomenon was plaguing the other tenant living there. (I had just graduated college and was sharing the house with a roommate to help pay the rent.) Over a period of several months Carlos kept complaining that records from his sizeable collection were missing. He shared some of my compulsiveness and kept his records in alphabetical order by composer, so it seemed unlikely that they had been misplaced. Nor did he ever lend them to our friends. Since we rarely entertained guests in those days (we couldn't even cover our *own* expenses), theft was an unlikely explanation for the incidents.

Eventually, these disappearances became more overt, as if the force behind the infestation were deliberately challenging or mocking us. I can well remember the most dramatic of these incidents. I was suffering from a bacterial infection in my throat for which I was taking medication. When I was almost done taking the pills, I deliberately left the last two capsules for the following day since I was lecturing. But when I went to take the medication in the morning, only a single capsule remained. Carlos denied taking the pill, and I believed him, for there was absolutely no reason for him to have done so.

These mysterious disappearances might not strike the reader as forcefully as they did me when I originally experienced them. Describing these little enigmas today, so many years later, it is difficult to convey the puzzlement I felt when I confronted them. Remember, too, that these incidents took place within a wider range of phenomena that continually occurred in the house, including the sound of mysterious footsteps, beds being shaken under me, and the strange behaviour of our dog. The haunting did not occur continuously, but broke out every so often and lasted for a few days before the 'energy' behind the poltergeistery ebbed.

Because these spontaneous dematerializations seemed linked to the infestation plaguing the house, I was genuinely shocked when the last incident literally *followed* me when I finally moved. When my career and finances began to improve, I decided to leave Canoga Park, and at the beginning of 1974 I rented a newer home in the neighbouring community of Reseda. In order to facilitate the move, I packed my library into large cardboard boxes and placed them in the new house's smaller bedroom. Now one of these boxes contained a collection of scientific journals and my prize possession—a large print of a famous 'psychic' photograph I had specially ordered. The print showed the faces of two dead seamen photographed in 1924 following the ship on which they were killed. The case is something of a classic in psychical research and can be found described in several books on maritime mysteries. (The case is covered in considerable detail, for instance, by Vincent Gaddis in his fascinating book *Invisible Horizons*, and I retold the story and reproduced the photograph in 1974 in *An Experience of Phantoms*). The strange case of the S.S. *Watertown* was originally reported by the owners of the ship in 1934 in their publication *Service*, which was distributed to their employees. The tragedy struck while the ship was sailing to the Panama Canal. Two seamen on board were cleaning a cargo tank and were overcome by gas fumes. They were buried at sea in true maritime tradition, but their faces began continually following the ship and were successfully photographed. The strange faces in the ocean represent the best 'ghost' photograph ever taken, and it has never been successfully debunked.

Since I had been able to track down a copy of the print, I ordered two large blow-ups of it and gave the first to Raymond Bayless as a gift. The second had hung in the dining room of the Canoga Park house for several weeks before I packed it for my move.

Now I *know* I placed the box with this oversized print in the Reseda house. It was hard to overlook, for on two separate occasions I bumped into the print, which stuck up several inches from the box in which it had been placed! The box was near the bedroom door, and since the poster protruded into the doorway I eventually turned the box in the opposite direction.

Early the next morning, I began unloading my books and setting up my library. But the box containing the journals and the poster had disappeared and it never turned up. To this day I still lament the loss of that S.S. *Watertown* poster.

My feeling was that perhaps the Canoga Park house was bidding me a last goodbye. Perhaps the force behind the infestation wanted to supply me with a final mystery before we parted company for good. I offer this suggestion rather facetiously, since I never really felt that there was a specific 'intelligence' behind the haunting there. It struck me instead that some strong emotion was linked to the building because of the weddings conducted there. It is also possible that some 'force' linked to the place was interacting with some psychic disposition within my own mind—in other words, that some power within my psyche liberated or reinforced 'something' lodged in the little stucco house. I'll probably never know the real reason the house was haunted. Two years after I moved, I revisited it and spoke to the new tenants and told them of my mysterious experiences there. They seemed interested but reported nothing unusual during their own stay. Nor did my landlords (the second owners of the house), whom I interviewed in depth in 1974. Whatever mystery resided in the building was destroyed when the property was cleared in the late 1970s.

When I lived there, I really didn't think that my own psychic powers contributed to these bothersome dematerializations. For one thing, I didn't feel I possessed any such skills! But I had to reconsider this position a few years later when the dematerializations made their unwelcome return.

When I made the move from Canoga Park to Reseda, I figured that I had seen (or *not* seen!) the last of these crazy spontaneous dematerializations. I had bought a large supply of sheets and no longer suffered from that damnable sore throat! But in the strange world of psychic phenomena, never become too smug or you'll probably be sorry. Perhaps that's what happened to me beginning in the summer of 1975. Before describing these incidents, though, I'll have to explain a curious psychic pattern that often crops up in my life.

Over the course of several years, I've gradually discovered that I will encounter any form of psychic phenomenon upon which I am currently writing. Either people will start writing or spontaneously calling me to report similar experiences, or I'll encounter the phenomenon itself. To cite just a few examples:

- While writing a book on UFO reports and contacts, a renter of mine experienced a dramatic UFO encounter while driving through a canyon near Los Angeles.

- A year later while I was writing a book on psychokinesis, a friend of mine dropped by for a visit and a dining room chair hopped towards him by itself. The chair moved a good foot from its original position and scared the life out of the guest.

- While writing a chapter for a book on the powers of the mind, I was sifting through several reports on Uri Geller and his purported powers to bend metal psychokinetically. During the week in which I was writing my chapter on paranormal metal-bending, a heavy key on my keyring bent upwards some 30 degrees, rendering it useless. (I was eating in a restaurant when the episode occurred, demonstrating for a friend the 'ritual' Geller goes through when trying to bend keys, when the key warped.)

I have witnessed this pattern so often that I've dismissed coincidence as the probable explanation. I've come to believe that my own mind orchestrates these events subconsciously in order to psychically validate whatever I'm writing.

I believe something of this sort can best explain the following events, which—as I said earlier—took place in the summer of 1975. My goal for that summer was to produce a book on the role the psyche plays in some mysteries of nature, such as UFO sightings and so forth. I decided to devote the first chapter of this book (published in 1977 under the title *The Haunted Universe*) to the subject of teleportation—i.e. the fourth-dimensional transference of a physical object from one location to another, sometimes instantaneously and through physical barriers such as walls. In order to market the book, I took the first draft with me to New York and presented it to my publisher. My editor was interested in the book but requested three changes. She wanted me to strengthen the book's introduction and to replace a rather weak chapter she didn't particularly like, and she suggested I contribute more information to the chapter on teleportation. This chapter briefly covered the phenomenon of spontaneous dematerialization, but not in much detail. As I flew back to Los Angeles, my mind raced over the changes I needed to make in the manuscript. One of my plans was to present the suggestion that our minds subconsciously orchestrate these strange disappearances more forcefully.

When I finally got back home, it was precisely ten o'clock on a rather muggy summer night, and I didn't feel like retiring. Instead I immediately set about making the revisions to the manuscript for *The Haunted Universe*. No sooner had I begun work than, to my considerable annoyance, I spotted a large Oriental cockroach staring into my study from the hallway. Now I am personally opposed to killing any living creature (even insects) unless it is absolutely necessary. (The only exception I make to this rule is in the case of mosquitoes, those devilish little bloodsuckers!) But I was edgy from my flight, just settling down, and the house was in a shambles thanks to a friend I'd let use it. I was annoyed and just couldn't bring myself to chase the cockroach, lasso the critter, and let it loose outside. So against my better judgement I decided to step on it. A sprightly chase ensued, and finally I backed the tiny villain into the wall, where I dealt the fatal blow. My foot came down speedily and I could both hear and feel the resulting crunch of the roach. There could be no doubt but that I had successfully crushed the poor insect, but simultaneously I felt remorse for murdering it. I slowly removed my shoe, realizing that I had succeeded only in creating a small, obnoxious mess to clean up. But to my complete surprise, the cockroach had completely disappeared and there wasn't a speck of blood or fluid on the floor. The insect had vanished from under my foot! Nor was there any place for the cockroach to run without revealing itself.

I probably could have dismissed the incident but for the peculiar 'coincidence' of the disappearance and my complete preoccupation with spontaneous dematerialization when it took place. Could I have somehow used psychokinesis subconsciously to spirit the insect to some psychic never-never land, while at the same time relieving myself of the guilt for my shameless moral transgression? Nor did I miss the implication that, by orchestrating the incident, I gave myself a perfect example of the point I had decided to make in *The Haunted Universe*: that these disappearances probably result from the power of our own minds.

I encountered this same phenomenon in the spring of 1977 while corresponding with a fellow parapsychologist on poltergeist outbreaks. My colleague had written me to request some references to poltergeist cases in which the 'geist' steals objects from the infested house and never returns them. Such a phenomenon is commonly reported in these cases. I began the thankless job of digging out the proper references when a rash of spontaneous disappearances began plaguing me. Credit cards started to vanish from my wallet, shirts disappeared from my closet, and so forth. Sometimes the objects reappeared in strange places days later.

Spontaneous dematerializations in everyday life
These bothersome incidents were so frequent in 1977 that I finally decided to prepare an article on them for *Fate* magazine, a popular periodical in the United States that reports on psychical research and other borderlands of science. This little piece was published in their May 1978 issue under the slightly humorous title 'Are You a Victim of Psychic Theft?'. (The title was chosen by the publication's editor, not by me.)

I didn't really know what the readers' response to the piece would be, since most of the material I publish in *Fate* deals with mainline parapsychology. I was rather worried that the readers would consider me some sort of credulous fool—or at least someone of rather unstable ratiocination.

The response to the article astonished both me and the editors. In my entire career writing on the paranormal, no single piece of mine has generated so much personal mail. Some of it was puzzling, some of it was provocative, informative, or downright funny. Most of the readers described similar incidents from their own lives, but usually not in any detail. Probably the most interesting letter was contributed by a reader who informed me that spontaneous dematerialization was known in Russian folklore and belief. She explained that her Bessarabian grandmother had told her that when she 'lost' or misplaced something, she should tie a string to a chair leg and place closed scissors in a corner of the room. She should then say out loud, 'Chortik, poigrai, i otdai.' Roughly translated, this little exhortation means 'Little devil, play a bit [with the stolen object] and return it.'

My correspondent ended her letter by saying, 'If I remember correctly, when I was a child the formula worked. I haven't tried it recently.'

More serious, though, were several letters from people with truly impressive stories of spontaneous dematerialization to report. Some of these were simple, straightforward events where 'logical' explanations don't seem to fit—like the strange disappearance and reappearance of my car keys when I was 16 years old or so.

Since writing that seminal piece, I have kept a file on reports of such cases of spontaneous disappearances. Most of these reports are merely stories given to me by the original witnesses. Nobody can prove the episodes actually took place as recorded, but I don't think we can just dismiss them either. Two of these cases were reported from within my own family, and I have no reason to call into question the integrity of the witnesses. Since my file is rather large the following sample represents what I feel to be particularly strong examples of this strange and unrecognized phenomenon. In most of them, the target object's strange dematerialization was followed by a similarly inexplicable rematerialization.

Case No. 1   The mystery of the disappearing glasses
My first case was submitted in response to my *Fate* article by a lady from Arizona, whose report resembles the story Fred Keating originally told Hereward Carrington back in the 1920s. My correspondent was reading Carlos Castaneda's book *Tales of Power*, which are obviously fictional tales of his experiences with a shaman pos-

sessing paranormal powers. She felt that reading the book somehow prompted her bizarre experience. She writes:

> I was taking my dogs to the little park beside my home and, while they romped, I sat [on the ground] reading some of the book. I wear glasses and cannot read without them. When it was time to leave, I gathered up my book, cigarettes, lighter and glasses and was calling the dogs, when I dropped my glasses straight down in front of me. I looked down but no glasses!

The lady explained that, when this incident took place, she was sitting in a clearing at some distance from any benches or trees. What happened next was even more bizarre:

> Only a worn earth area was under my feet with nothing on it—nothing at all for a circle of perhaps 10 feet in diameter. The earth was hard packed and light brown and my glasses are black-rimmed. I turned around, looking everywhere. Of course, I went over to the bench about 12 feet away to look under it but, you'll have to admit, a 12 foot bounce is just as hard to believe as a disappearance. They weren't there so I turned back to where I had believed they had fallen and there they were, exactly where I would have guessed they were, in plain sight, standing out clearly on the packed earth.

My correspondent was convinced that the incident was designed by her own subconscious mind in order to prove its supernatural powers in true Carlos Castaneda style. She didn't feel it had any deeper meaning. She explained further that a similar incident occurred some time later when a spice can disappeared from her kitchen cabinet. She and a friend dismantled the entire cabinet looking for it, but could find no trace of it. The other lady casually opened the cabinet the following day, only to find the can directly in front of everything else on the shelf, with its bold label conspicuously turned outward. The can seemed to be deliberately announcing its return!

Case No 2 A vanishing Christmas tree ornament
My second case dates from several years later, when I received a detailed letter on the incident from Mrs Pauline Eble Campanelli, an excellent still-life painter in New Jersey. She and her husband witnessed the strange disappearance/reappearance and, remembering my *Fate* article, wrote to me to report the experience:

> On 15 December 1982, my husband Dan and I drove up to the Christmas Tree farm in northern New Jersey where we have cut our own

trees for years. After lunch with the folks who own the farm we headed home with the tree in the back of the car. Half way home it began to snow making driving dangerous, and by the time we got home, there were three inches of snow on the ground. We were tired but our holiday spirits intensified with the snow storm and we brought the tree right into the house and spent the rest of the afternoon decorating it with our collection of antique Victorian and reproduction ornaments. When we finally finished, we lit the tree and sat back to admire it. As we gazed at it, we heard the sound of an ornament falling down through the branches, but we never heard the dreaded smash of it hitting the floor. We carefully removed and examined all the gift wrapped packages under the tree, then the antique linsey-woolsey coverlet with which we had wrapped the base of the tree, but we found no ornament. So we assumed that it had fallen hook and all, and had gotten hung up on a lower branch. We had no idea which of the two hundred carefully collected glass ornaments it might have been, but we were sure we'd find it when we packed them away after the holidays.

Mrs Campanelli explained that, by this time, six inches of snow covered the ground and continued to cover it until January. That's when the denouement to this strange dematerialization occurred.

We took the tree down on 9 January and as I packed the ornaments away for another year, all the valuable antique ones were present and accounted for, but there was an empty compartment in the moulded plastic liner of a new box of reproduction miniatures that we had opened the day we decorated the tree. At least now we knew which ornament was missing.

Dan carried the dry empty tree out the front door to the curb, then he walked up the driveway to come in the back door. There, not two feet from the back door, which gets used 10 times a day, on bare brown earth that had been exposed for a week, was the brilliant red, bright, shiny, missing ornament!

Apparently it had been out of doors for at least some of the time that it was missing because the cap on top was quite rusty. Even now, years later, it is still possible to distinguish the runaway ornament from its boxmates by the rusty cap.

No one has yet come up with a 'logical explanation' that could not be disproven.

Case No. 3   Discharged from a hospital bed
My third case is probably the most impressive since it comes from an impeccable source: my mother!

Owing to some serious problems with her back, my mother entered St Joseph's Medical Center in Burbank, California, in August 1988 for surgery. When the physicians examined her spine after making the incision, they realized that she needed extensive reconstruction of two discs, which necessitated doing a bone graft. The result was that, during her recovery, she was secured in a body cast which prevented her from moving her body for several weeks while the graft took effect. In order to pass the day she engaged in two main pastimes: reading novels and listening to classical music. During this time I was outlining the present book and was planning the chapter on spontaneous dematerialization. Since my mother had read the initial outline of the book in late July, she knew I was incorporating information on spontaneous disappearances.

Never underestimate a Jewish mother's devotion to her son. In true synchronistic fashion, while recovering she experienced the exact phenomenon with which I was once more preoccupied. The strange disappearance took place on the morning of 23 August 1988 while she was engrossed in a popular novel. While reading the following report, remember that my mother was completely immobilized. Any object she held could *only* be deposited within her immediate reach—unless she decided to hurl it to the other side of the room!

> I had just had back surgery and was recovering in the hospital flat on my back in a body cast. My only sources of entertainment were my Walkman radio and some books. I refused to watch television.
>
> I was deeply engrossed in a mystery story one morning and had laid it next to me on the bed when I had some medication to take. I put my hand down to pick it up again, and it was gone! During the day at least three different attendants searched the bed and floor for that book and no one could find it. (Actually, the only linen on the bed was a single sheet.) By that evening I'd given up trying to find it and had started on another book. Then later, I put that book down and when I picked it up again, there were *two* books. The one I had just laid down and the mystery story that had been missing all day. The second was right by my side.

Under the circumstances, and in light of the fact that three hospital workers specifically searched for the book, a 'rational' explanation for the disappearance seems extremely unlikely.

Case No. 4   *Hijacking a blank tape recording*

My last case is probably the most bizarre and represents a personal story. I undertook an investigation into a complicated UFO abduction case in March/April 1987. The subject of the probe was a young man I'll call Sammy Desmond, whose story will be told in considerable detail later in this book. Sammy had suffered a series of psychic experiences which led to a mysterious loss of time, and he wanted my help in remembering what occurred during the missing hours. So, on the evening of 7 April, Sammy and I drove to the Los Angeles home of a clinical psychologist I knew who had agreed to hypnotize him. I took with me a previously used tape to make a recording of the promising session. While the regression went reasonably well and the tape equipment worked correctly, the recording came out completely blank—even the previously recorded interview on it was wiped clean! I checked the tape recorder and found nothing wrong with it. Sammy was extremely annoyed and I was left scratching my head.

When I returned home later that evening, I was still puzzled by the mysteriously blank tape—especially since other UFO investigators have reported similar mechanical problems while gathering their evidence. Since a friend of mine was a recording engineer, I decided to keep the tape and have him check to see if it had been demagnetized. So I placed the tape in a folder in my study in which I was filing the material on the Desmond case. The folder was sitting on top of a small bookcase by the study door.

I went to fetch the folder the next morning and found the tape gone! The folder was still in its place on the bookcase and my notes were completely in order, but the tape had disappeared and, to this day, has not resurfaced.

I might add that, several weeks later, I successfully recorded a regression with Sammy in which he recalled a typical UFO space-napping from his suburban home in Los Angeles. I provided him with a copy, which similarly disappeared from his briefcase several months later—though it is, of course, impossible for me to determine whether he simply misplaced it.

A replication study reported from Great Britain

As I mentioned earlier, my collection of mysterious disappearance cases was the first of its kind, building on only three cases formally placed in the literature of psychical research in 1930. It came as a surprise, then, in March 1988 when I learned that a British investigator was keeping a similar and even more extensive file.

A barrister by training, Mary Rose Barrington is a spokesman for the right to die (euthanasia) movement, a proponent for animal rights, and a long-time council member of the Society for Psychical Research in London. Addressing the Society's annual conference in Oxford in 1987, she reported on her collection of JOTT ('just one of those things') cases, which included 60 cases of disappearing/reappearing household objects surprisingly similar to my own.

The British researcher began collecting reports of these cases in 1983 by placing a letter requesting information on the subject in the newsletter of the Society for Psychical Research. She soon found herself placing the reports she received into several different categories, and she ended up with a six-factor codification system:

- Simple spontaneous dematerialization cases were placed under the category of *flyaway* reports.

- *Windfall* cases are those in which a previously unknown object suddenly materializes in the house, seemingly from nowhere.

- *Comeback* incidents are those in which the object disappears and then reappears later and just as mysteriously.

- Probably more bizarre are *rollover* events, in which some psychic packrat steals an object but replaces it with a similar (but not identical) item.

- A few of Ms Barrington's cases represent *turn-ups*, in which a familiar household object shows up in a place where it shouldn't be.

- The last type of case is the *walkabout* phenomenon, where the article—securely left in one location—inexplicably reappears in another place.

In each of these types of cases, of course, the implication is that the item spontaneously dematerialized during its strange travels.

Ms Barrington realizes that many of her cases could be suspect, but she doesn't feel that the 'carelessness' of everyday life can explain them. The only counter-explanation she can find in psychology is the concept of the 'negative' hallucination. This is a well-known phenomenon usually linked to hypnosis, in which the experimental subject is programmed through suggestion *not* to see an object—such as a chair—in the room. (Negative hallucinations are not completely successful, however, for the subject will carefully walk around the chair if instructed to run into it!) Maybe, she suggests, negative hallucinations occur more frequently in everyday life than psychologists realize. But she is sceptical of this explanation. (It certainly cannot explain my Case No. 3 reported earlier, in which three separate people searched for my mother's lost book.) The British researcher finally opts for the suggestion that these psychic translocations result from the way the psyche dynamically interacts with consensus reality. Speculating that the world around us is held in place by corporate acts of will, she suggests that:

If the items in the material world are not effectively willed into existence by the mind of the observer—by a process akin to positive hallucination —the object lapses into an altered state as if it were something in the nature of a toy balloon elephant that loses its elephant identity when the air is allowed out of it. Which means that it is our business, or the business of one part of our mind, to give our personal stock of images the breath of life and keep a thumb and finger on the mouthpiece.

She also suggested during the conference that these disappearances and reappearances could be symbolic in nature.

Explaining spontaneous dematerialization

The meaning behind these strange psychic episodes is difficult to decipher. I think that Ms Barrington is correct in saying that these disappearances could be symbolic. If we properly understood the psychological dynamics behind the incidents, they might make better sense to us. Explaining some of these cases isn't difficult, in fact, if we shed a little psychological light on them. A prime example would be those crazy happenings with Sammy Desmond's regression tapes. It was clear to me during the investigation that Sammy suffered severe conflicts over his possible spacenapping. He broke into a cold sweat during his first regression even though he didn't fully recall his kidnapping by the UFO entities that entered his suburban home in 1984. Those complete memories surfaced during a subsequent session. Some part of Sammy's psyche probably sabotaged the tape equipment to 'destroy' the evidence which was beginning to substantiate his experience, perhaps permanently programming the tape to disappear completely later on.

Similar dynamics could explain some of the cases I've encountered in my own life. When I stepped on that defenceless cockroach in 1976, I was immediately racked with guilt. Could its instantaneous disappearance have been my psyche's way of destroying the evidence of my crime?

It wouldn't be hard to postulate similar deep-seated psycho-dynamics behind some of the other cases reported in this chapter. Maybe we could speculate that Fred Keating's grandmother didn't really want to read to her grandson when her glasses strangely vanished. Perhaps there was something in that mystery novel my mother didn't like, so she temporarily teleported the book into some fourth dimension. I certainly know that while in college I hated laundering my sheets, so perhaps I used some psychic power to shirk the responsibility. But while these speculations sound plausible and probably can explain some cases of spontaneous dematerialization, I don't think they can resolve every case reported in these pages. There seems little reason for the Campanellis to dematerialize their Christmas tree ornament right after decorating their tree. Or why would I use some subconscious power to dematerialize a box of expensive science publications and a beloved print? These little events seem to be completely senseless.

Of course, a related puzzle is why these disappearing objects oftentimes suddenly reappear. One possibility is that the subconscious psychokinetically causes these disappearances by somehow 'imbuing' the objects with its force. When this force (or whatever it is) wears out, the objects may instantaneously reconstitute back to their proper forms and positions.

There is a final possible explanation for these disappearances, however, which is more bizarre and far-reaching. This suggestion is so disturbing that I hesitate to broach it, but the possibility can't be ignored. Could these disappearances take place when somebody *else's* mind surreptitiously probes into our own environment and reality?

I first began developing this theory thanks to my colleague Raymond Bayless and to an incident he witnessed in 1957. Raymond explains in his book *Experiences of a Psychical Researcher* that he and a friend were walking down Hollywood Boulevard (in Los Angeles) and had entered a shop that looked interesting. While the friend was talking to the proprietor, Raymond spotted a peculiar Canadian penny on a desk which he picked up and examined. The coin was scratched on its reverse side. Raymond liked the coin and tried to purchase it from the owner, who refused, saying he was keeping it for himself. Raymond was disappointed but placed it back on the desk, glancing back at it while leaving the store. The remarkable part of the story came as Raymond and his friend were walking further down the street. Something suddenly struck his trousers. 'I looked down in surprise and found on the sidewalk by my feet the identical penny,' he reports in his book. 'To make sure that it was indeed the same coin I looked on the reverse side, and there was the scratch I had noticed on its surface in the leather store.'

The implication of this incident should be obvious. While the teleportation of the object makes complete sense from the perspective of Mr Bayless and his desire for the coin, the shop owner probably experienced an otherwise inexplicable spontaneous disappearance —though I'm quite sure he suspected a more prosaic explanation for the dematerialization!

'To this day,' Raymond likes to say, 'I'll bet the proprietor still thinks I swiped his coin.'

During the course of my research on spontaneous dematerialization, I was contacted by some people who claimed to be able deliberately to conjure up objects in similar fashion. This claim has been made before in the psychic literature, and a complete report on such a case was given by Mr Louis H. Van Loon in a paper delivered to the First South African Conference of Parapsychology held in Johannesburg in October 1973. Mr Van Loon described several impressive cases in which important household items disappeared, or were stolen from his residence or from his relatives' homes. Many of these objects mysteriously reappeared in bizarre places when his wife deliberately conjured them back by visualizing them. The objects tended to return hours or a few days later, but sometimes reappeared in distant cities. Mr Van Loon's report is fascinating and should be closely studied by readers interested in this phenomenon. (See references at the back of this book.) My point, however, is that this power may be more widespread and used more commonly than we think. Mrs Van Loon's strange power to conjure forth lost objects seems similar to the following story. The letter reproduced below came to me from a reader of my original *Fate* report on psychic theft:

> I had a very dainty pill box which had been given to me by my son's girl friend, a girl I was very fond of. One day I filled it with dimes and took it to the laundromat. I came home without the pearl inlaid pill box and could not find it, although I went back to the laundromat. At home, when I had given up the search, I sat down and addressed the empty room. I said:
>
> 'This is my pill box and I am very attached to it. I am not asking for something that isn't mine, or something that will hurt someone. Please return my pill box to me. I have cleared a place on this shelf. Will you please put it right there so that I will know you returned it. Thank you.'
>
> I went about my work putting the laundry away. When I returned to the space on the shelf, there was my pill box.

Did my correspondent simply overlook the small box? That's certainly possible, but I later received a more impressive letter from a different reader. I was first contacted by this individual through my publisher. The gentleman's letter was brief but emotional. He claimed that certain psychic experiences were bothering him and requested my help in dealing with them, but he offered precious little information about the incidents. He claimed only that he could occasionally materialize objects he particularly wanted or needed, and he wanted an explanation of the episodes. Since the letter was emotional but straightforward, I immediately wrote back and requested him to describe his experiences for me. I received a second letter in due course in which the gentleman described two purported sudden materializations.

The first incident took place when the writer was a child and wanted a dime to buy a pretzel during school recess. 'Mom said there was no money so I forgot about it and started for school,' he stated. 'About two blocks from school I said a prayer to my grandfather in heaven. At a usually crowded corner I realized I was alone just about the time I finished talking to Grandpop. There was a flash of silver in the air heading toward the ground in front of me.' Of course, it was a shiny new dime and the boy was delighted. There were no trees or buildings nearby from which it could have been flung.

Despite this unusual 'coincidence', my informant could have dismissed the incident were it not for a repeat performance many years later. He was on combat duty in Vietnam in the 1960s when the following event took place:

As a point man in a RECON unit there is not much between you and death. The item I depended on was my St. Michael medal (patron saint of paratroopers to protect us in battle), a specific medal at that time you could only purchase at Ft. Benning. Just before Thanksgiving 1967 I lost my medal on a patrol in the south area of our basecamp. I was devastated. There was not another available. The following week we were on a long distance patrol near the Cambodian border. About midday we were on a meal break and I kept wishing I had my medal. I finally said a prayer to my grandfather. Again before I could finish the prayer there was a flash of silver above my head. I reached above me and brought my hand back down closed around the object. When I opened my hand there was a St. Michael medal. The same kind.

Most likely it was the soldier's psyche that materialized the medal and not his grandfather's spirit. The prayers he offered on those two occasions were probably focusing rituals by which he liberated some force from his mind that teleported the small objects. These prayers could have served the same psychological purpose as the invoking techniques used by Mrs Van Loon. The important point to remember, however, is that the mysterious dime and medal had to be teleported from some place else. So I'm forced to wonder whether their original owners witnessed 'senseless' spontaneous disappearances when the objects were 'stolen'. Did my correspondent's mind omnisciently roam through time and space to find the desperately needed objects?

The implications suggested by this line of reasoning are frightening. Every day during our lives, could it be that our offices and homes are being continually probed by somebody's liberated and rampaging mind?

Of course, each of the suggestions presented in this chapter represents nothing more than speculation. The cases themselves rest solely on the reporter's word, and the sceptic could easily dismiss them, but I find it difficult to sweep inconvenient cases and facts under science's powerful but soiled carpet. (That's a bad habit I've picked up from 20 years of studying the byways of psychical research.) Maybe there really *is* no meaning behind these little events. Maybe the lady who lost her glasses in the park was correct when she suggested that these incidents represent subconscious games. She speculated in her letter to me that the psyche could be producing these disappearances merely to say, 'Hey, look! See what I can do!'

More important, though, is whether the psychokinetic power behind these disappearances can be tapped or developed. This is the subject we'll explore in the following chapter.

2
Psychokinesis: East and West

I know only one person who ever 'learned' to develop psychokinetic (PK) powers. Her story represents a brief diversion in the cluttered but fascinating history of psychical research. The story began in the early 1970s when several parapsychologists from the West were running off to the Soviet Union to see what the Russians were up to.

Worldwide interest in Soviet psi research had been ignited in 1970 when Sheila Ostrander and Lynn Schroeder published their blockbusting *Psychic Discoveries Behind the Iron Curtain*. Their popular volume included sensational claims for the sophistication and funding behind Soviet parapsychology. Interest in the truth or fiction of their claims was even greater when films showing Soviet scientists working with a psychic named Nina Kulagina, who could move small objects by concentrating on them, were smuggled out of the country. Researchers in the United States and England hadn't seen such a phenomenon for years. It was partially to document this form of 'stable-system' PK that so many parapsychologists decided to get their passports in order.

Some of these films were eventually shown in the United States, where they were viewed by the staff of the Maimonides Medical Center's parapsychology laboratory. Among those present was Felicia Parise, a young woman in her thirties who worked in the hospital's haematology unit. She was also a star ESP subject at the lab. When she saw the films, something snapped inside her and she immediately knew she possessed the same capability.

'When I went home that evening,' she explained in a tape she prepared in 1975, 'I tried to move something with the power of my mind. I had no idea what Kulagina was thinking while she was moving objects. It was obvious from the film that she wasn't in any meditative kind of situation. She was trying very hard and focusing her attention on the object and nothing else. I just had to try to get into a similar state and find the right condition that was necessary for me to move objects. I happened to have a little plastic pill vial on my coffee table and I began to concentrate on it. I had no success at all for a long time, but was so interested that I kept on trying.'

Since Felicia didn't have a teacher to guide her development, she worked by trial and error. Working with the bottle became an obsession with her, but there was a method in her madness. She was extremely close to her grandmother, who was dying, and her private PK experiments became her only diversion. 'I could hardly wait each night to get home [from the hospital] for a quiet period with my plastic bottle,' she explained on the tape. 'That was the only time I could stop thinking about the heartache and tragedy that was coming at the time. It became such an obsession that I took my plastic bottle to work and tried to move it during lunch hours and coffee breaks.'

This ritual extended over several months, but Felicia never succeeded in moving the bottle. Then one evening her mother called her, telling her that her grandmother had taken a sudden turn for the worse. Felicia dressed quickly and reached out to place a small bottle filled with rubbing alcohol back into a cupboard. The vial suddenly moved before she touched it.

Several weeks later (after her grandmother's death) Felicia returned to her experiments and found that she could now manipulate her little bottle through PK, but it wasn't easy for her. She has stated that producing this form of psychokinesis 'is extremely stressful, and continually putting one's physical body under such stress can only result in poor health and shortening of one's natural life'. In order to produce her psychokinesis, Felicia tensed her muscles and body until she nearly shook.

Ms Parise only exhibited her PK for a couple of years. Films of her phenomena were eventually taken in New York, and her PK was scientifically studied at the Institute for Parapsychology in Durham, North Carolina. She soon discovered that she couldn't live a normal life and practise PK simultaneously. Like a great musical virtuoso, she felt she had to practise continually in order to keep her skills in shape. Nor did she enjoy the fact that incredulous friends sometimes suggested she was faking her psychokinetic feats. So she just stopped. Today she still works in the medical field in New York, but few of her co-workers know of this strange episode in her life.

The critical issue is not that Felicia Parise successfully exhibited remarkable PK powers. The real puzzle is why she succeeded. Was the New York lab worker in some way special, or did she merely liberate a psychic potential each of us shares deep within ourselves?

A case for each of these positions could be made. Even before she developed her psychokinetic skills, Felicia was a star ESP subject. Perhaps she was particularly gifted with psychic capabilities which she simply rechannelled into PK. She once told me that her extra-sensory powers seemed to decline when she practised PK work, which supports this suggestion.

On the other hand, considerable research is showing that PK may be a capability common to mankind, but this discovery has only recently been made in parapsychology.

Before the late 1960s, testing people for PK in the scientific labora-tory was a rather cumbersome task. The basic method was to throw dice inside a special cage while the subjects focused on making them land on certain faces, or positions, more often than by chance. The problem was that this research was tedious, the subjects were easily bored with it, and it took considerable time to collect enough data to publish. The situation changed in the 1970s when parapsychology entered the space age and took physics with it. Thanks to the pioneering research and technological innovations of Dr Helmut Schmidt, then of the Boeing Laboratories in Seattle, parapsychologists started using high-speed generators in their work. These devices incorporated oscillators which were run by electrical noise or radioactive decay. Researchers wanted to see whether their subjects could influence the oscillators by PK. Since the oscillators were working at enormously high speed, even the weakest PK force would disrupt them. The tests worked! (These gadgets are generically called random event generators and will be discussed in further detail later in this chapter.) A team of researchers headed by Dr Dean I. Radin, then of SRI International in Menlo Park, California, found that there were 332 such experiments reported in the literature between 1969 and 1984. They took a detailed look at 188 of these experiments (which met special criteria) and found that 58 of them showed significant results—an extremely impressive figure not easily ex-plained away by the sceptics.

Now most of these studies were not conducted with gifted subjects. The experimental participants were everyday sorts of people who volunteered to take part in them. So one implication gathered from this research is that some sort of PK is possessed by many people, but is only detectable by extremely sensitive equipment. The force required to deflect an oscillator flipping between two positions thousands of times per second is obviously different from the power that can levitate a table! But could this form of micro-PK represent the seeds of a greater PK potential within us? Did Felicia Parise succeed with her bottle-moving experiments because of the impressive time and energy she deliberately devoted to them?

Looking back over the work carried out with Felicia in the 1970s, it is unlikely that the stress and strain she used to produce her phenomena were really essential. They were probably little more than rituals she learned by watching the original Russian films showing Kulagina engaged in the same practices. Remember that when she first moved her bottle, Felicia was not consciously trying for PK but moved it spontaneously. My feeling is that, through her practice with the bottle, she somehow *programmed her mind for PK*, and that perhaps we can similarly succeed.

But how?

Psychokinesis and the traditions of the East

There is some evidence that PK capabilities can manifest as a side effect of practising yoga. Certainly there is some scattered evidence that gifted practitioners of the discipline can sometimes perform impressive psychokinetic feats.

Nobody knows exactly when yoga originally evolved. According to tradition and legend, its basic essentials have been taught in India for over five thousand years. The practice of some forms of yoga— consisting primarily of specific exercises for body control, breathing, and meditation—were originally systematized in the *Yoga Sutras* of Patanjali, who codified them some time in the second or third century BC. Most scholars agree, however, that Patanjali edited and structured his material from a previous oral tradition that predated him by a thousand years or more.

When one glances through the *Sutras*, there doesn't seem to be anything too mysterious or esoteric in these practices. Psychic abilities and their development are barely mentioned. But there is a more mystical and supernatural side even to these traditional Eastern teachings. Later writings such as the *Hatha Yoga Pradipika* (which dates from the twelfth century) discuss such psychic phenomena as extrasensory perception, psychokinesis, and out-of-body travel and their development more fully. These were the topics Patanjali had merely touched upon unenthusiastically several centuries earlier. These writings teach that through the proper mastery of yoga, the student will simultaneously develop impressive paranormal powers. Some forms of yoga, such as Kundalini and Tantric yoga, even teach that a dormant energy resides at the base of the spine. If properly released through breathing, this energy purportedly has the power to travel up the spine, progressively stimulating several psychic centres (*chakras*) of the body. The awakening of each centre gives the practitioner certain prescribed psychic powers.

So despite the fact that yoga is primarily concerned with the proper control of both mind and body, it also entails a system of psychic development. Now the traditional wisdom is that these powers should not be emphasized or deliberately cultivated, since such an emphasis would distract the practitioner from focusing on his or her spiritual development. But in reality, this wisdom may be more lip-service than real, despite the fact that it is constantly stressed by contemporary writers on Eastern philosophy. The late Arthur Koestler, for example, was a celebrated writer and a keen student of the East. Before his death through self-euthanasia in 1983, he became a public proponent of parapsychology. His interest in the paranormal may have resulted from his travels in India during the 1950s, which he describes in his book *The Lotus and the Robot*. Although he didn't witness any psychic displays there, he certainly heard of them:

> While in India, I talked to more than forty people who, at one time or another, had practiced Hatha Yoga. They included elderly men, highly placed in the administrative hierarchy, young journalists and office workers, Yogic researchers and their professional subjects, religious believers and agnostics, Gandhians, Marxists, and one ex-Communist. Leaving professions aside, their records of sustained practice ranged from three weeks to twelve years; and the time spent on practicing from half an hour to several hours a day. The only common element shared by these people of diverse age, profession, and social background was the belief that if pursued with sufficient will-power, and persistence, Yoga conferred siddhis, supernatural powers, on the practitioners. Only a few averred having actually exercised such PK powers at one stage; but all without exception believed that only slackness or inconstance were preventing them from attaining to that state.

These gifts represent a hodge-podge of psychic, legendary, and super-natural powers, and Patanjali lists eight of them in his *Yoga Sutras*:

- Learning to shrink to the size of a single atom
- Expanding the self into space
- Levitation
- Leaving the body through out-of-body travel
- Developing the omnipotence of the will
- Creating thought-forms or physical matter by willpower

- Developing physical control over people and matter
- Perfect control over the body's needs and personal needs

In other words, there is certainly a strong tradition that mastering yoga should result in concurrent psychic development. This tradition suggests further that both extrasensory perception and psychokinetic capabilities will be the reward. While specific techniques for psychic development are not readily discussed in the literature, this is a relatively minor point: for paranormal powers represent by-products of the spiritual path rather than developable gifts.

In his book *The Lotus and the Robot*, Koestler harshly criticizes the popular belief that traditional Eastern literature steadfastly warns students against deliberately focusing on psychic powers. 'In books on yoga written by, or for, Westerners,' he writes, 'it is usually asserted that miracles are not the aim of Yogic training, but merely a by-product, and that every good guru would discourage his pupils from using them.' Koestler is willing to concede that Patanjali issues such a warning in the *Sutras*, but he finds this fact rather unconvincing. Patanjali merely states that 'these powers of the spreading (or out-going) mind are injurious to contemplation', but Koestler points out that:

> This aphorism is the only warning in the entire text; and it only refers to certain psychic powers mentioned in the preceding paragraphs, whereas the powers which are listed after the warning, such as entering into another's body, omnipotence, and levitation, are held out as legitimate rewards to those who master the high forms of contemplation. As for the later sources, the *Hatha Yoga Pradipika* and its companion texts, the eight siddhis are promised on practically every page in remuneration for the more difficult mudras [hand positions]. All disclaimers notwithstanding, the siddhis are an integral part of Yoga.

But do these traditions teach that anybody can develop PK powers merely by practising these skills? This is a difficult issue to resolve, but there certainly exist many 'traveller's tales' telling of great Eastern masters and their psychic powers. Some of these reports seem to be more than simple hearsay evidence.

The observations and experiments of Louis Jacolliot
The longest and best of these traveller's reports was published in a remarkable book, *Occult Science in India and Among the Ancients* by Louis Jacolliot. Such a title would certainly not endear the book to many parapsychologists or students of the East today. Originally

published in 1875, the book describes some of the secret supernatural traditions behind Indian philosophy, including the writer's
own experiences with Eastern holymen and fakirs. Not that the writer
was some sort of miracle-monger, for Louis Jacolliot was a high-
ranking French official who spent several years in India as a tough-
minded jurist. While he was not initially interested in the paranormal,
his encounters and experiments with Eastern holymen converted
him.

The first of these encounters took place when Jacolliot was living
in the city of Pondichéry, the capital of the French enclave in India.
One morning his valet-de-chambre informed him that a fakir wished
to see him. Jacolliot was unfamiliar with the paranormal, but he had
heard of these fakirs and considered them nothing but tricksters. He
was intrigued enough, however, to let the fakir enter the house. During
the cryptic conversation that followed (repeated in the book) the fakir
claimed that he was guided to the residence. He didn't understand the
reason, so the Frenchman suggested that perhaps it was to demonstrate his psychic powers. The fakir replied that he possessed no
paranormal powers other than summoning spirit entities who could
make their presence known through some poltergeistery. Jacolliot was
ever the gentleman and duly invited his guest to summon the spirits
without realizing what the upshot would be.

The fakir promptly squatted on the floor and requested a household servant to fetch seven earth-filled pots together with stakes and
leaves. When these items were brought to the room, the fakir
instructed the servant to plant a wooden stick in each pot with a leaf
impaled on each one. The holyman then offered an invocation and
stretched his hands towards the pots. By this time he was in a trance.
Jacolliot was entertained by the performance, but took it more
seriously when he felt a mysterious current pass over his face. The
mild gusts continued for 15 minutes while the fakir remained
motionless. Then the leaves began to move up the sticks, seemingly
by themselves.

The Frenchman was so surprised by the movement that he deliberately walked between the fakir and the pots to disrupt any surrep-
titious connection. The leaves continued their motion despite this
commonsense experiment. When the mysterious visitor later
emerged from trance, Jacolliot disengaged the sticks and leaves and
ordered his servant to bring in duplicate props. These sticks and pots
were placed over four yards from the fakir, and Jacolliot bade him to
repeat his performance—which the holyman did without blinking an
eye! The fakir eventually performed the telekinetic display some

twenty times for the Frenchman under different experimental conditions.

Oddly enough, though, Jacolliot came to some rather strange conclusions about these little demonstrations. He doesn't state in his book that he witnessed remarkable psychokinesis, but that the fakir had somehow (psychically?) controlled his mind.

Later that same day the fakir demonstrated a second inexplicable power for his host. While the jurist randomly and verbally designated letters of the alphabet, the fakir caused the leaves to move periodically. The letters formed by the movements spelled out a communication from a deceased friend of the French official.

Louis Jacolliot concludes his description of the fakir's visit by describing similar experiments he conducted for 15 days with him. These included primitive seances in a (probably) darkened room in which objects moved by themselves. A partial materialization was seen by the Frenchman during one session. These experiments are not described for the reader in any detail, even though the report ends with the claim 'I may say that I never detected the slightest deception and I applied the severest tests in order to discover any fraud.'

The modern reader will probably scratch his head when reading *Occult Science in India* (the book's shortened and more commonly used title). The lengthy description of the writer's meeting with the fakir certainly *reads* like a series of conjuring tricks. The fact that it was Jacolliot's servant who brought the fakir into the house and fetched the props suggests collusion on their part, but for what purpose is not evident. On the other hand, the fact that the fakir apparently permitted Jacolliot to manipulate the conditions of the demonstrations is impressive. Not many magicians today would permit such latitude to their observers, except for some performers who specialize in 'close up' prestidigitation.

The modern reader might also ask if we, today, can even believe Jacolliot's book. Could the Frenchman have invented the report in order to sell his book in Europe? Remember that by the end of the last century, Europe was bedazzled by the mysteries of the East and eager to read such books—the more remarkable, the better! This possibility does not seem likely, however, when we examine Jacolliot's life and work.

Louis Jacolliot was born in 1837 and became a jurist. He was later sent to India to become the chief justice of the French colony, Pondichéry. He served in a similar capacity in the French East Indies and in Tahiti. He began his career opposed to organized religion, which explains the critical reception he originally gave the fakir in

Pondichéry. Eventually, though, his opinions softened when he became a student of Eastern thought, and he even translated some important Hindu religious texts into French. His dislike of conventional Christianity never abated, and he suggested in his writings that Christianity originally borrowed heavily from Brahmanism. Even more controversial were his writings on sexology. The common belief that late nineteenth-century views on sexuality were repressive and prudish is only partially correct, since sexual issues were openly discussed in medical and psychological literature throughout this period. Sexual topics, in other words, had a specific place in those days, but it wasn't in the home. This is precisely where Jacolliot came in with his popular books on sexology, which were expressly written for the general public. His most notable works include the two-volume study *Untrodden Fields of Anthropology*, and his posthumously published *L'Amour aux Colonies*. These books were probably rather explicit, for in 1970 a biographer of Jacolliot stated that 'libraries which possess either or both titles still keep them in locked cases, inaccessible to the public'.

In light of his impressive and eclectic career, it seems unlikely that Jacolliot invented the miraculous stories he recounts in his book. Obviously he was a keen and serious student of Eastern religion and ethnology. This isn't to say that he wasn't tricked by the fakirs with whom he worked, only that he probably didn't deliberately hoax his readers.

Louis Jacolliot's life has been examined extensively, since the stories he recounts don't end with his meeting with the leaf-bending fakir in Pondichéry. Even more stunning were his experiments with a second fakir named Covindasamy, whom he met in Benares in 1866. The fakir was visiting the city to take charge of some funerary remains. Since the holy man was renowned for his miraculous powers, Jacolliot initiated contact with him and the fakir often visited the Frenchman's residence. Some of his own powers resembled those of the first fakir with whom Jacolliot experimented. During their first session together, for instance, he took Covindasamy on to the terrace and invited him to perform. The fakir immediately raised his hands and extended them towards a large bronze water-filled vessel:

> The Fakir was already in position with both hands extended toward an immense bronze vase full of water. Within five minutes the vase commenced to rock to and fro upon its base, and approach the Fakir gently and with a regular motion. As the distance diminished, metallic sounds escaped from it, as if some one had struck it with a steel rod.

At certain times the blows were so numerous and quick that they produced a sound similar to that made by a hail-storm upon a metal roof.

The Frenchman was obviously impressed by the display, but decided to take personal control of the experiment. The results were likewise impressive:

The vase, which was still under the performer's influence, advanced, receded, or stood still, according to my request.

At one time, at my command, the blows changed into a continuous roll like that of a drum; at another, on the contrary, they succeeded each other with the slowness and regularity of the ticking of the clock. I asked to have the blows struck every ten seconds, and I compared them with the progress of the second hand upon the face of my watch.

Then loud, sharp strokes were heard, for a minute and two-thirds.

Later in the demonstration, the fakir produced raps in rhythm with a tune played by a musical box. Even more remarkable was Covindasamy's skill of levitating the large vessel by merely touching it. Jacolliot carefully notes that, even though the vase rocked back and forth, the water inside refused to slosh 'as if there were a strong pressure that prevented its regaining its equilibrium, which the motion of the vessel containing it had disturbed'.

Probably the most sensational psychokinetic feat reported by Jacolliot came during a later set of experiments in his home. He and the fakir had been experimenting and were preparing to break for lunch when Covindasamy offered the following demonstration:

. . . the fakir stopped in the doorway opening from the terrace into the back-stairs, and folding his arms, he was lifted—or so it seemed to me—gradually without visible support, about one foot above the ground. I could determine the exact height, thanks to a landing mark upon which I fixed my eyes during the short time the phenomenon lasted. Behind the fakir hung a silk curtain with red, golden and white stripes of equal breadth, and I noticed that the fakir's feet were as high as the sixth stripe. When I saw the rising begin, I took my watch out. From the time when the magician began to be lifted until he came down to earth again, about ten minutes elapsed. He remained about five minutes suspended without motion.

So many (purported) psychic displays were recorded by Jacolliot that it is impossible to explore them further in this book. *Occult Science in India* was republished in 1971 but is currently out of print. The original English-language translation is extremely rare since it was published in a limited edition.

Some parallel present-day claims and reports

If the detailed records kept by Louis Jacolliot in the 1860s were unique, perhaps the sceptical reader could dismiss them. Similar travellers' tales have, however, been reported from modern times and match those published in the 1800s. Such reports tend to be rare, but I don't think this necessarily renders the older reports suspect. Remember that, during colonial times, travellers and officials to the East often remained there for several years and had a better opportunity to meet gifted holymen. The experiences of people such as Louis Jacolliot stand in understandable contrast to the relatively short stay in India of Arthur Koestler, for instance, whose *The Lotus and the Robot* is more an indictment of the East and its wonders than a homage!

Other keen students of the paranormal have reported better luck in the mystical East, and some fascinating eye-witness accounts of psychic wonders appear in *Jadoo*, a travelogue written in 1957 by journalist John Keel.

Throughout the 1950s, Keel spent months guru-hunting in the East, and his book is a fascinating and entertaining record of his travels. Keel was initially disappointed with his little expedition since he ran into every confidence trick and rip-off scheme the Indian fakirs had to offer. But he witnessed one truly mystifying demonstration while hunting for the legendary Abominable Snowman in Sikkim. Though he never came face-to-face with a real live Snowman in the Himalayas, the journalist fortunately encountered something even stranger. It happened on a day when his search led him to a monastery located north of the little town of Changthang:

. . . lamas were beating drums and blowing trumpets when I arrived. They'd seen the *Yeti* only a few hours before, running along the trail I was following. I lingered there awhile because they had an interesting oracle who was supposed to be able to summon up ghosts and do strange things. He put on a special demonstration for me in the little temple dimly lighted with oil lamps. About fifty lamas gathered and sat twirling prayer wheels while he went into a trance in front of a huge Buddha. He sat cross legged, his mouth open, his head thrown back, his eyes closed, mumbling incoherent phrases over and over.

After fifteen or twenty minutes of this, things started to happen. The flame of one of the lamps wavered and went out as if a wind had blown it. Something thumped loudly on the roof overhead, then a small stool in a corner of the temple started to move slowly across the floor toward me. It came within a foot of me and then slowly circled around. I passed my hands all around it. There didn't seem to be any threads or mechanisms of any kind. It was just a plain three-legged stool. It moved on to another corner and stopped. Later I examined it carefully but couldn't find any sign of trickery.

As a sidelight to this story, several years ago a fellow writer on the paranormal told me that Keel had never witnessed any miracles during his travels in the East and made up stories such as this one to better sell his book. So while writing this chapter I tracked down Mr Keel, reported this claim and asked for his response. I received an immediate reply in which he stated for the record that 'for all the silly rumours circulating about me, this is the silliest. Nothing in *Jadoo* was fabricated.'

When he was in India, Keel also witnessed a fakir levitating himself, but could not determine whether the demonstration was genuine or not.

Keel is not, however, the only Westerner to remain puzzled by these displays. The noted scholar Ernest Wood writes in his book *Yoga* that 'levitation, or the rising of the body from the ground and suspension a few feet in the air above the seat or ground, is a universally accepted fact in India'. Later in the book he states: 'I remember on one occasion when an old Yogi was levitated in a recumbent position about six feet above the ground in an open field, for about half an hour, while the visitors were permitted to pass sticks to and fro in the space between.'

As far as I can determine, Wood was probably referring to a much less impressive stunt performed and photographed in India in 1936. The reporter and photographer was an Englishman named P. T. Plunkett, and his description and pictures were published in the 6 June 1936 issue of the *Illustrated London News*.

According to the sketchy report in the paper, the performance (witnessed by dozens of bystanders) took place on a plantation owned by a friend of the photographer's. It was held early in the afternoon under a tent supported by four poles, set up in a compound. Before levitating himself, the yogi marked out a circular space under the tent, forbade anyone to enter it, soaked it, stepped inside, braced his hand on his walking stick, and then—while hidden from view by a blanket—rose sideways into the air. The ultimate effect was that the fakir seemed to be floating on his side without any support—except for the stick, which was heavily blanketed. The performer then let the witnesses examine him closely before descending to the ground.

The British photographer was so impressed by the display that he stated in his *London Illustrated News* story: '. . . as I have witnessed the performance with several of my planters, I am quite convinced of the total absence of trickery.'

The more sceptical reader probably won't be similarly impressed by this stunt. In his published report, Plunkett admits that upon completing the display the yogi's body was extremely rigid, possibly indicating that the 'levitation' was little more than a clever balancing act mastered by the performer through muscular control. The walking stick employed by the fakir to support himself might likewise have been a trick device. While preparing for the demonstration, he could have surreptitiously secured it to the water-soaked ground. By attaching it (under the drapery) to a metal rod conveniently hidden up his sleeve, he could have balanced himself the way Plunkett described. Recently, in fact, two books on the paranormal have described this trick and the methods for its execution.*

PK and yoga enter the laboratory

While tales of levitating fakirs and psychic swamis were often reported by visitors to the East in days past, it wasn't until recently that Western psychologists and scientists began taking an interest in examining these self-proclaimed miracle workers under controlled conditions. The famous Soviet brain specialist L. L. Vasiliev reported in the 1960s that Russian scientists were interested in the purported powers of the Indian fakirs, including their legendary psychic prowess. Whatever research resulted from this interest, however, has never been widely published. The situation is a little different in the United States, where some similar research has been both successful and well-publicized.

The first scientific experiment ever conducted in the West specially designed to test the psychokinetic powers of an Eastern holyman was, to my knowledge, conducted in 1970 by Dr Elmer Green. Dr Green, who enjoys a lively interest in the paranormal, was at that time director of the Voluntary Controls Program at the Menninger Foundation in Topeka, Kansas. This institute is a leading centre for psychological research in the United States. Dr Green is also a past president of the Biofeedback Society of America and is generally considered a pioneer in this field of research. The subject for his brief series of tests

* See, for instance, *The Spiritualists* by Ruth Brandon (New York, Knopf, 1983, p. 273) and *Anomalistic Psychology* by Leonard Zusne and Warren H. Jones (Hillside, NJ: Lawrence Erlbaum, 1982, pp. 85-6). I would like to thank George Hansen of the Psychophysical Research Laboratories in New Jersey for reminding me of these references.

was Swami Rama, a well-known spiritual teacher from India.

Swami Rama made his first visit to the Menninger Foundation in March 1970 when Dr Green was primarily engaged in biofeedback research. The swami was originally invited to Kansas, in fact, so that his powers of voluntary bodily control could be examined with scientific precision. Before he returned to the East, he successfully demonstrated remarkable control over his heartbeat, body temperature, and other unconscious physiological functions for the Menninger staff. But that was hardly the last the Foundation heard from Swami Rama, for he wrote to Dr Green the following month that, on a return trip, they should get together and conduct some PK tests. Dr Green's chance came the following September when the guru returned to the United States.

Swami Rama's first demonstration was informal and took place in an office room at the Menninger Foundation. Dr Green described the incident in his book *Beyond Biofeedback* (written with Alyce Green) published in 1971:

> One day when one of the physicians and I were interviewing the Swami in my office, he mentioned the fact that he could move objects by mind. Instantly, the doctor said, 'You mean you can do it just like that, right now?' The Swami said, 'Yes, there's nothing to it. I can do it in five minutes.' The doctor said, 'Show me.'
>
> The Swami jumped up and said, 'I'll do it in your office.' I interrupted and said, with some irritation, 'I though you said none of this would take place except in the laboratory. We are not planning any such demonstrations until next year. We are not set up to do any of this.'
>
> The Swami looked very bothered, but said, 'I have been challenged. I have to do it now.'
>
> So the three of us went to the doctor's office. At the Swami's request, I hung a pencil on a string from the corner of the desk. He knelt down close to the pencil and began saying a mantra very fast with considerable breath force. Soon the pencil rotated.
>
> Before my colleague could say anything, I pointed out that obviously the pencil would move, if for no reason other than because his breath was pushing it. To conduct the experiment properly, I said, we would have to make certain that no air currents were involved.
>
> The Swami jumped up and said, 'All right, I will do it again.' I could set it up, he said, under laboratory conditions, and he would wear a mask to prevent air currents and would be several feet away from the object. And he would 'make it move.'

Dr Green was, of course, intrigued by the Swami's pledge to repeat his psychokinetic demonstration under better-controlled conditions. By mutual agreement, they decided to conduct the test a week or so later, which gave Swami Rama plenty of time to prime himself and the Menninger staff time to prepare. Because of some scheduling problems, however, the demonstration wasn't conducted until some time later. This delay may have been fortunate since it gave Dr Green time to plan the exact strategy he would ultimately use to examine Swami Rama's psychokinesis.

During this break, Dr Green invented a special apparatus which he believed would be extremely sensitive to PK. This little device was elegantly simple. It consisted of two aluminium knitting needles, 14 and 7 inches in length respectively, placed crosswise to form an X. A hole was drilled where they intersected, and the needles were set on an axle connected to a plastic block. This block was, in turn, placed on a 360° protractor. The needles were delicately balanced so that any pressure reaching them would cause their movement. Dr Green next specially prepared a basement room at the Menninger Foundation for the coming session by carefully closing the incoming vents. This precaution was taken to offset any uncontrolled currents from entering the room which could possibly interfere with the experiment.

When the day for the long-awaited experiment finally came, Dr Green placed a foam mask—complete with a plexiglass mouth and nose guard—over Swami Rama's face. This mask prevented him from deliberately or inadvertently blowing on the needles during the test. The Swami sat cross-legged on a couch three feet from the PK device, which was placed on a table in the middle of the room. He faced the target with his back to a solid wall. Several observers were invited to witness the experiment, and they were seated far to the side of the Swami.

During the course of the test, Swami Rama sat quietly and simply chanted a mantra while concentrating on the needles. Dr Green reports in *Beyond Biofeedback*:

The mantra was quite long, possibly fifteen seconds, and was concluded with a loud exclamation, a word of command, at which time the needles rotated toward him. The point he was focusing his eyes on moved toward him. We sat for a moment in silence, and then got up and examined the needles. They had moved ten degrees.

The Swami asked if I wanted him to do it again. I said yes and the performance was repeated. The needles moved another ten degrees toward him. We talked for a while in the group, looked at the mask again, glanced at the protractor, and went back upstairs.

This experiment is, to date, probably the most intriguing exploration into the psychic power of yoga ever conducted by Western science. It was obviously well thought out, cleverly designed, and ingeniously executed. Unfortunately, though, the results of Dr Green's experiment can only be considered suggestive of psychokinesis since there was a complicating factor in the experiment.

It is clear from his report that Dr Green figured that Swami Rama could only fraudulently or inadvertently move the knitting needles by blowing on them. There is, however, a second possibility that the researcher overlooked. Note that Dr Green states in his report that the guru shouted a word of command before the needles moved. The noise probably surprised everyone present, since Swami Rama had been silent and motionless until that point. The onlookers might not have noticed whether he simultaneously jerked his body or shoved the couch. Such a movement could have vibrated the floor with enough force to jiggle the needles. This suggestion is purely conjectural, but it is a possibility never mentioned in *Beyond Biofeedback*.

This theory might strike the reader as unlikely, but I've watched a purported PK demonstration faked in just this manner. So I cannot completely dismiss the possibility that Swami Rama accomplished his stunning feat by using similar means.

For the sake of argument, let's work from the premise that Swami Rama really does possess remarkable psychokinetic powers. Can the experiments Dr Green carried out with him reveal any specific relationship between PK and Eastern spiritual exercises? Did the psychokinesis develop as a by-product of the Swami's training in yoga? It is certainly possible, but it is equally likely that the psychokinesis had little to do with Swami Rama's other remarkable capabilities. Perhaps the guru is a born psychic or his paranormal powers merely *blossomed* when he began practising yoga. So the interesting case of Swami Rama, though it remains provocative, doesn't indicate that everyone can develop PK by studying Eastern meditation skills. It merely suggests the possibility.

PK and meditation in the lab: the search continues
This possibility was, in fact, being simultaneously explored in more conventional parapsychology when some experimental parapsychologists in the United States tried to see whether meditators, in general, made especially good subjects for laboratory PK experiments. The results of these experiments could feasibly resolve the types of issues Dr Green failed to answer with his work with Swami Rama, since these parapsychologists worked with unselected subjects. The results

of this project were a curious mixture of success and failure, even though only a few of them were conducted.

The first of these experiments was undertaken by Francine Matas and Lee Pantas (himself a seasoned meditator) and was reported to the Fourteenth Annual Convention of the Parapsychological Association held in Durham, North Carolina, in September 1971. The two researchers were serving on the staff at the Institute for Parapsychology in the same city and conducted their research there. The two experimenters were not primarily interested in discovering whether certain *forms* of meditation—Zen, yoga, Transcendental Meditation, or the like—are linked to the development of psychokinetic abilities. They simply wanted to determine whether seasoned meditators would perform better in laboratory PK tests than non-meditators. They eventually tested 25 meditators by seating them in a dark room in front of a small globe light. This light was connected to a generator which caused it to flick on and off randomly. (In other words, the generator was programmed so that during any given time period, the light would remain on for a total of 50 per cent and off for the other.) The subjects were instructed to focus on keeping the light on for as long as possible. The only way they could succeed was by using psychokinesis to interfere or bias the inner workings of the generator. Each subject was tested separately and then several control subjects were tested—i.e. subjects with no background in meditation, who were challenged with the same task. The results of the experiment were strictly in keeping with the researchers' predictions. The meditators were capable of keeping the light glowing slightly more than 50 per cent of the time to a statistically significant degree. The control subjects merely scored at chance level.

Nobody, unfortunately, followed up this important lead by trying to replicate the experiment. But a more elaborate exploration into the PK/meditation issue was later designed by Dr William Braud, a brilliant psychologist engaged in full-time parapsychological research at the Mind Science Foundation in San Antonio, Texas. This organization is a top research centre for parapsychology in the United States. Not only has Dr Braud been employed there for several years, but Dr Helmut Schmidt—who pioneered the use of random event generators in parapsychology—currently works out of their facilities. It is probably the only parapsychology lab in the United States that simultaneously employs two acknowledged leaders in the field.

Dr Braud recruited 10 subjects experienced in Transcendental Meditation for his little project. (TM is a pleasant form of meditation in which the student focuses on a mantra, or sound, which is repeated continuously.) Each subject was individually tested either by Dr Braud or by his co-worker, Janice Hartgrove, to see whether he/she could use psychokinesis to disrupt a random number generator. This generator had an internal oscillator that switched randomly to either of two positions. (For convenience, these positions can be labelled $+1$ and -1.) The generator oscillated a thousand times per second. Fifty per cent of the time it switched to the $+1$ position and 50 per cent of the time to the other. Each subject was instructed to meditate for 20 minutes while keeping in mind that they were being tested for PK at the same time. One half of the subjects were instructed to make the REG oscillate to the $+1$ position, while the other experimental subjects tried to score in the -1 position. Dr Braud then tested 10 control subjects with the same procedure but found no difference in scoring between the two groups.

Perhaps it was ironic, in light of the poor results of Dr Braud's experiment, that the leader of the TM movement was later involved in a serious imbroglio regarding the movement's paranormal claims. In the spring of 1977 the founder of the movement, the Maharishi Mahesh Yogi, publicly announced that his techniques could help meditators learn to levitate! As reported in the 13 June 1977 issue of *Newsweek*, Robert Oates—the Maharishi's biographer and a spokesman for the TM organization—told the press that several TM teachers had mastered the skill. The press went wild with the story, but not a single TMer ever publicly levitated, nor were credible photographs ever circulated. Some people felt that the Maharishi's claims were a publicity stunt, since there were rumours at the time that the TM movement was floundering. Even though the Maharishi's claims were based on a genuine yogic tradition, the resulting controversy probably caused more damage to the TM movement than anything else. (A complete and entertaining history of this scandal is given by Steve Richards in his book *Levitation*.)

So whether or not meditation and yoga can help people develop psychokinetic powers remains a puzzle. Not nearly enough laboratory work has been done to explore the question, nor have researchers systematically experimented to discover whether specific types of meditation/yoga seem linked to the phenomenon. Such practices as mantra yoga (the practice of repeatedly chanting a certain phrase or word) and Kundalini yoga have, for example, purportedly been used by Eastern spiritual masters specifically for psychic development. There even exist (allegedly) secret mantras which, when chanted, supposedly make psychokinesis happen!

Research into the relationship between Eastern spiritual skills and psychokinesis is only in its infancy. It was unfortunate that the early explorations into this relationship conducted in the early 1970s were soon dropped by experimental parapsychologists when public interest in Eastern religion began to fade. With the 'New Age' upon us, however, perhaps it is time to re-examine the interrelationships between psychokinesis, yoga, and meditation. The observations of Louis Jacolliot in the 1860s and Dr Green's work with Swami Rama today certainly suggest that some relationship might exist, even though the nature of this connection remains elusive.

3

Living Ghosts

What exactly is a 'ghost'?

What factors produce a conventional 'haunting'?

Does a traditional 'ghost' possess any real existence beyond the witness's own mind?

Parapsychologists and other students of the paranormal have been debating these issues for years, yet they still remain completely unsolved. Some of the first psychical investigators believed that ghosts were exactly what they purported to be—i.e. spirits of the dead psychically trapped in their former homes because of some dire misfortune. Murder or suicide were the popularly ascribed causes in many instances. Other researchers believed that ghosts were merely three-dimensional picture shows somehow 'impressed' on to the house, which merely depict the people who once lived there. Even scientists in the Soviet Union have their pet theory to explain the existence of haunted houses. Dr Genady Sergeyev, a physicist and the current doyen of contemporary Soviet parapsychology, has suggested that our bodies continually radiate a hyperphysical emanation he calls 'bioenergy'. This radiation is capable of imbuing furniture and other physical objects in our immediate environment. If this bio-energy is not completely dissipated when somebody dies, he suggests, the 'free-floating' psychic energy could organize itself into a 'ghost'.

A good case could be made for each of these theories, even though none of them can explain several inconvenient facts about ghosts and hauntings.

Why, for instance, can ghosts sometimes infest residences which the original people never inhabited or even visited during their terrestrial lives? Why do some houses suddenly become 'haunted' even though they have no history of violence or tragedy? But most important, can we explain the fact that a *living person* can haunt a house just as easily as the 'spirit' of a dead person? This is the most inconvenient fact with which students of the paranormal must contend.

In Chapter 1, I suggested that some aspect of the psyche can invade a distant environment—i.e. to find or 'steal' objects needed back home for some (probably psychological) reason. I showed in Chapter 2 that we psychically possess the innate capacity to materially interact with the physical world. This force has been traditionally called psycho-kinesis by contemporary parapsychologists. In this chapter, these two findings will be expanded. My central thesis will be that the mind possesses the power to invade a localized environment and make itself known or otherwise interact with other people located there. Such a phenomenon seems linked to so-called 'haunted houses', though the underlying mechanism is somewhat different.

Some historical cases of 'living ghosts'

Ever since the turn of the century, psychical researchers have known that the phantoms sometimes seen in 'conventional' haunted houses really represent living people. Very few students of the paranormal, however, seem cognizant of these cases, even though they promise to help us to understand the force behind hauntings in general.

One of the most famous cases of a 'living ghost' was recounted by Dorothy Grenside in her book *The Meaning of Dreams*. The case has become a classic and concerns an English woman who reported a series of strange dreams to her husband. She would invariably find herself driving in a carriage and travelling down a tree-lined country lane to a large stone house. One day—or so the story goes—the lady was visiting some friends in the country, who suggested she join them when they called upon some friends who lived nearby. The lady consented but was in for a considerable surprise, for Mrs Grenside writes:

> As they were approaching their destination the woman began to experience a curious sense of familiarity with the district. Now she remembered! No wonder the country had seemed familiar. This was the approach to the house of her dreams. In one moment they would sweep round sharply to the left, and she would see the grey stone house with the big portico that she knew so well.
>
> Sure enough all happened as she suspected. Every detail was exactly as in her dream, except that a woman, her hostess, was standing on the steps, waiting to greet them. Silent, amazed, the woman got out of the car, trying to collect herself: but she was not the only one who was shaken out of her composure, for the hostess, on seeing her, started,

turned pale, and looked almost as if she would faint. Asked the reason, she said to the woman, 'Why, *you* are the ghost who has been haunting our house for the past two years.'

This is a fascinating story, but it is hardly more than that. Even though the case is recounted in several popular books on ghosts and hauntings, this particular *version* of the incident is probably not the original.

I first began tracking the history of this story in the 1970s when I became interested in the study of living ghosts. I soon discovered that the case has been published several times, but in different guises, ever since the turn of the century. The Grenside version of it, for instance, was probably lifted from a letter to the editor which appeared in a British periodical, the *Spectator,* close to the turn of the century and which was subsequently republished in the *Revue des Etudes Psychiques* in 1902. According to this earlier rendition of the story, the incident really occurred in 1882, several years before the Grenside story was written. The letter's anonymous writer claimed to be a member of the London-based Society for Psychical Research and reported that, many years before, his wife had constantly dreamed of a country house. Some time later, claimed the writer, he was travelling the English countryside looking for a summer residence to lease when he ran into a suitable house which the proprietress said was haunted. When the writer's wife finally visited the house she immediately recognized it from her dreams. The proprietress obviously concurred, for upon seeing the woman she exclaimed: 'Why, you are the lady who haunted my bedroom!'

Although the *Spectator* version was written in the form of a personal story, it seems likely that it, too, was lifted from a story originally recounted by the well-known English author Augustus Hare in the sixth volume of his autobiography *The Story of My Life,* which was published in 1900. In this perhaps original version of the story, the dreams occurred to an Irishwoman named Mrs Butler in 1891. Hare explains that a year later, the Butlers decided to move to England, where they were informed of a promising residence in Hampshire and immediately travelled to see it. While driving by carriage to the house, Mrs Butler recognized the gate-house as similar to a structure located near the house in her dreams. The Butlers ultimately decided to buy the house, but were rather surprised by the low asking price. The real-estate agent (not the proprietress) then admitted that the house was haunted, but that they shouldn't worry—for he recognized Mrs Butler as the ghost!

It is pretty obvious that each of these stories is based on a single incident, but we will probably never know the real facts or fiction behind the tale. Nor is even Augustus Hare, the most obvious originator of the story, a very credible source either, since he sometimes incorporated obviously fictional ghost stories into his books or borrowed them from true incidents he had read about. (His most obvious fabrication was in offering in his biography a first-hand account of the 'monster' of Croglin Grange purportedly given to him by an informant familiar with the case. The monster was a vampire-like ghost that reputedly plagued a manor in Cumberland. The legend of the monster/ghost is genuine enough, but the version published by Hare borrowed heavily from a popular penny-dreadful novel of the 1700s.) The story of the lady who haunted her own future home is probably based on a true incident—but when, where, and to whom it happened are pieces of information most likely permanently lost to history. But whatever the case, the story shows that even the first psychic investigators knew that the living, not merely the dead, could 'haunt' houses. By the turn of the century, several well-documented cases of these living ghosts had been placed on record.

One of the most extraordinary cases of this type was collected and investigated by the Society for Psychical Research, an organization founded in England in 1882 for the scientific study of reports of the paranormal. This particular case was published in a huge 1894 report prepared by the Society which documented several cases of haunting and related phenomena. The case was originally investigated by Mrs Eleanor Sidgwick, a well-known pioneer of women's higher education and one of the Society's most critical researchers.

The infestation was reported between 1886 and 1887 by a British gentleman referred to as Dr E. in the report, who claimed it took place in his own home. The haunting began in October when a caller to the house saw a pretty young lady with reddish-gold hair reading on the settee. She was wearing a brown dress with a lace collar. The visitor thought little of the seated figure until she later discovered that the lady had mysteriously vanished from the house. She then learned that nobody else there had seen the phantom. The ghost was seen on two occasions several months later by another visitor and by a servant. The guest, only called Mrs R. in the published report, told Mrs Sidgwick that the phantom silently entered her room one night and took down its hair. Mrs R., who merely presumed that the night caller was a regular member of the household, walked up to help her. But when she tried to touch the figure, her hand passed through it and the figure vanished.

This incident concluded the first chapter in this strange episode. The denouement wasn't to come for several months yet, when the son of Dr E. returned from Australia in the summer of 1888, having been gone for a considerable time. He had found romance on his travels and was proudly bringing his bride back to England. She had recently been ill and was extremely gaunt when the family first met her, so they did not initially link her to their former 'ghost'. Several days later, however, she appeared for a family dinner in perfect health with her red-gold hair perfectly coiffured. She was wearing a brown dress with a lace collar—whereupon Mrs R. and the servant (who had seen the ghost a year previously) recognized her. She was the mysterious 'brown lady' who had 'haunted' their peaceful home!

Dr and Mrs E. never told their daughter-in-law of their 'brown lady'. But during a casual conversation, the young lady herself mentioned that during her lingering illness in 1886, she often tried to visualize what her new relatives' house looked like.

Possibly related is a very different but no less interesting case of a 'living ghost' recounted by E. Katherine Bates some time later. Miss Bates was herself a gifted psychic and she reports the incident in her book *Seen and Unseen*, originally published in 1907. She had encountered the curious haunting in 1896 while visiting Cambridge, where she boarded in some rooms seemingly pervaded by an evil force. The force never congealed into a traditional ghost, but the psychic intuitively felt that the 'haunting' was in some way linked to a gentleman she had known some years before. When she checked, she discovered that this (still living) friend had once lived in the same rooms she was currently using. Miss Bates didn't think that she was just picking up past impressions from the room, but firmly believed that some aspect of her friend's psyche was present there.

She writes in her book that 'the impression of his presence did in some way cling to the surroundings; that my sleeping there, even in complete ignorance of his tenancy, enabled me, as a sensitive, to pick up this special influence from many others presumably present; and that the memories of the past galvanized the impressions into some sort of temporary astral existence.'

A similar explanation for the case was suggested by J. Arthur Hill, in his day a well-known psychic investigator and prolific writer on the paranormal. While reviewing Miss Bates's book in 1907 in the *Annals of Psychical Science* he pointed out that 'it would be rash to take it for granted that the whole thing was elaborated by Miss Bates' own mind'. He suggested further that 'the subliminal consciousness or "astral self" of the "haunter" might be taking part in the affair'.

These remarks are extremely provocative. So far as I know, Hill was probably the first student of the paranormal to realize that these living ghosts might be related to the out-of-body experience. Can a person 'haunt' a distant location either through out-of-body travel or by projecting a thought-form to the place? While this suggestion is the stuff from which good science fiction is crafted, I think the possibility certainly exists.

A modern case of a 'living ghost'

I was initially drawn to consider the possibility of 'haunting' through out-of-body travel or thought-form projection several years ago, when I personally investigated a fascinating case in Los Angeles perhaps linked to a 'living ghost'. Some time in February 1973 I received a call from the University of California, Los Angeles, requesting that I look into a case brewing in a local suburb. A friend of the victimized family had reported the case to the University. Since the family lived in my neck of the woods, some sympathetic people in the psychology department contacted me and I immediately phoned the family (whom I'll call the Carters). I drove to their fashionable middle-class home in the San Fernando Valley that same day, and talked with several witnesses to the strange events.

The case turned out to be extremely difficult to interpret since it combined features of both a conventional haunting and a poltergeist. (A poltergeist is a short-lived or violent haunting, in which objects are moved or thrown repeatedly in the infested place. Such cases tend to be linked to a person living in the house, usually a child or teenager, who is repressing severe hostility. Such cases seem to be the result of psychokinesis running rampant, but they burn themselves out within a few weeks or months.) Mr and Mrs Carter shared the house with their five children, who were between 10 and 17 years old. With so many children in the household, the Carter residence was a perfect place for a poltergeist outbreak. Any one of them could have been psychically responsible for the disturbance. The family explained that their problem had broken out suddenly and unexpectedly in typical poltergeist fashion. On the other hand, though, the particular phenomena reported were *not* typically poltergeistic, but resembled the effects more commonly associated with haunted houses. The family had heard mysterious footsteps stalking the house during the night. Cold breezes were felt by some of the witnesses, who also reported that a radio once turned itself on and then back off. Even a traditional ghost was occasionally seen in the place.

One of the strangest incidents the family reported to me occurred the day before I first visited them, and it concerned their resident 'ghost'. Mark, the Carters' 13-year-old son, revealed that he had seen a strange apparition in his room that night. The phantom was little more than a vague shadowy figure, and Mark initially thought that it was a burglar. The figure soon moved out of his sight and into his sister's room, whereupon he heard strange shuffling sounds emanating from her closet. The boy didn't think much of this bizarre incident until the next morning when Sharon, Mark's 16-year-old sister, woke up to discover that someone or *something* had been in her closet. Some of her clothes were lying on the floor and several empty clothes-hangers were carefully positioned outwards to a 45° angle, braced on either sides by clothes.

I only stumbled across the most provocative aspect of the case, however, when I spoke with Stan, another of the Carter children. He once spotted an apparition while lying in bed one night. But interestingly enough, he told me that the figure—while undoubtedly spectral—*bore an uncanny resemblance to his father*!

Stan's remarks provided me with a partial solution to this perplexing suburban haunting. The sudden outbreak of ghostly phenomena and psychokinetic disturbances was probably both a haunting and a poltergeist. It was a poltergeist in the sense that Mr Carter was probably psychokinetically generating the disturbances. But it was a haunting in the respect that he was probably creating these disturbances by somehow producing a living ghost, thought-form, or etheric duplicate of himself capable of interacting with the environment. In other words, my feeling was that Mr Carter was literally haunting his own home! This possibility became even more tenable when I learned that the Carters' problem became bothersome when my prime suspect was either sleeping or missing from the house.

Fortunately for the Carters, their haunting was short-lived and ended as suddenly and mysteriously as it had begun. The outbreak seemed to be linked to the family's frustrated desire to leave California and move to South America where they had lived previously.

I become a living ghost!

As I mentioned earlier in this chapter, few researchers have seriously considered the implications of these 'living ghost' cases—i.e. that a living psyche can invade and infest a localized environment. I became especially interested in such phenomena only upon running into the Carter case. What I didn't know in 1973 was that I would eventually end up becoming a living ghost myself and haunting my own home several years later—from the great metropolis of New York!

The events behind this strange story began on 8 August 1977 when I had to fly from my home in Los Angeles to New York on publishing business. Now, I fully enjoy my sojourns to New York, which I had to make often in those days before I began working with my publishers by phone. The only problem I continually faced when planning these trips was trying to find somebody to care for my house while I was gone. This problem had become especially severe by 1977; for in the past, I had usually rented a room in my three-bedroom house to a college student or to a financially strapped friend. This arrangement provided me with both a caretaker and a tenant for the place. But for several months before my trip that summer I had been in the house by myself, so I eventually had to recruit a friend to take care of the house while I was back East. Dave Ostovich was relieved to be able to move into the house temporarily and enjoy a respite from his three roommates, with whom he shared a rented flat nearby. Dave was a 21-year-old printer whom I had met through his brother Mike, a research assistant of mine while I was carrying out some research at UCLA. Mike had previously rented from me while he was still in college.

Everything was working out fine for this trip, or so it seemed. I was no longer concerned about the house since I had a competent caretaker, and I didn't have a care in the world when I stepped on board my jet. This trip seemed little different from many others I have taken. So when I arrived in New York, I settled right down to scheduling business meetings, visiting parapsychology laboratories on the East Coast, and so forth. I was staying in a relative's apartment in Long Island City, which was only a short subway ride from downtown Manhattan.

But this trip was bound to be different from my others to the Atlantic coast. During the first week of my stay I started experiencing 'sinking' sensations when I was falling off to sleep. Since I always retired at 11.30, these experiences invariably occurred near midnight and would sometimes evolve into full-blown bouts of paralysis. The experiences didn't bother me, though, since I was familiar with them and their meaning.

As a teenager, I had experimented with out-of-body travel and had enjoyed several etheric experiences which were usually preceded by similar episodes of paralysis. It didn't take long for me to realize that I was beginning to have out-of-body experiences once more, even though I hadn't undergone chronic projections for years.

The second week of my stay in New York (the week of 15 to 22 August) was replete with more such experiences, and each night I would seem to be leaving my body. These episodes rarely changed. When I retired I would fall into a deep sleep. Some time later in the night I would suddenly find myself back in Los Angeles standing in my hallway by the door to the study. I would then proceed to walk (or 'float') up the hallway, systematically entering each of the bedrooms to make sure everything was in order. When these examinations were concluded, I would lose consciousness and wake several hours later back in New York. I could remember these experiences in the same manner I often remember dreams; but these experiences were different since I would wake up with the strong subjective feeling that I had literally been projecting to Los Angeles. I initially thought these experiences could be dreams, but I was soon forced to change my mind.

Any suggestion that I was merely enjoying a series of peculiar recurrent dreams was dispelled on 19 August when I had an especially vivid out-of-body projection to Los Angeles. Upon retiring that night, I woke up later out-of-body and took a good look at myself. I saw that I was occupying a whitish, amorphous-looking body and I was standing in the hallway of my home in California. For some inexplicable reason my eyes focused on my telephone, which was on a small stand towards the back of the hall. The notion struck me, crazy as it sounds, to ring up my colleague Raymond Bayless, so I moved towards the phone and tried to manipulate the dial. My mind 'cleared' when I failed to make contact with the instrument, and I then fully realized that I was functioning in some sort of out-of-body state.

'Wait a minute,' I thought to myself. 'I'm in New York. I can't call Raymond. I must get back.' I blacked out and woke up back in New York some time later with a complete and stunning memory of this whole etheric episode.

'No way was that a dream,' I mumbled to myself before getting out of bed and beginning my busy day of business meetings.

The final and dramatic conclusion to these unusual out-of-body projections took place a few days later on the evening of 22 August. I had retired that night at my customary eleven-thirty and, predictably enough, I soon found myself pacing the hallway in my Los Angeles home. But instead of merely walking down the hall like a robot, for the first time I felt a mischievous urge to make psychic contact with Dave! This urge puzzled me somewhat since never previously during my out-of-body experiences had I encountered him in the house, but I soon found myself searching the bedrooms for him. My search came to a halt when I wandered into the spare bedroom and spied a figure sleeping there. I immediately made the assumption that the figure was

Dave and tried to make my presence known to him by concentrating on him. My 'vision' is usually blurred during my out-of-body experiences (I don't take my glasses with me!), and when I looked closer, I saw that the figure wasn't Dave at all but his brother Mike. The sleeping figure stirred suddenly and I felt curiously uncomfortable and left the room. My out-of-body excursion ended and I returned to New York even more puzzled than ever.

When I woke up in the morning, I was still wondering whether I could have really been dreaming. I just couldn't understand why I had seen Mike in the spare room. Seeing him in the house seemed consistent with the dream hypothesis since, as I explained earlier, Mike had previously lived in the house—and dreams tend to be constructed from past experiences. But that explanation didn't make sense to me, since during the experience I saw the room the way it was currently furnished. The decor was completely different from when Mike had rented it several months previously. If the experience were only a dream, it struck me, I should have seen the room (with Mike sleeping in it) the way it was furnished in the past.

Even though I remained totally baffled by this episode, I resolved to enquire if Dave had detected my presence in the house during my New York stay. For despite the fact that I had only seen Mike in the house, inwardly I felt that I *had* established some sort of contact with his brother.

This incident represented the last out-of-body projection I enjoyed during my East Coast trip. My sinking sensations and etheric projections ended that night and I returned to Los Angeles a week later, arriving at my house close to eight o'clock in the evening.

Dave was still working at his print shop when I arrived, and I had nearly forgotten my experiences. But my memories returned with a vengeance when Mike stopped by to see me.

'Some mighty strange things have been going on here while you've been away,' he blurted out even before saying hello.

My erstwhile roommate proceeded to explain, with no prompting from me, that the house suddenly became haunted. My excitement grew when he made this sensational claim, but I didn't encourage him to describe the events in further detail. I knew that Dave would be returning to the house soon and I wanted to get the story directly from him. When he finally returned later that night, he immediately told me the entire, fascinating story of the haunting. (Suffice it to say that this house was a relatively modern tract home with no previous history of being haunted or otherwise infested.)

Dave began his story be telling me that strange noises, mostly consisting of peculiar rappings and humanlike moanings, erupted in the house the same day that I left for New York. The printer didn't initially pay much attention to the sounds. Los Angeles was going through a sizzling summer spell that week so he had been keeping my creaky forced-air evaporative cooling system on when he was home. He merely rationalized that the strange sounds were being produced by the system which, sad to say, had seen much better days and tended to emit creaks and other sounds on occasion.

Even though Dave didn't realize that the sounds were possibly paranormal, they were relatively loud and he heard them every evening. They usually began about 6.30 p.m. and he gradually became increasingly puzzled by them. Then on the evening of 22 August (the night of my final and most vivid out-of-body experience in New York) a series of events took place in the residence that so alarmed him that he ran from the house in pure panic.

Dave had come home from work that Monday still euphoric from a lazy weekend. He planned on immediately returning to work so stopped by my house to just change clothes and freshen up. But at a little after eight o'clock he heard an unexpected knock at the door while casually slipping into his shoes in the master bedroom.

'For some reason,' he told me 'something just flashed and I thought to myself, "There's nobody at the door." Instead of getting up and answering it—you know, making a move to answer it—my first instinct was that nobody was at the door. Before I could even begin to start to think why I felt that, I heard it again distinctly and loudly enough to rattle the brass door-knocker that's on the door. So at that time I got up and walked to the front door and opened it. There was nobody at the door and the screen was latched.'

Dave looked around the porch to see if a prankster was hiding or walking away from the door, but nobody was in sight. He assured me that he hadn't previously heard anyone walking up or down the steps leading to the door, either before or after the knockings.

'About that time,' Dave continued, 'I decided that something odd was definitely going on. And I walked back to the house into the master bedroom again, to put on my other shoe. This was a matter of a few seconds. But then things started really moving in my mind.'

It was then that Dave again heard the familiar moanings. The sounds were made by a deep masculine voice which emitted two groans, which constituted long and unsettling wails. The groans so frightened him that he literally began to shake and couldn't even tie his shoelaces! Panic finally got the better of him and he rushed to the front door to escape.

'I was as close to running as you can get in the house,' Dave admitted. 'I went out the front door, and didn't close it hard enough to latch it. At that time, I opened it approximately a foot and a half to two feet in order to slam it closed. At that time, something—you know, a figure—went by the hallway [doorway]. It was just "something" going by the doorway. It's very hard to have to describe. It's just the way it would look if you caught somebody who was about out of view walking by a doorway. After that, I slammed the door and it latched.'

Dave's reaction to these events was predictable enough: he jumped into his car and began driving from the house in panic. Then his natural psychological defences took over and he mysteriously forgot why he was running. He experienced a sudden sereneness and blocked out the events that had just taken place. His uncomfortable memories didn't return until his brother dropped by the print shop later that evening and mentioned my name. This provided Dave with the catalyst he needed to remember his paranormal experience earlier that evening. He became so shaky when he recalled the sounds and the spectral figure that he asked his brother to return with him to the house when he finished work. *That night Mike slept in the spare bedroom just as I had seen him while projecting out-of-body to the house.*

Looking back at those events in retrospect, there is little doubt in my mind that I somehow produced this short-lived haunting. The length of the haunting, which extended roughly between 8 and 22 August, tallied with the time of my bizarre projection experiences in New York. It was more than coincidental, too, that the figure seen by Dave materialized in the same location where I continually found myself while out-of-body in Los Angeles. The icing on the cake came when I correctly saw Mike sleeping in the house, and in the correct room on the same night he stayed there while I was gone. The fact that Dave experienced the haunting so vividly the same night that I had undergone my strong desire to establish contact with him is also revealing and provides further evidence that I was the ghostly intruder that so frightened him.

Only one aspect of the haunting still puzzles me. Dave's encounter with the raps and vocalizations usually began early in the evening and long before I usually retired in New York. Even the critical events of 22 August took place after eight o'clock in Los Angeles, which would have been several minutes before I fell asleep in New York. So either some component of my mind was projecting to Los Angeles while I was still conscious, or somehow my out-of-body projection transcended both time *and* space. Perhaps my friend was somehow being influenced by my *future* etheric journeys. Such a suggestion shouldn't strike you as strange, since many gifted psychics claim that they can out-of-body themselves into the future. So why couldn't I have projected my way back into the immediate past? While too complex to detail in this chapter, there is some experimental evidence that a present event (such as the output of a random event generator) can be psychokinetically influenced by a future attempt by the experimental subject. This phenomenon is called retroactive psychokinesis and has been demonstrated widely by Dr Helmut Schmidt, whose work was briefly mentioned in the previous chapter. Perhaps the experiences I shared with Dave represented a similar sort of reaction between my mind and his physical environment.

Whatever the explanation, cases of living ghosts prompt us to take a hard look at wraiths and hauntings in general. It seems obvious that even conventional hauntings may not necessarily be caused by spirits of the dead, nor by *representations* of the dead. 'Living ghosts' imply that each of us possesses the potential to generate hauntings during the course of our daily lives! Perhaps this fact explains why some houses suddenly become infested for no discernible reason.

The last implication that can be drawn from these cases is more unsettling, however. If the human mind possesses a faculty that can invade a physical location and exert some sort of influence on physical matter, could it likewise influence a living brain? Do some people possess the power to invade other people's brains and 'haunt' them with compulsive thoughts or psychotic thinking? This frightening subject will be discussed in the following chapter.

4

Scientific Evidence for Psychic Self-Defence

Paranoid schizophrenia is probably the most frightening mental illness to which mankind is prone. The patient not only loses contact with reality, but often suffers from both disordered thinking and frightening hallucinations. These disturbances usually focus on self-perceived threats. The patient may, for example, hear inner voices warning that his/her life is in continuous danger. Schizophrenic breaks are generally classified into one of two categories: either *reactive* (which occur suddenly in response to a stressful life situation) or *process* (which are long-term chronic problems that seem unrelated to a specific psychological cause). These latter cases are extremely resistant to therapy, and the patients rarely make full recoveries. Cases of paranoid schizophrenia can be either chronic or transitory reaction conditions.

The specific delusions of the paranoid schizophrenic can be bizarre. Patients typically complain that their thoughts are being stolen from them, that invisible rays or telepathic messages are being beamed into their brains, or that they are being persecuted by some secret organization. It is not known why these specific types of persecutory syndromes so frequently develop, though several theories have been put forward over the years.

The specific cause of schizophrenia is also relatively unknown. While it appears that genetic factors play some role in the disease, some researchers feel that biochemical disorders or a slow-working viral infection of the brain produces the illness. Other researchers feel that schizophrenia probably consists of several different diseases which are erroneously lumped together because they share symptomology.

But could some cases of 'schizophrenia' be caused by thought-insertions really 'sent' by a second person just as some schizophrenics have claimed for years? This was the possibility that Dr

James McHarg faced in 1964. Dr McHarg is today retired from his psychiatric post at the University of Dundee in Scotland, but he retains his strong interest in the paranormal. When the following case first came to light, he was a staff psychiatrist at Royal Dundee Liff Hospital.

Driven crazy by telepathy

The patient's history originally read like a typical case of paranoid schizophrenia, process type. Mrs Mary Leeds* was 58 years old and living reclusively in her apartment when her illness first developed. The first symptoms appeared in the summer of 1958 when she became depressed over the course of her life. (She had separated from her husband some time earlier.) Hallucinatory voices began plaguing her, which she immediately blamed on evil spirits invading her flat through the chimney and roof. She was particularly terrified that the spirits would possess her. Despite the severity of these symptoms, she lived quietly in her flat for a year before seeking admission to a hospital. She entered Royal Dundee Liff Hospital in July 1959.

The voices were not the only symptoms that eventually plagued the patient. Five months later the hospital staff observed her spitting into ashtrays and plant pots. Mrs Leeds's explanation for her peculiar behaviour was that 'beasts' were living in her throat which she was trying to hawk up. This belief was so persistent that she complained of the beasts for 14 months before the delusions mysteriously subsided. The patient remained disturbed but stable for the next two and a half years, until September 1963 when her illness seemed to get worse. Bizarre hallucinatory sounds started to bother the patient in her left ear, which she told the staff were being caused by a 'beast' eating its way into her brain. She naturally grew exceedingly agitated when she found that her doctors couldn't excise the monster, and she persisted in her belief until early in 1968. Other complications set in during this time, for towards the end of 1965 she began developing a similar delusion concerning a beast living in her right ear. This delusion also seemed to abate after 1968, and the patient—who remained continuously hospitalized because of the severity of her illness—remained stable until her death a few years later.

This case report is a sad one. The patient was so deluded that little could be done for her. But even though she remained paranoid, Mrs Leeds was always pleasant to the staff and stayed in the hospital voluntarily.

* This is a pseudonym used to protect the patient's family. Her real name is on file at the hospital where she was treated, as well as in Dr McHarg's private files.

So far there is nothing extraordinary about this case, which reads fairly typically for a paranoid schizophrenic. That was certainly Dr McHarg's reaction to it. But he began changing his mind in 1964 when he discovered a strange series of synchronicities related to the case.

The fact that there was more to Mrs Leeds's problems than simple paranoia came to light when Dr McHarg learned that a second patient in the hospital was complaining of unusual sounds in his right ear. No cause for the complaint could be found, though the gentleman was obviously not psychotic. Dr McHarg became interested in the patient's problem when he learned of him from a colleague, and was doubly surprised to find out that he was Mrs Leeds's estranged brother! They had not been in contact for several years, and neither patient knew that the other was being treated in another ward of the same hospital. This gentleman was psychologically stable, and Dr McHarg suspected that the man was suffering from an undiagnosed organic condition.

Dr McHarg kept tabs on this patient until the man's death in November 1969 from an (unrelated) abdominal condition. Through a post-mortem examination, it was discovered that the patient had suffered from an acoustic neurinoma (tumour) in his left ear pressing against his brain. Then came the real surprise. By checking the patient's records, Dr McHarg discovered that the patient's first symptoms and Mrs Leeds's delusions concerning the beast in her left ear (eating into her brain) *both* developed in September 1963. It began to look as if Mrs Leeds's delusion was somehow telepathically triggered by her brother's medical problems. By digging even further, the psychiatrist subsequently learned that Mrs Leeds's delusions subsided during the same critical months that her brother was reconciling himself to his imminent loss of hearing in his left ear.

These coincidences were so extraordinary that Dr McHarg spent considerable time tracing the medical history of Mrs Leeds's brother. Stunning synchronicities gradually came to light as he proceeded, which served to connect each of Mrs Leeds's delusions directly to her estranged brother.

It turned out that some time between 1957 and 1959, Mrs Leeds's brother developed what would later become a growing bronchial carcinoma (a malignant spreading tumour). These months curiously corresponded to the time in 1958 when Mrs Leeds first developed the delusion that 'malignant' spirits were invading her home through her chimney. Dr McHarg rightly feels that there exists an obvious symbolic connection between Mrs Leeds's symptom and her brother's illness, since they both concerned a spreading malignancy channelled through a passageway. The brother's condition worsened and in 1960 he developed a productive cough. This was only a month after his sister came to believe that *there were beasts in her throat which she had to cough up*! More suspicious, too, was the fact that Mrs Leeds's delusion mysteriously subsided in 1961, close to the time her brother's tumour was surgically removed.

This chain of synchronistic events extended into 1963 when—as I described earlier—Mrs Leeds started complaining that beasts were living in her left ear. This bizarre delusion obviously corresponded to her brother's complaint with regard to the strange noises in *his* left ear, which resulted from his unsuspected neurinoma. There was also a connection to Mrs Leeds's subsequent affliction (dating from December 1965) regarding a similar beast possibly living in her right ear. It turned out that, fearful of his hearing, her brother had started complaining towards the end of 1965 of strange noises in his right ear as well. (These symptoms turned out to be imaginary, caused by the greater sensitivity in his right ear upon losing his hearing in the other.)

'These findings,' explains Dr McHarg '[are] therefore very suggestive of the whole psychosis having been based on a synchronistic partial personation by the patient of her totally estranged brother.'

Despite this fact, the patient failed to improve after her brother's death. Dr McHarg tried to explain the connection between her symptoms and her brother's problems to Mrs Leeds, but she could never comprehend the relationship. This situation could have been foreseen, for schizophrenics often possess serious defects when it comes to such abstract reasoning. It would have been extremely difficult for her to see any connection between her 'beasts' and her brother's tumours.

Do cases of psychic attack really exist?

Of course, this report prompts us to consider a series of related issues. Was this poor woman literally 'driven crazy' by telepathy? Or would she have become psychotic even had her brother never become sick? Do schizophrenics tend to be gifted psychics, or could some people who seem insane really be psychic?

It is difficult to answer any of these questions definitively. While it is well known that schizophrenics can be phenomenally sensitive to non-verbal forms of communication, considerable laboratory research has failed to show that they are particularly psychic. While some of this research has shown that psychotics can score reasonably well in experimental ESP tests, there is no evidence that they are *more* prone to flashes of telepathy than any other group of people.

This general finding may, in fact, give us a clue to Mrs Leeds's strange psychosis and its curious and chronic transformations. Mrs Leeds suffered from a condition any competent psychiatrist would diagnose as chronic schizophrenia. Since her condition lasted well beyond the death of her brother, it would seem that her relative's illnesses merely *influenced* the development of her delusions, but probably did not originally cause her psychosis. While the course of her sickness may have been modified by her brother's conditions, it probably wasn't programmed by them.

There is, in fact, some related and provocative evidence that psychotic delusions can be manipulated (if not produced) by telepathy. This is certainly the view of Dr Elizabeth Mintz, a clinical psychologist with a private practice in New York, who makes this point in her book *The Psychic Thread*. Dr Mintz explains that she and some of her fellow therapists once began experimenting with extrasensory perception at the hospital where they worked. To contribute to their experimentation, on one occasion Dr Mintz decided to send one of her colleagues a psychic message while taking a break from her ward duties. So she sat in her office and tried to send the name 'Johnny Walker' (meaning the whisky) to him, since he was known for his temperance concerning such beverages. She was focusing on the name when one of the hospital's schizophrenic patients came running down the hall. He was extremely agitated, and kept complaining that he was being called Johnny Walker!

Whether such incidents will contribute to our understanding of the case Dr McHarg has so thoroughly studied is, of course, not known. But in the long run, such incidents suggest that we should be looking deeply into the dynamics of the disturbed mind while studying the roots of telepathy. The more frightening implication of these cases is that occasional cases of 'psychosis' or 'disordered thinking' might be *produced* by some people's sensitivity to psychic messages, and even some conventional parapsychologists have seriously considered this possibility. Writing in their recent and acclaimed book *The Mind Race*, for example, Russell Targ and Keith Harary, two parapsychologists formerly of S.R.I. International in Menlo Park, California, suggest that 'it seems quite likely that an unethical psychic practitioner could deliberately put thoughts into a potential victim's head in such a way as to disorient him, confuse him, or make him feel depressed'.

As if this weren't enough, they proceed to argue that 'with regard to unethical uses of psi, we think it is quite likely that some people will think of a variety of uses of psi that most people would consider an invasion of privacy. If individuals or governments have developed psi abilities enough to feel that their awareness can transcend both space and time, there is no telling what kind of information they might try to gather.'

The concept that we could be prone to this sort of psychic 'attack' is certainly not novel, and this possibility crops up repeatedly in occult and magical literature. But if such a phenomenon genuinely exists, is there anything we can do to counter the invasion? We know that telepathic messages or psychic functioning is neither obstructed nor shielded by such physical factors as distance or physical barriers. Even brick walls will not keep a telepathic message from reaching the person to whom it is directed. So does there exist any method people can employ to ward off possibly hostile psychic intrusions projected into their minds and/or brains? Some occultists and writers on the paranormal in the Victorian age certainly believed that there were. The well-known British psychologist Violet Firth (who wrote books on the occult under the pseudonym Dion Fortune) even published a book on the subject. She suggested in her famous work *Psychic Self-Defence* that rituals of self-purification could protect an individual from such psychic intrusions. She didn't believe that the rituals caused the shielding in themselves, but that the energy and intention *behind* their execution were filled with power. Dion Fortune also suggested that the student should cease experimenting with psychic functioning while trying to inhibit hostile psychic energy projected his/her way.

Fascinating though these suggestions and opinions may be, until recently little scientific evidence existed that such procedures were efficacious or more than rank superstition. But the situation has now radically changed.

Scientific evidence for psychic self-defence

San Antonio, Texas, is the present home of the Mind Science Foundation. This institution is a privately funded research centre that houses a parapsychology laboratory and library, and employs two senior researchers and several assistants. Their current experimental projects include research on psychokinesis, remote viewing, and psychic healing. It was the existence of this third phenomenon that first led researchers there to posit the possible reality of 'psychic attack', and to begin pondering whether techniques could be established for warding off such influences. For when they realized that psychokinesis could be used to heal, it also struck them that it could simultaneously be used to harm people.

That is certainly the opinion of Dr William Braud, who relinquished his faculty position with the University of Houston to devote himself to parapsychology full-time in the 1970s. The soft-spoken, bearded psychologist is probably the most creative experimental parapsychologist in the field today. During the early 1980s, he and his colleagues began taking a critical interest in what they called 'psychic shielding'.

Dr Braud presented the results of his initial research at the 1984 Annual Convention of the Parapsychological Association, which convened that year on the campus of Southern Methodist University in Dallas, Texas. Dr Braud had previously mentioned his exciting research to me when he visited Los Angeles a month earlier, so I was eager to hear his report.

The impetus behind this fascinating project resulted from Dr Braud's interest and research into psychic healing. Back in the mid-1970s, he began studying a phenomenon he christened *allobio-feedback* or bio-PK. Today it is generally accepted that an experimental subject can influence his/her own body by receiving feedback monitoring involuntary physiological functions such as heart rate and electrical skin resistance. But Dr Braud began wondering whether a subject could influence a *second* person's body in the same way, presumably by way of telepathy or psychokinesis. It didn't take long for him to begin exploring the possibility. Soon he began experimenting to see whether his experimental subjects could *psychically* influence a second or 'target' person sitting in a separate room in the building. The experimenters relied upon a relatively simple design. No contact was permitted between the two people, of course, and the experimental subject—placed in a second room—was instructed solely to focus on the target individual and influence his galvanic skin response. (The GSR gauges the skin's fluctuating power to conduct an electrical current. The more relaxed you become, the less electrical activity is picked up by electrodes connected to the skin.) Sometimes the experimental subjects tried to relax their own bodies at the same time.

In order to provide some feedback to the experimental subject, he/she and the experimenter watched a graph that kept continuous track of the changes in the person's skin resistance.

Dr Braud first successfully employed himself as both experimenter and experimental participant, but soon learned that many people possess this strange power.

This little experiment might seem pointlessly pedagogic, but it really wasn't. For like most provocative experiments, it is teeming with important implications—implications that were certainly not lost on

Dr Braud. His discovery of allobiofeedback/bio-PK indicates that probably many people possess some power similar to psychic healing.

'We conceived of these experiments as healing analogues,' Dr Braud explained to me during a break in the conference. We were standing together in a small meeting room while our colleagues were examining some new computer software. 'In fact,' he continued, 'in most of our studies the psychic influence was in a medically and psychologically beneficial direction. We were calming people.'

But these tests suggested to Dr Braud that psychokinesis could possibly *harm* people if projected to them with negative thoughts. He became rather circumspect when our conversation proceeded further.

'Once we had demonstrated that we could influence a distant person, especially in those bio-PK experiments,' he told me, 'the obvious question was how well that individual could *prevent* that influence if it were unwanted. Physical methods of shielding fail, but psychological and psychic methods of shielding have been strangely ignored [in the laboratory]. There was a gap there, so we decided to look into it.'

Dr Braud conceded, however, that there was a more empirical and pressing need to know whether psychic self-defence strategies had a practical reality. This concern stemmed from his own day-to-day involvement in the field of parapsychology. It is a concern many researchers have expressed and confronted while exploring the sixth sense and psychokinesis.

'Another input into our research had to do with counselling,' Dr Braud continued. 'We receive reports in from people who claim that they are being psychically controlled and that their thoughts are being influenced.'

These people usually call parapsychology laboratories for help, and Dr Braud feels that researchers in the field have an ethical responsibility to respond to their concerns. 'We usually tell them some things that we believe to be the case,' he told me. 'We explain that they have some veto power over the situation and that they can block and not co-operate with these influences if they choose.'

But since he is primarily an experimental psychologist, Dr Braud was not willing to base his response to these people solely on such personal beliefs or occult teachings. The enterprising researcher decided to explore his theories in the cold environment of the scientific laboratory. Three fascinating experiments exploring 'psychic shielding' have so far been completed, with promising results.

Formal experimentation to study the effects of psychic shielding was undertaken by the Mind Science Foundation in 1983. Dr Braud's main project employed 16 volunteer subjects, each tested separately. None of them, by the way, knew that they were participating in an experiment on psychic blocking. They were merely instructed to call out the symbols on a standard set of ESP cards (each printed with one of five geometric symbols). Each subject completed two runs consisting of 25 'calls' each. It was a co-worker of Dr Braud's who focused on the blocking. While testing each subject, she randomly chose to block the subject's ability to clairvoyantly call the cards for one run, but exerted no such influence when the subject responded to the other series. To accomplish this blocking, the experimenter subjectively constructed a huge monolith between the subject and herself. During the other run she tried to remain perfectly neutral.

The results of this experiment were encouraging but not statistically significant, so Dr Braud decided to replicate it. The results of this second experiment were more decisive.

The problem with this experiment was obvious, however. It was difficult to isolate the cause of the blocking effect. One possibility was that the experimenter really succeeded while trying to interfere psychically with the subject's ESP. But it is also possible that the experimenter was cueing the subject when to 'fail' through slight facial expressions. This problem, called sensory cueing, commonly takes place when the experimenter/sender remains in the same room as the subject. This problem wasn't crucial in these studies, however, since Dr Braud was merely interested in learning whether ESP could be blocked by either psychic *or* psychological factors. Such 'cues' could, therefore, be considered an important part of effective psychological blocking.

So in order to focus on the shielding effect more concisely, Dr Braud designed a new study. This time the subjects were requested to clairvoyantly 'see' into opaque envelopes and describe the target pictures hidden there. The targets used for these trials ranged in complexity, and the procedure was specifically designed to let the subject ignore the experimenter's presence. Each of the subjects was tested with two envelopes and they were encouraged to sketch their impressions of the targets. The experimenter (yet another lab assistant) tried to block the subject's power to clairvoyantly 'see' one target, but not the other. Drawing upon principles from folklore and occult literature, Dr Braud instructed his co-experimenters to imagine a bright pulsating oval of white light between the subject and the target envelope.

The instructions worked. Dr Braud found that the subjects were much better at psychically exploring the sealed envelope when nobody interfered with the process.

Dr Braud has also employed his bio-PK research design in his explorations into the possible existence of psychic self-defence. For yet a third experiment, the psychologist experimented to see whether 16 (individually tested) volunteer subjects could successfully block an 'influencer' who was trying to increase their galvanic skin response (GSR). Each subject was tested in a sealed experimental room while the 'influencer' was placed elsewhere in the lab. The 16 subjects were instructed to ward off the 'sender's' psychic influence, while 16 control subjects were told to co-operate with the influencer. The experimenter for this series of tests was either Dr Braud or a long-time staff member at the Foundation, Marilyn Schlitz, who also served as the psychic 'influencer'. To keep the test as strict as possible, they kept themselves unaware of whether the subjects were trying to help or hinder them. The only feedback they received came by watching a graph keeping track of the subject's GSR activity. Only when each session was completed did they learn which of their subjects were blocking their psychic efforts.

The results of this experiment were somewhat mixed, since the subjects only succeeded when Dr Braud was trying to influence them.

Some further issues complicating psychic self-defence
More important for our purposes than the technical features of Dr Braud's current research are the implications of these curious findings. I was personally interested as to whether Dr Braud feels that people can be trained to be proficient psychic self-defenders. When I broached this subject to him, the psychologist instantly responded.

'I think the ability is there,' he said. 'It would be very much like training people in psychic functioning—in other words, that perhaps such functioning is already there in all of us. Maybe it is functioning all the time beyond our awareness and it's a matter of learning to look and recognize it. I think we all know how to do this [psychic blocking] and we do it rather well. So it's a matter of learning by practice and by some hints from other people about what it is, what the techniques are, and practising it.'

The San Antonio based researcher isn't interested in simply proving the reality of psychic self-defence, however. 'I'm interested in the possible limits of it, also,' he reminded me. 'Are there, for instance, some things that can't be blocked? Just as blocking imposes a limit on psychic functioning (it would seem), are there limits on blocking itself?'

Since his first tests seemed so encouraging, Dr Braud is confident that further research will provide him with even more information regarding the reality of psychic self-defence. Of special concern to him is the elimination of sensory cueing and other psychological elements from his experiments—i.e. the factors that rendered his initial tests so difficult to interpret. His research into the existence of bio-PK blocking has provided him with a good start. He is also fascinated by the possible selectivity of the shielding effect. Could a subject, for example, set up a shield with the capacity to eliminate the influences sent by one particular person, but not by somebody else? The possible temporal capacity of these shields is yet another provocative issue. Dr Braud hopes to learn whether psychic shields last indefinitely or only temporarily. Or do they dissolve when the subject's concentration begins to falter?

Perhaps the most intriguing research, however, will relate to the site-specific possibilities of psychic shielding.

'Could psychic shielding be used as a kind of physical sense?' Dr Braud pondered as our conversation came to a close. 'Could we surround a place, or a location, or an object? I'm speaking almost metaphorically, but can we shield a specific target site against all psychic intruders?'

The problem with studying nebulous concepts such as psychic shielding is the same problem that repeatedly crops up in parapsychology. Researchers in the field often find themselves searching for physical parameters which regulate a process (extrasensory perception or precognition) that in itself is *non*-physical. It is a contradiction in terms to speak of measuring something that could be, by nature, invisible or undetectable. So it certainly looks as though Dr Braud will have a difficult time probing and isolating the laws regulating psychic shielding. I would be more interested to see whether psychic blocking is a personal or an interpersonal process. In other words, will the psychic shields erected by one person exhibit the same features as those conjured up by somebody else?

Dr Braud will probably be exploring this issue sometime in the future. If nothing else, these experiments in psychic shielding look both promising and provocative, and enormous implications can be drawn from them. Several years ago I received a call from a tabloid press reporter, requesting a statement on the possibility of psychic shielding. He wanted to know whether I believed a psychic (or team of psychics) could shield the President's mind from being psychically tapped by a foreign power! My first response was to laugh, since the suggestion sounded so preposterous to me.

I don't know whether I would laugh if I were asked the same question today.

PART II
Realities beyond Death

5
Children and the Afterlife

Mexico was the setting in the 1970s for some fascinating and original research into extrasensory perception. The experiments were conducted by Michael Winkelman, a blond and bearded social science student from sunny California (then) working towards his doctorate from the University of California, Irvine. With the help of a grant from the Parapsychology Foundation in New York, the enterprising experimenter trekked south of the border to test native Mexican children for clairvoyance. The experiments were especially designed to spark the interest of the youngsters, since the children were challenged to guess the colour of a package of gum concealed in the experimenter's hand. For other tests the children were requested to guess the colour of a marble hidden inside a box.

After several field trips to Mexico and experiments with dozens of children, the primary finding of the study became clearer and clearer. The children performed progressively *worse* on tests for psychic functioning the more formal education they possessed. In other words, the Western educational process seems to stifle the child's innate sensitivity to the psychic world.

The psychic and extrasensory world of children has fascinated students of the paranormal for years. Early in the heyday of experimental parapsychology at Duke University (in Durham, North Carolina) in the 1930s, several successful projects were undertaken with children. Books on the care and nurturing of psychic children still show up on the bookracks periodically, and I often receive calls from bewildered parents reporting their children's psychic experiences to me. Most of these people expect me to explain these experiences for them, or want to know methods for coping better with their youngsters' psychic gifts.

Children and their inner sensitivity to the Universe

The fact that children live in a special world filled with psychic and spiritual realities has been repeatedly emphasized in the work of Dr Keith Harary—who is himself a psychologist, psychic, and psychical researcher. Keith has been a psychic since childhood, and during his undergraduate years at Duke University he was the primary subject and co-experimenter for some very innovative explorations into the out-of-body experience. (Keith can induce the experience consciously, and these experiments were described in some detail in my previous book *The Return from Silence*.) When he left Duke with a master's degree in experimental psychology, he worked in parapsychology laboratories in New York and California before turning to more clinical interests.

Keith is currently the research director of the Institute for Advanced Psychology in San Francisco. One of his favourite projects is to educate the public on parapsychology and especially concerning the problems faced by psychic children. In the spring of 1987, I was fortunate enough to interview Keith (whom I have known for close to 20 years) on the subject of children and their spiritual world for *Science of Mind* magazine. This periodical is the official publication of the United Church of Religious Science, and its editor was intrigued by my colleague's work. Sitting together in the kitchen of the apartment he shares with his wife near San Francisco's colourful Polk Street, Keith spoke openly about his own troubled psychic childhood and the need for such education. I began the interview by asking him whether he felt children were linked to the Universe in special ways.

'By the time you can ask children about their intuitive perceptions of the world,' he replied, 'they've usually been so enculturated that they're busier fulfilling their sex roles. They're too engaged in the culturally determined activities of growing up—engaged in meeting the expectations of their peers, parents, and teachers. So it's rather difficult to figure out what their original state was.'

Despite these problems, Keith feels that some children experience a special connection to the world, which he describes in terms of 'a very close affinity for nature, a kind of sensitivity to the world around them merging on the mystical'.

But this inner knowledge that personality transcends the self soon becomes disenfranchised. 'If a little boy feels that way in this culture,' the psychologist explained from his personal experiences, 'he's apt to get such feelings beaten out of him very quickly. Such a child will have to fight very hard to maintain that sort of sensitivity in the face of cultural forces that work to make him tough and insensitive.'

Our *Science of Mind* interview together ranged over a significant number of topics, including Keith's own childhood experiences and the reactions of school officials and formal religion to children reporting psychic and spiritual experiences and so forth. The important point to remember is that, from a clinical perspective, Keith's experiences are completely consistent with the findings of the Winkelman research summarized earlier. Children simply become brainwashed by contemporary culture to ignore or lose their sensitivity to the spiritual dimensions of life. This same theme has cropped up consistently over the years in psychic literature, most recently in such books as Samuel H. Young's *Psychic Children* and *Is Your Child Psychic?* by Dr Alex Tanous and Katherine Fair Donnelly.

Perhaps this point of view is best summarized by Keith Harary in some of his concluding remarks in the interview:

> Who is to say there isn't some connection between your thoughts and the experiences you have in the world around you? Many philosophers believe this to be true, and that idea serves as the basis for much New Thought philosophy. Psi researchers—parapsychologists—have experimentally demonstrated that the mind can directly interact with the world and perceive information at a distance, through time, or from mind to mind when this information is blocked from 'ordinary' perception or analytic inference. For all we know, we might be intuitively responding to one another's thoughts on a regular basis. If this turns out to be the case, wouldn't we say that our thoughts are directly influencing events in the world around us—as well as being influenced directly by those events on more than a simple, mundane level?
>
> I think children often feel that sort of connection between their inner experiences and the outer world. It may not be magical thinking but rather an expression of an understanding of how reality operates. They may experience this connectedness because they specifically *don't* set up culturally determined ego-boundaries between their inner experiences and the outer world.

Children's special sensitivity to death

In light of the preceding discussion, it isn't strange that children sometimes show a special sensitivity to the realm beyond death. Most people in Western societies fear death with a phobic terror. This lamentable situation isn't strange since we live in a death-denying culture where death is constantly divorced from the everyday realities of life. Popular illustrations of this widespread denial don't seem difficult to find. Death is a subject most people refuse to discuss in polite conversation, while the dying are usually shunted off to hospitals or rest homes, conveniently out of sight and out of mind from the standpoint of their relatives. We even try to shield our children from the simple reality of death on the misguided premise that we're doing them a favour. This particular fact was recently illustrated by a legal battle in 1987 reported from the city of West Hollywood, California. A hospice organization had secured a small home in a residential community to care for six dying AIDS patients. There was a terrible outcry from the neighbours, who tried to block the hospice with a legal suit, which they eventually lost. The well-meaning neighbours weren't frightened of catching AIDS, but they still didn't want a hospice on the block. One lady explicitly told court officials that the hospice would 'force her children to grow up familiar with death'.

No wonder the very thought of life's passing is so threatening to most people. According to conventional psychological theory, the fear of death is instinctive to mankind, but this shibboleth of psycho-analytical thinking has been recently challenged. In an essay on death education published in 1987, Gary J. Grad (from Columbia University) and Sir Stephen V. Gullo point out that 'we are not born with a fear of death; we learn it from the taboos of silence and fear transmitted by our families and society as a whole'.

Now if that position is correct, it could be that children have a special capability to see beyond life's barrier. People who have worked with dying children have often noted the youngsters' complete openness to death, and their instinctual knowledge that life lasts beyond its welcoming silence. These findings have been published as part and parcel of psychical research's literature dating back to the late 1800s. Perhaps the first researcher to bring widespread attention to this fact was Sir William Barrett, a Dublin physicist and co-founder (in 1882) of the Society for Psychical Research in Great Britain. In his posthumously published and celebrated book *Death-bed Visions*, he cited an unusual incident reported from the United States. The story concerned two small children who were dying of diphtheria—then a serious bacterial disease usually resulting in death. Jennie and Edith were close friends and both contracted the disease in June 1889. Jennie died first, but little Edith's parents and physician took pains to keep the information from her. Three days after the first child's death, though, Edith reported a welcoming figure by her bedside. She instantly realized she was dying and suddenly stared towards the invisible presence in the room.

'Why papa, I am going to take Jennie with me!' she exclaimed. 'Why papa, you did not tell me that Jennie was here!' She then reached towards the phantom and said, 'Oh Jennie, I'm so glad you are here.'

She died soon after reporting the figure to her surprised parents.

Cases of such deathbed visions could be dismissed if they weren't so commonly reported. A serious and detailed study of similar deathbed phenomena was undertaken by Professor James H. Hyslop, who republished his results in his book *Psychical Research and the Resurrection* in 1908. (The professor began his career teaching philosophy at Columbia University and later helped found the American Society for Psychical Research in 1907.) While engaged in his research, he uncovered a curious book published by the parents of Daisy Dryden, a little girl who died in Marysville, California on 9 September 1854. Some sort of progressive enteritis caused her death, and she expired four days after becoming ill. During those critical days, she became so clairvoyant that her mother constantly sat by her side taking copious notes. The little patient reported seeing a series of 'spirit' visitors at her bedside. Often these figures claimed to be her deceased relatives, but Daisy also perceived deceased friends and relatives of her neighbours and delivered evidential messages from them.

Such stories read like sentimental nursery school or campfire tales. But similar reports were commonly reported when child mortality was still severe in the United States, and when the dying usually expired peacefully in their own homes, surrounded by their friends and relatives.*

Children and death revisited:
the findings of Dr Elisabeth Kübler-Ross

Dr Elisabeth Kübler-Ross is probably the world's best known and respected expert on the psychology of dying and death. Born in Switzerland, she had first-hand experience of the nightmare of the Second World War through her work helping to rebuild human lives shattered by its ravages. After taking her medical degree she came to the United States to specialize in psychiatry, and soon found herself drawn to the problems faced by dying patients. She began talking with these people in depth while she slowly mapped out the 'stages' of the dying process—to the exasperation of her medical colleagues in Chicago. They were firmly opposed to her work, despite the fact that the patients liked to talk about death and their emotional responses to their terminal condition. After working with some 200 patients, Dr

* The research of Sir William Barrett and James H. Hyslop has been described in more depth in my book *The Return from Silence*. It seems wise to briefly repeat this information to help introduce the more current findings of Dr Elisabeth Kübler-Ross.

Kübler-Ross finally decided to publish her substantial findings in a series of books.

Her first book on the subject was *On Death and Dying*, which was published in 1969 and soon became a best-seller. Her primary discovery was that people exhibit four stages or reactions before finally accepting death. Usually they first deny the fact, then display anger towards their fate, try to bargain with God for more time, and finally enter into a deep state of depression. Once they survive this dark night of the soul, they emerge prepared to face life's final journey.

Whether these stages of dying are predictable and sequential reactions to terminal illness, or even whether they really exist, is still being debated by psychologists. But by bringing her experiences before the general public, Dr Kübler-Ross gave contemporary society a new appreciation of the complexities of death. She took the subject out of the closet and converted it into a subject of popular debate.

The work of this pioneering psychiatrist didn't end with the publication of the book. She followed her seminal studies with a sequel entitled *Questions and Answers on Death and Dying* in 1974. Seven years later her *Living with Death and Dying* was published. This book represented a significant change in Dr Kübler-Ross's thinking and research. The Swiss-born psychiatrist had previously been concerned primarily with people coming to the end of long and productive lives. But in *Living with Death and Dying* she devoted a significant chapter to the care of dying children. Beginning in the late 1970s, she began refocusing her private practice, and became fascinated with the challenge of counselling these young patients. She is, today, specializing in their psychological care, which serves as the topic for her latest book. *On Children and Death* explores the psychological world of the dying child with its many facets. What is so surprising is that the book doesn't merely cover the psychological aspects of this inner world, but also deals in part with the dying child's psychic perceptions and experiences.

Parapsychologists have long known that some people become extremely psychic when faced with death. Children hardly represent a significant exception to this general rule. Please remember that death has been progressively robbed of its spiritual essence by the consistent mechanization of society, and today it is rare for a patient to return home to die. As I pointed out earlier, people more commonly die in hospital rooms, often unconscious, and usually hooked up to several life-support systems. Luckily, though, Dr Kübler-Ross refuses to champion this impersonal approach and lack of regard for the dying person. She prefers to counsel the dying wherever they remain most comfortable, and she has gradually rediscovered the psychic world of dying children through this practice. She reports openly about this inner world in *On Children and Death*. Children seem intuitively conscious of death and sense its presence whether it comes from disease or from sudden accident.

'One couple shared the story of their little eight-year-old girl who died from a freak accident during a trip overseas,' reports Dr Kübler-Ross, 'and how they missed the cues that they might have been better off not going on the trip at all.'

The little girl was killed when she fell and struck her head. Her parents rushed her to a hospital, but the facility was several miles away and the child survived for only 20 minutes. Later the parents realized that their daughter had intuitively sensed her death. Even during the flight the child was seen writing a thank-you note to the family's (future) hosts. She had never written such a note before. She then gave the letter to her sister, asking the girl to deliver it in her stead. She seemed to realize she wouldn't live to deliver the letter personally.

Remarkable, too, is a letter Dr Kübler-Ross received from a similarly distraught parent. Two days before her daughter was killed in a traffic mishap, the correspondent took the girl to dinner. During the meal they discussed their future, and the girl's mother expressed some concern regarding her daughter's declining school grades. That's when the girl suddenly said that it simply didn't matter. 'My life is almost over,' she explained to her startled mother. She expressed herself in a disarmingly matter-of-fact style.

What was even more bizarre was the way the girl obviously *prepared* for her coming death, since she left significant clues for the mother.

'She spent the last couple of days ironing everything,' the mother wrote in her letter to Dr Kübler-Ross. 'I couldn't believe the order in her room . . . This is a fifteen year old child, you know. I was just amazed. And she didn't take any identification with her [the day of the accident], and so I see it as an act of love because she knew. She knew when she left to go in the car that she would not be coming home again; she didn't want me to be awakened at one in the morning to be told that my daughter had died, and I didn't find out until 3 o'clock the next day.'

These important comments become clearer when the entire letter is read. The child always took her ID with her when she left the house, so this singular oversight was significant in the mother's opinion. She left the ID by her bedside right next to her diary, and when her mother explored further she found an important passage inscribed in the book. The message was written for her benefit, and it exhorted her to self-heal the pain she felt. The girl obviously expected her mother to find the passage after her death.

Children's experiences with the afterlife

The fact that children are sensitive to the coming of death is not Dr Kübler-Ross's only discovery, for the psychic world of the dying child is more complex.

She cites additional cases where children suddenly began talking about death, reincarnation, and other spiritual issues just before life-threatening accidents. These cases do not always represent simple precognitions or intuitions of death, though, for sometimes the children actually received some kind of spiritual revelation concerning their future state. The most sensational letter the psychiatrist ever received came from a parent on the East Coast and fits directly into this category. She explained to Dr Kübler-Ross that her daughter woke up early one morning in a state of extreme euphoria and excitement. She had slept in her mother's bed that night, and she woke her by spontaneously shaking and hugging the sleepy parent.

'Mom, Mom!' she kept saying, 'Jesus told me I'm going to heaven! I enjoy to go to heaven [sic], Mama, and it's all beautiful and gold and silver and shiny, and Jesus and God are there.'

The girl was talking so quickly and excitedly that her mother couldn't remember the entire speech.

'It was affected mostly by her excitement,' the correspondent wrote to Dr Kübler-Ross. '[My daughter] was by nature a calm, almost contemplative child, extremely intelligent, but not a child much given to wildness, bounding-about-silliness that many four-year-olds get. She was verbally skilled and very precise with her speech. To find her so excited that she was stammering and tripping over her words was very unusual. In fact, I don't remember *ever* seeing her in such a state, not at Christmas, birthdays, or the circus.'

The mother tried to calm the child, but the little girl's enthusiasm couldn't be quashed. She kept talking of the angels, the jewels she saw in heaven, and the beings she would meet there. Finally, and almost in despair, the child's mother reasoned with her the best she could.

'If you went to heaven, I'd miss you,' she explained. 'And I'm glad you had such a happy dream, but let's slow down and relax a minute, OK?'

But the girl ignored her and kept talking about her experience. 'It was *not* a dream' she insisted, 'it was *real*.' She emphasized the claim in that dejected way little children sometimes do. She said further that she would take care of her mother from heaven. This conversation continued for several minutes before the child finally relented, went out to play, and wasn't seen for the rest of the day. Some time later in the afternoon the girl was found murdered. Her life came to its tragic end seven hours after she received the revelation.

The subject of dying children and their psychic world will probably depress many people. We usually feel bitterness when a child's life is so suddenly cut short—either by accident or as a result of diseases such as leukaemia. But I think there is a spiritually uplifting side to this dark picture. Dr Kübler-Ross's cases indicate that some power was preparing these children for their deaths, and the children seemed intent on sharing this information with their parents. In fact, this process of sharing seems to be a consistent feature of such cases—i.e. death comes to those prepared for it. Because I personally believe in a life after death, it is difficult for me to feel too bitter when a child dies. My feelings are based on cases similar to Dr Kübler-Ross's already placed in parapsychology's rich literature. Take this last case published by the psychiatrist, for instance. Though the murder was both tragic and senseless, the child openly welcomed her death and looked forward to her future life in the beyond.

This fascinating and uplifting case brings us to Dr Kübler-Ross's second important finding on children and death. The psychological process of dying can be spiritually edifying for us, and the psychiatrist has collected several cases reminiscent of those reports previously published by Dr William Barrett and Professor James Hyslop. While conducting her interviews and therapy, Dr Kübler-Ross is primarily concerned with helping dying children accept and deal with life's end. Sometimes, though, she finds her work hampered by the family's primary care physician. Physicians (even today) remain reluctant to tell their patients the sad truth concerning their terminal illnesses. Because of their perhaps understandable bias, they have at times refused to let Dr Kübler-Ross work with her clients in a completely open fashion. She feels that these children intuitively know when they're dying, however, and don't really need to be specifically shielded from the fact. The dedicated psychiatrist has stayed by the bedside of these young patients sometimes to the end of their short lives. What she has experienced could serve as a lesson to the medical profession in general.

'Shortly before children die there is often a very "clear moment" as I call it,' writes Dr Kübler-Ross in *On Children and Death*. 'Those who have remained in a coma since [their] accident or surgery open their eyes and seem very coherent. Those who have had great pain and discomfort are very quiet and at peace. It is in these moments that I asked them if they were willing to share with me what they were experiencing.'

The results of these enquiries eventually contributed to Dr Kübler-Ross's personal belief in spiritual immortality. The psychiatrist was summoned during one such crisis to the bedside of a traffic accident victim. The boy's mother was killed in the crash, but his brother (who was named Peter) survived and was being treated in a different hospital where the facilities included a better burn centre. When the psychiatrist asked her charge whether he felt okay, the boy replied with a surprising comment.

'Yes, everything is all right now,' he told Dr Kübler-Ross. 'Mommy and Peter are already waiting for me.' The little boy gave a contented little smile and slipped back into a coma from which he failed to recover.

'I was quite aware that his mother had died at the scene of the accident, but Peter had not died,' reports the psychiatrist. 'He had been brought to a special burn unit in another hospital severely burnt, because the car caught fire before he was extricated from the wreck. Since I was only collecting data, I accepted the boy's information and determined to look in on Peter. It was not necessary, however, because as I passed the nursing station there was a call from the other hospital to inform me that Peter had died a few minutes earlier.'

Cases such as this resemble the incidents which opened this short survey. Psychologists know that shortly before dying, terminal patients often see welcoming figures coming to greet them. The widespread incidence of this phenomenon was first formally documented in 1961, when Dr Karlis Osis—then a researcher with the New York based Parapsychology Foundation—published his monograph *Deathbed Observations by Physicians and Nurses*. This study reported the results of a survey taken from 5,000 physicians and 5,000 nurses in the United States. Those health care professionals responding to the survey disclosed that their dying patients commonly reported seeing either beautiful landscapes or phantom visitors in their sickrooms. These apparitions usually represented spirits of the dead or were interpreted to be religious figures, such as messengers from heaven and so forth. Later, and after he became research director for the American Society for Psychical Research (also located in New York), Dr Osis decided to expand his research. His goal was to compare deathbed experiences reported from this culture to those reported from another country. So in order to implement this important research, the Latvian-born psychologist conducted similar surveys among physicians and health care professionals in both

America and India. His results proved that those deathbed reports collected in both cultures conformed to consistent patterns. Since few of these patients were taking drugs when the visions occurred, Dr Osis and his collaborators came to believe that their data pointed directly to survival of death.

Despite this prolonged research, however, some psychologists and even parapsychologists still remain sceptical of Dr Osis's conclusions. While deathbed visions and revelations probably don't result from brain dysfunction (such as progressive oxygen starvation), there remains the possibility that these experiences represent a curious form of psychological phenomenon. Some sceptics put forward the theory that the brain can artificially produce such experiences in order to reduce the patient's fear of death. Such visions might help dying patients become reconciled to their fate so that they don't fight a futile battle with their own mortality.

It is for this reason that evidential cases such as those reported by Dr Kübler-Ross are so important. They indicate that the patient *is* experiencing a real visitation—an experience that conventional psychology cannot explain or explain *away*.

'In all the years,' the psychiatrist says in *On Children and Death*, 'that I have quietly collected data from California to Sydney, Australia; from white and black children, aboriginals, Eskimos, South Americans, and Libyan youngsters, every single child who mentioned that someone was waiting for them mentioned a person who had actually preceded them in death, even if by only a few moments. And yet none of these children had been informed of the recent death of the relatives by us at any time. Coincidence? By now there is no scientist or statistician who could convince me that this occurs, as some colleagues claim, as "a result of oxygen deprivation" or for other "rational and scientific" reasons.'

It is because these cases provide such impressive evidence that Dr Kübler-Ross believes in a life after death. She links the importance of deathbed vision cases to the many NDE (near-death experience) reports she has collected from her patients—i.e. people who journeyed into the next world during close brushes with death. This emphasis on the spiritual dimensions of the death experience is reflected in Dr Kübler-Ross's thinking in a third important way. She does not hesitate to collect and publish purported cases of children who *returned* from death to comfort their grieving parents. She writes in her book, for instance, about a mother who returned home one day in total despair. Her little daughter had been sexually assaulted and killed shortly before, which struck fear in the small community where she lived.

Her mother was lying down when a bright light suddenly came through her bedroom window. Within the light appeared her six-year-old child smiling radiantly. The figure disappeared within a few moments but the contact significantly comforted the mother.

'The sight filled her with such peace and love,' says Dr Kübler-Ross, 'that she was in a much better mental condition after this incident than the rest of the still frightened community!'

Dr Kübler-Ross is presently continuing her work into the private worlds of dying children. But she is expanding her work to include the spiritual, psychic, *and* psychological issues uncovered by her research. Probably her best advice, which she repeats consistently in each of her books, is that society should learn to live with death. By accepting that death is more of a psychological potential than some sort of dark enemy, we can learn to let go of the dying and not encumber them with our own fears and denials. Perhaps we can learn to appreciate death as a final chance for our ultimate personal growth. The courage and spiritual fulfilment so many children find during the process of dying represents an important lesson for us. They don't seem to show the fears so many of us display when facing the prospect of death. Dr Kübler-Ross has actually redirected us to a wise and ancient truth first pointed out in the Bible—that when it comes to matters of the spiritual, children can sometimes be our best teachers.

The Harmonies of Heaven

Richard Rolle (1290-1349) has been called the 'father' of British mysticism. He originally studied at Oxford to be a scholar, but decided to follow a religious life and left the college before obtaining a degree. Rolle was a strict contemplative and was highly critical of the established clergy, whom he often roundly rebuked in his writings. He never became licensed as a hermit by the Church, but his mystical writings were very influential in England, and he eventually became the spiritual director of the Cistercian nuns at Hampole, near Dorchester. While he was never canonized, Rolle was widely revered throughout England until the Reformation.

The British mystic's most famous prose is contained in his short book *The Fire of Love*, which dates from 1343. These ruminations rival the burning fervour more typical of the Spanish mystics, and they contain several descriptions of Rolle's spiritual encounters. He believed that deep within the soul lies an inner music that the contemplative can 'hear' while in ecstasy. This music, he explained, was infinitely more beautiful than any earthly sounds. It is obvious from his book that Rolle was not speaking metaphorically and that he often personally heard this music.

'I was sitting in a certain chapel, and while I was taking pleasure in the delight of some prayer or meditation,' he wrote, 'I suddenly felt within me an unwonted and pleasant fire . . . Now from the beginning of this fiery warmth, inestimably sweet, till the infusion of the heavenly, spiritual harmony, the song of eternal praise, and the sweetness of unheard melody, which can be heard and experienced only by one who has received it, and who must be purified and separated from the earth, nine months and some weeks passed away.'

A second description of this fascinating music is offered later in *The Fire of Love*.

'For while I was sitting in the same chapel,' Rolle writes several pages later, 'and was reciting psalms as well as I might before supper, I heard above me the noise of harpers, or rather of singers. And when with all my heart I attended to heavenly things—prayer, I perceived within me, I know not how, a melody and a most delightful harmony from heaven, which abode in my mind. For my thought was straightway changed into a song, and even when praying and singing psalms I gave forth the selfsame sound. Thenceforth I broke out within my soul into singing what previously I had said.'

What exactly was this strange music that Rolle found so enthralling and comforting? Was it some sort of genuine spiritual grace, or was it the result of some form of hallucination from his feverish mind?

In the previous chapter, considerable evidence showing that dying children can sometimes look through death's doorway was cited. They can literally perceive 'properties' of the afterlife. That chapter was not meant to prove that *only* children possess this capability. Many people occasionally experience the higher worlds. This was the conclusion I reached several years ago, when I began studying the type of experiences Richard Rolle placed on record back in the fourteenth century.

The belief that our purely terrestrial music is based on some type of 'cosmic' harmony generated by the Universe or sent to us by God is of long standing, and similar doctrines emerged from several early cultures. The great Greek mathematician and philosopher Pythagoras (582-507 BC) first popularized the concept in the West with his doctrine of the 'music of the spheres'—celestial music produced by the spinning of the planets and other heavenly bodies. While most modern scholars believe that Pythagoras was speaking metaphorically, it is possible that he once had a spiritual experience similar to Richard Rolle's. The belief that the heavens produce their own personal music is not merely a Western philosophical tenet, for the same concept crops up in Eastern philosophy as well. According to some schools of yoga, there exists a life stream in the Universe that expresses itself through cosmic sounds, into which a person can enter during meditation. The music expressed within this life stream is called *Nad* or *Nada*, with the final vowel remaining silent.

To the best of my knowledge, the first detailed description of this doctrine offered in Occidental literature was published in 1939 by Julian Johnson in his book *The Path of the Masters*. Dr Johnson was a keen student of Eastern philosophy and explained that *Nad* is 'the giant symphony out of which all other symphonies flow. It is the primal music of the Universe. Every musical chord of this world is

an echo of that primal chord . . . the all-creative NADA is that sound
out of which all other sounds arise, while at the same time its heavenly
strains linger in all material worlds as echoes of the original melody.'

The British scholar notes, however, that this music isn't heard
through the physical ears, but through some inner perceptual faculty.
He also notes in *The Path of the Masters* that a similar concept exists
in Islamic mysticism, where the cosmic music is called the *Sultan-
al-Azkar.*

First-hand reports of the Nad

The fundamental cohesiveness and consistency of these metaphysical doctrines first sparked my interest in 1968 when I was a college
student in Los Angeles studying music. Even though I planned to
enter the music business professionally, my true and consuming
interests were parapsychology and mysticism and I constantly read
up on the subjects. I first read the Julian Johnson book during this
time, when my colleague Raymond Bayless lent me his copy.
Raymond thought I'd be interested in the *Nad* doctrine because of my
musical background, and I was surprised when he explained that his
interest in the subject stemmed from a personal experience. It seems
that he once heard the music himself while living in Los Angeles.
Unlike the experiences of Richard Rolle in the fourteenth century,
however, his encounter was spontaneous and didn't result from
meditation or other similar spiritual exercises.

The following report is Mr Bayless's description of the incident,
which he prepared for me in 1968 for my files:

> One evening after I had gone to bed and was still awake and fully
> conscious (I was about thirteen years of age), I heard apparently in the
> distance the sound of what I believed to be a radio playing. At first the
> music—at the very beginning I realized that it was music I was hearing—
> was barely heard, but it steadily gained in volume until it was clearly and
> distinctly heard, and it then diminished until it faded out completely.
> It was impossible to estimate the duration of the incident but I would
> guess that no more than a few minutes actually passed. It was also
> impossible to locate the music in space.
>
> I was interested in music greatly, but at the time possessed no 'formal'
> knowledge of type or origin. In spite of this lack, I became completely
> aware that the music was totally unearthly and inconceivably beautiful
> and majestic. The greatest music on earth, be it Brahms or Bach, is
> nothing but an inharmonious jangle of crude sounds by comparison.
> It was literally celestial and at the time I believed it to be associated with
> religious matters, and I still believe this to be so. It seemed to be pro-

duced by vast numbers of players, singers; I do not know, but the sense of a great number of units was felt. I cannot say that the music was vocal or that it was instrumental; it was on an inconceivably higher level than such distinction, and all that can be said is that it was incredibly beautiful, clearly superhuman, and could not possibly originate from earthly instruments and voices. In spite of the time that has passed—I am almost 49—the memory of the experience is powerful and unforgettable.

I was doubly surprised when Raymond told me that he knew somebody else personally familiar with the phenomenon!

It turned out that this friend was a gifted psychic with whom he experimented during the 1950s. Attila von Sealay (simply called Art by his friends) originally hailed from New York and first developed his remarkable powers while studying yoga. Never interested in becoming a professional psychic, Art earned his living in the photography business until his retirement in the early 1970s. Since I had previously met Mr von Sealay, I lost little time in asking him to contribute his personal experience with the 'music of the spheres' for my files. It is interesting that his experience took place while he was still living in New York, long before his psychic gifts developed:

It was approximately during the mid-1930s as near as I can remember. I was very much the materialist at this time . . . a complete nonbeliever in anything psychic, spiritistic, or religious. I was walking down a hill smoking a cigar when suddenly I began to hear faint music in the distance. However, instead of actually being in the distance it was in my ears, in both ears, sounding as does stereo today . . . It seemed to be in my head. I just stood still and the music welled up into my consciousness; this is the only way that I can describe it. I became overwhelmed by it. I could not distinguish any particular musical instruments or any particular melody and I could not identify any human voices. I just stood there and the tears came into my eyes and I think that I became entranced, for at least ten minutes. I was oblivious to a crowd of people around me but I only became aware of them when I recovered from this state. There is no way of describing the music except to say that I was overwhelmed by something so majestic that any music heard here on earth is nothing, absolutely nothing in comparison to it.

The two cases contributed to my files by Raymond and Mr von Sealay were certainly interesting enough, but they hardly constituted a case collection! So I decided to explore the subject further by amassing more cases. It was probably more than coincidence that, the same week I made this decision, I received a surprising letter from Washington State. It came from a woman in Edmonds who, having read something

I had written, wanted to share some of her psychic experiences with me. During the course of her long letter, Mrs Grace Russell mentioned that she had once heard 'beautiful music coming from nowhere, divine music' and wondered if I was familiar with such a phenomenon!

I certainly couldn't pass up the opportunity, so I asked Mrs Russell to send me the complete story of her experience. She sent me a return letter nine days later, in which she detailed the incident.

It was very early one summer's morning that I heard the music. I had, if memory serves me, slept very soundly, as was usual with me. But suddenly I was awake and there was music, wonderful music, coming in through the only open window in the room. This room was on the first floor of a small house. Others in the house were asleep. All was quiet within. I got up, went to the window, and knelt before it looking into the morning light. I saw the large house across the way, perhaps fifty feet away. A widow and her daughter lived in this house. Neither cared for music. The music could not have come from there. It came from the air outside the window. It poured in, seemingly against my face as though some of the musicians were as close as ten feet from me—or so it seemed at the time and so it seems in memory.

I felt spellbound. I did not try to move. But I listened, and this is what I heard: *A very large group of instruments being played in a way I had never heard music played before.* It was as though the instruments were not far apart, but close together, at least that is the impression that I got.

Speaking retrospectively, Mrs Russell tried to describe the mysterious essence of the music:

I have thought about this music with sincere effort, trying to decide what instruments must have played it, but I have never come to a conclusion other than I did not know then and do not now. No one instrument played solo at any time. All played in unison. All played as one. But I felt there were many because of the variety of tones. *There were no wild clashes of sound, no beating of drums, no shrill high tones.* But there was definite melody, wonderful harmony. Back of the melody, which seemed an endless song without words, I heard a deep roaring sound something like the ocean's roar. This was not louder than the rest, but it was there. The melody seemed to be carried by a *great* many instruments of high pitch expertly played. This music was of an intensity most unusual. It had meaning and great beauty. Not charm as some music, but a beauty that enthralled me.

As experienced by many other people graced with hearing *Nad*, the music reached a climax and then softened—dying out in the distance as if the celestial musicians were floating higher into the heavenly realms.

With this third case contributed to my files, I decided to implement a full-scale search for similar cases within the combined literature of parapsychology, Western mysticism, and Oriental religion. Raymond Bayless helped me, and together we searched through every issue of *Fate* magazine back to 1950. Several independent reports of this cosmic music had been contributed to the publication's 'True Mystic Experiences' and 'My Proof of Survival' sections, where readers regularly reported their personal psychic encounters. But I still needed more cases. Finally I decided to write brief letters both to *Fate* and to the well-known British publication *Psychic News* in which I described my interest in the phenomenon and specifically requested readers to send me details of their first-hand experiences.

The result was an impressive batch of letters from both the United States and England. While many of them were rather eccentric (to put it kindly), several intelligent and sober witnesses stepped forward to describe their personal experiences. Some of these were identical to the reports submitted to me by Bayless, von Sealay, and Mrs Russell. The percipients usually claimed that the sounds surpassed even the music of the great Romantic masters, and that it invariably faded into the distance.

Nad cases related to death

I soon learned that the critical study of this celestial music did not begin with my own survey. For when I started looking for *Nad* cases within psychical research's historical literature, I found that several cases in which the dying heard this same music had been collected by earlier researchers in Great Britain and Italy. Several reports had been collected by Ernesto Bozzano in his 1923 monograph *Les Phénomènes psychiques au moment de la mort*, while similar incidents were discussed by Sir William Barrett in his unfinished book *Death-bed Visions*, published in 1926, to which I referred in the previous chapter.

These cases didn't impress me initially, however, since it was impossible to evaluate them. The percipients were usually close to death, so perhaps they either imagined the music or suffered from hallucinations caused by their illnesses. But the deeper I delved into those cases, the more impressive they became, since Barrett, in particular, published some incidents in which *several* people heard the music in the dying person's room!

It is unfortunate that he published reports of only a slim handful of these cases, mostly drawn from the publications of the Society for Psychical Research issued during the 1880s and 1890s. My favourite of these reports concerned the clinical death experience of a British gentleman named John Britton, an intelligent but deaf-mute witness dying in his family home from rheumatic fever. Because his hands were extremely swollen, he could no longer signal to his relatives, and everyone expected him to die. The patient's brother-in-law, Mr S. Allen, joined the household vigil when he was summoned by the family doctor. He was the first person in the household to hear the music, when he and his wife heard beautiful singing while staying in the room directly below Britton's chambers. They determined that it came from upstairs but could find no normal source for it.

Mr Allen later stated in writing:

> We found Jack lying on his back with his eyes fixed on the ceiling, and his face lighted up with the brightest of smiles. After a little while Jack awoke and used the words 'Heaven' and 'beautiful' as well as he could by means of his lips and facial expression. As he became more conscious he also told us in the same manner that his brother Tom and his sister Harriet were coming to see him. This we considered very unlikely as they lived some distance off, but shortly afterwards a cab drove up from which they alighted. They had sent no intimation of their coming, nor had anyone else. After Jack's partial recovery, when he was able to write or converse upon his fingers, he told us that he had been allowed to see into Heaven and to hear most beautiful music.

The fact that the witness 'saw' his relatives coming implies that he experienced some sort of out-of-body experience, which he obviously survived.

The original records of this case were collected by the Rev. L. A. Milford, the master of Haileybury College, who turned them over to the Society for Psychical Research. Since both the primary witness and his wife heard the music, it is difficult to maintain that Mr Allen's perceptions were simply hallucinations.

Some of the cases Sir William Barrett included in his *Death-bed Visions* read even more impressively, since occasionally several people have reported similar music from such deathbed scenes! The physicist even published the statement of a physician who heard the music while waiting for an elderly patient to expire.

When I undertook my own case collection towards the end of 1968, I was hoping to find some similar contemporary cases of collectively perceived psychic music heard in sick-rooms. Such cases would constitute an important confirmation of Bozzano's and Barrett's earlier studies. But I'm afraid this goal was never realized, since none of my informants reported cases similar to those wonderful Victorian reports. Looking back on my case collection today, however, I'm really not surprised by this. It didn't dawn on me in 1968 that people today don't die the way they did in Victorian times. In those days, a sick or elderly person usually died a comfortable death at home, often surrounded and supported by both family and friends. The love and intimacy of the parting moments probably gave rise to extraordinary displays of psychic phenomena—such as significant outbreaks of psychic music with the soul's passing. But today the situation is very different, since roughly 80 per cent of people die in sterile hospital rooms—usually hooked up to life-support systems and deserted even by the medical staff. People who expire in a hospital setting usually die by themselves, often without the support of their close relatives and friends.

The fact that I didn't find any deathbed cases in my contemporary collection of *Nad* cases probably stems from changes within the sociology of the death experience, and has little bearing on the objective existence of deathbed music.

But even though I couldn't replicate William Barrett's research, my 1968 survey did reveal some surprises of its own.

Nad and the out-of-body experience

The most significant single finding I made was that this music— whatever its nature—is particularly heard by people during out-of-body experiences. While it has been described in various ways by different people, the other-worldly beauty of the harmonies is often mentioned, and I traced such reports back to the turn of the century. Probably the earliest case I found in the literature was published in 1918, some 50 years before my own research was undertaken. The report was published by J. Arthur Hill, an early member of the Society for Psychical Research, in his excellent book *Man Is A Spirit*:

About five years ago I woke from sleep to find 'myself' out of the body. I was conscious of two places—in a feeble degree, in the body which was lying in bed on its left side; and to a far greater degree, away from the body (far away it seemed), surrounded by white opaque light and in a state of absolute happiness and security.

The whole of my personality lay 'out there' even to the replica of the body—which like the body, lay also on its left side. I was not conscious of leaving the body, but woke up out of it. It was not a dream, for the consciousness was an enhanced one, as superior to the ordinary waking state as that is to the dream state. After lying in this healing light *I became conscious of what, for want of the better term, I must call music; gentle and sweet it was as the tinkling of snapping water in a rocky pool and it seemed to be all about me.* I saw no figure, nor wished to, the contentment was supreme. *The effect of these sounds was unutterably sweet,* and I said to myself, 'This must be the voice of God.' I could not endure the happiness, but lost consciousness there and returned unconscious to the body and woke next morning as though nothing had happened. (Emphasis added.)

This early case is nearly identical to several I collected between 1968 and 1969. The following incident, for example, was first given to me by Mr Louis Nelson, whom I met during a lecture I gave in 1968 to the 'experimental college' of UCLA. Mr Nelson wanted to speak to me because I had mentioned my interest in psychic music cases. When he explained that his mother (Mrs Emma Powell) once heard the music, I expressed my interest and he contacted her for me. Since she didn't live in California, she kindly sent me a tape-recording describing her experience:

I had an out-of-the-body experience in 1926 in November. My daughter was a baby, I had been ill but was out of bed and doing pretty well. But this night, I lay down to go to sleep and I left my body and went straight up, very slowly, *but all the time I could hear music and the higher I got the louder the music became. It was the most beautiful music I have ever heard.* But I could hear my baby crying and it seemed like she was a way, way off, and I asked the Lord to let me come back, she needed me. And instantly I was back in my body, and then I could feel my mother and father's hands working with me and saying that I was cold and that they could hardly find a pulse. I knew I had been close to heaven or another world.

A further report closely resembling Mrs Powell's was sent to me from Great Britain by Dr Robert Crookall, whom I consulted on the project. Dr Crookall was a noted British geologist interested in the out-of-body experience, who between 1964 and 1971 wrote several books on the subject. This report had been previously sent to him by Mrs Kathleen Snowden, whose musical out-of-body experience took place when she was a teenager:

I was only sixteen years old, ill in bed. I told mother I thought I was going to faint . . . I felt myself drifting away from her. Suddenly I realized a feeling of great excitement, wonder and delight surpassing anything I had ever experienced as I felt my body weightless and floating upwards in a golden glow towards a wonderful light around hazy welcoming figures *and the whole air was filled with beautiful singing.*

I floated joyfully towards the voice and the light and then I heard my mother's voice calling me . . . My whole being revolted against going back. Her voice grew nearer and to my great distress, I felt myself slipping away from that wonderful light and merging into a dull black cloud where my heaviness of body returned . . . My mother thought I had died; I had seemed to stop breathing . . . I am now forty-two and the wonder of it still remains.

Of course, the experiences reported by both Mrs Powell and Kathleen Snowden would today be called near-death experiences or NDEs. NDEs are out-of-body experiences which take place when the percipient is nearly dead or perceives himself in a life-threatening situation. Some people undergoing NDEs even experience themselves travelling to the Great Beyond where they might meet their deceased relatives. Music is often heard during these otherworldly journeys.

The existence of the NDE was first popularized in 1975 by Dr Raymond Moody in his famous book *Life After Life.* The result of Dr Moody's success was that several researchers began publishing NDE reports. The most notable of these were published by Dr Kenneth Ring in his *Life at Death*, by Dr Michael Sabom in his *Recollections of Death*, and by Margot Grey in her *Return from Death*. It is notable that every one of these researchers—including Dr Moody—described NDE cases in which the 'music of the spheres' was heard. None of them, however, specifically commented on these heavenly sounds. The only brief exception was Ms Grey, who noted in her British study of 41 cases that 11 per cent of her informants reported this music.

Explaining the experience

By the middle of 1969, I had amassed over 100 reports from people who had experienced the 'music of the spheres', and I included these cases in my first book on the subject *Nad, a Study of Some Unusual Other-World Experiences.* I continued collecting cases when several other individuals sent me their personal reports after reading the book. So in 1972 I published a second book, *Nad, Vol. 2: A Psychic Study of the 'Music of the Spheres',* which incorporated 58 further cases.

So what is this music?

After pondering this question for several years, my general conclusion is that the metaphysical speculations of the Greek philosophers and the Eastern sages probably point obliquely to a great spiritual truth. Perhaps the 'music of the spheres' is some sort of property of the higher spheres—spiritual realms existing within the

Universe that interweave with the physical world in which we live. Perhaps this is the realm we enter when we die. When a person comes close to death, perhaps a rift opens between our terrestrial dimension and the Great Beyond, so that the patient can momentarily experience its pleasures and music. People sharing the intimacy of death with a close friend or relative could perhaps share in this experience. People enjoying out-of-body experiences might perceive the music, since a similar rift in the fabric of reality could easily take place during these mysterious excursions.

Finally, some lucky people—such as Richard Rolle—may simply be highly attuned to the higher spiritual realm of existence and can spontaneously experience its properties.

Whatever its nature, the 'music of the spheres' makes a considerable impression on the people who hear it. Their reports represent but a dim shadow of what the music must really sound like. One of my correspondents probably summed up her reaction to the music the best, for she explained to me that she would gladly die just to hear those harmonies of heaven for a second time. Perhaps each of us will personally hear these rapturous sounds when we make this great spiritual transition.

7

Reincarnation
Comes to the West

One of my best friends (let's call him Jay) survived a terrible ordeal in his teenage years. While his friends were dreaming of fast cars and Saturday night dates, Jay was preoccupied with strange 'memories' that kept surfacing and bothering him. He thought these were recollections of his previous incarnation in medieval England. The recollections were harmless enough and didn't interfere with his personal or scholastic life—until he made a fatal mistake. He detailed his memories to his parents. They were less than tolerant of their son's preoccupation and dragged him to an in-patient mental hospital, where they placed him under a 14-day psychiatric hold.

Luckily for my friend, the unit's psychiatrist was more open-minded. He listened to the story and freely admitted that he couldn't explain the reincarnation memories Jay was experiencing. But he realized there was certainly nothing wrong with his charge and released him when the two weeks were up. He recommended, however, that Jay could not talk to his parents about his strange experiences any further!

This little story demonstrates two important points concerning reincarnation beliefs in the United States. It shows that contemporary American children sometimes recall their (purported) previous incarnations, and also that few parents seem capable of handling such situations.

While it is well known that children in countries such as Burma, Thailand, Sri Lanka, and India often report such past-life recollections, similar cases seem rare and unusual in Western Europe and the United States. The reason is probably that reincarnation is a doctrine both foreign and bizarre to our culture. It is also a fact that most scientific research into reincarnation-type cases has focused on reports from Asia and the Middle East. This well-known research has been the special project of Ian Stevenson of the University of Virginia, who has spearheaded the study of children who recollect their previous lives in those cultures.

Despite this paucity of cases in the West, reports of children who recall their purported past lives come to light every so often. Probably the most famous historical example was reported by Dr Carmelo Samona of Italy, whose five-year-old daughter Alexandrina died on 15 March 1910. The child's death foreshadowed several psychic events in the physician's household. Three days after the little girl expired, for instance, Mrs Samona dreamt that the child came to her to reveal that she would be reborn to them. Since Mrs Samona suffered from a medical condition that made a future pregnancy unlikely, the couple dismissed the dream.

Even though they had little interest in reincarnation, it certainly seemed that some emissary from the spiritual realm was trying to contact them. Poltergeist phenomena (mostly consisting of raps) bombarded their house, which preceded the surprising information that Mrs Samona was pregnant—with twins! Two infant daughters were born to the couple on 22 November, and as they grew, the younger girl began resembling her deceased sibling more and more, both physically and psychologically. Like her deceased sister, the young girl—whom her parents renamed Alexandrina—suffered from hyperaemia of the left eye, slight sebhorrhoea of the right ear, and some facial asymmetry. She was also left-handed, while the other twin shared none of these problems or characteristics.

The physical resemblances between the two girls were surpassed by the psychic connections between them. In his detailed and careful report on the case, Dr Samona notes that the newly-born Alexandrina shared several behavioural traits with her deceased sister, including her calm disposition, which contrasted strikingly with that of her twin.

It is worth noting that this calm temperament and these particular occupations were special characteristics of the first Alexandrina . . . Alexandrina is indifferent to dolls and prefers to play with children of her own age; a preference which was equally noticeable with the other Alexandrina. Like her, too, she is always anxious that her little hands should be clean and insists on having them washed if they are in the least degree dirty. Like her predecessor again, she shows a singular repugnance for cheese and will not touch soup if it has the least taste of cheese in it.

Dr Samona proceeded to explain:

When she has a chance of opening the chest of drawers in the bedroom it is a great amusement to her to pull out the stockings and to play with them. This was also a passion of the other Alexandrina. We have also noticed that this one, like the other, always insists on putting one of these stockings—naturally a great deal too large for her—on her little foot and walking about the room with it on.

Another noteworthy fact is that the first Alexandrina, when about two years old, began to alter people's names, apparently out of sheer caprice. For example she turned Angelina into Angelanna or Angelona, while Caterina, the name of her aunt, became Caterana or Caterona. The second Alexandrina showed the very same peculiarity at the same age, which astonished us all.

The climax to the case took place when little Alexandrina began recalling significant incidents from the life of her departed sister. The most impressive of these episodes occurred when the family went to Monreale and were sightseeing. While Mrs Samona was discussing the significance of the local sites, Alexandrina suddenly claimed that she had visited the city before and mentioned seeing some 'little red priests' and a lady 'who had horns'.

This was true enough, but only if the information related to a visit the first Alexandrina had made. Dr and Mrs Samona had taken her to Monreale before her death, where they encountered some Greek priests wearing black robes with red ornaments. Accompanying them on the trip was a friend who was travelling to Palermo to consult some physicians. She suffered from disfiguring excrescences on her forehead and she wanted them surgically removed.

A recent case reported from England
A remarkably similar case was reported from Great Britain during the 1950s, which has since become a classic in the literature on reincarnation. This unusual case concerned two children tragically killed in a terrible mishap in 1957 in Hexham, Northumberland, when a driver under the influence of pills crashed her car on to the pavement killing Joanna (aged 11) and Jacqueline Pollack (aged 6) instantly. Mr Pollack was a strong believer in reincarnation, even though his wife was sceptical of the doctrine, so it was with special happiness that he learned his wife was pregnant in early 1958. Even though medical opinion indicated to the contrary, Mr Pollack was sure that his wife would bear twin daughters, and that Joanna and Jacqueline would return to earth. The expectant's father's first prediction was correct and his wife gave birth on 4 October 1958 to two daughters, whom they named Gillian and Jennifer.

It didn't take long for Mr Pollack to discover evidence linking the girls to his deceased daughters, for the younger twin (Jennifer) bore two birthmarks which corresponded to similar marks Jacqueline previously possessed. Even more impressive was a mark on the girl's forehead that matched a scar on the previous child, the result of a fall she suffered while playing. The twin girls eventually began to talk of their previous lives and even recognized some of their former toys.

Of course, evidence—like beauty—is oftentimes restricted to the eyes of the beholder. Since Mr Pollack had such an emotional investment in the possible rebirth of his daughters, it is difficult to know whether he could have 'leaked' some of this information to his children.

Some incidents in the case seem to be better documented, however. The Pollack family moved from Hexham before the girls were a year old, and they didn't return there for four years. But even so, while travelling through the town the twins spontaneously and correctly mentioned a school and some swings in a park before the places came into view. The girls also purportedly 'inherited' behavioural characteristics from their progenitors, sometimes becoming phobic when they saw oncoming vehicles while playing. On other occasions the parents would catch the girls discussing their past-life deaths in disturbing but graphic detail. On one occasion, for example, Mrs Pollack left the children in their playroom. When she returned later to make sure they were safe, she found them sitting together with Gillian cradling Jennifer's head with her hands. To her utter horror, she heard Gillian saying, 'The blood's coming out of your eyes. That's where the car hit you.' Such incidents greatly contributed to the mother's growing unease with the children's memories and their other links to her deceased daughters.

When the girls began to mature, their reincarnation memories faded and never returned. Today they are sceptical of their own case, though they openly discuss it with researchers interested in the reincarnation issue.

While a provocative case, the supposed psychic return of the Pollack girls is complicated by a number of problems which possibly limit its evidential value. Mentioned earlier was the sensory leakage problem—i.e. that the daughters could have picked up and internalized information concerning their progenitors from Mr Pollack, who was hoping and searching for evidence supporting his reincarnation beliefs. That the two little girls could have been internalizing information *telepathically* drawn from their parents is also a possibility. There is even the slim chance that, somehow, the information they possessed concerning the earlier Pollack children was genetically programmed into their brains during Mrs Pollack's pregnancy. But most critical investigators feel that the best explanation is that Mr Pollack unintentionally created it through his intense wishful thinking. A sceptical treatment of the case which follows this line of reasoning is offered by Ian Wilson in his book *Mind Out of Time?* While offering a reasonably complete summary of the case, the British researcher writes that 'despite all the openness and honesty which John Pollack displays when being interviewed, he cannot by any stretch of the imagination be regarded as an unbiased witness'. He then goes on to say that Mr Pollack 'is prepared to go to almost any lengths to prove his reincarnation beliefs, which seriously limits his reliability as an objective observer'.

Of course, Mr Wilson never considers that this exaggerated zeal resulted from Mr Pollack's personal experience. It is possible that his earlier convictions were more temperate and his observations perfectly valid.

Dr Ian Stevenson, for example, has written favourably on the Pollack case and has been following the girls' subsequent development for several years. Such cases must be refreshing for him, since the University of Virginia psychiatrist has conducted most of his research in countries where belief in reincarnation is strong. He has authored five casebooks on his better cases, summarizing reports of children with past-life recollections from Burma, Thailand, Sri Lanka, and other foreign lands. But more recently, he has begun publishing reincarnation-type cases reported from the United States. These cases generally lack the strong evidential features typical of foreign reports. Rarely, for instance, have the parents in these American cases taken pains to verify their children's recollections. Sometimes the reports don't even come to light until several years later, when investigating them is practically impossible.

Dr Stevenson has, nonetheless, reported on four recent incidents in his book *Children Who Remember Previous Lives*, published in 1987. The following three short summaries are taken from that source.

The case of Roberta Morgan

This case came to light in 1971 when Roberta's mother first contacted Dr Stevenson concerning her daughter's experiences. It seems that some years previously, little Roberta often talked of possessing 'another mummy and daddy' whom she wished to see. Her desire to establish contact with her 'other' parents often bordered on desperation. Roberta had been born in 1961 and was nearly 10 years old when Mrs Morgan contacted the psychiatrist from their home in Minnesota. The girl's past-life talk began when she was two-and-a-half years old, even though reincarnation had never played a role in the family's religious beliefs.

Despite her initial scepticism, Mrs Morgan told Dr Stevenson that sometimes her daughter behaved 'like an adopted child with full memory of her [previous] parents and their house'. She even gave precise details as to the location of her previous residence—i.e. on the top of a rise on a farm. The girl also presumably inherited some behavioural features from her past life and was immediately drawn to horses and fearlessly petted them when she encountered them. She explained to her surprised parents that she'd 'been on horses lots of times'.

Probably the most impressive features of the case occurred when Mrs Morgan and her daughter were driving outside of town. Roberta spontaneously recognized a dirt road and exclaimed that it led to her previous home. But her mother was scared that her daughter's descriptions could be correct, and refused to drive up the road. The child complained about the incident for several days and Mrs Morgan later came to regret her decision.

The child's memories eventually became extremely detailed. She spoke of her former toys, and her (past-life) mother's physical characteristics and cooking habits. Sometimes she interrupted her parents' conversation, reports Stevenson, 'with remarks indicating familiarity with some topic or object of which, in her mother's opinion, she could have known nothing'.

Several unusual and inexplicable features also cropped up. Roberta was inclined to dress like a boy, even though she never explicitly stated she had previously lived in that gender. Nor did the girl ever talk of her previous death, contrary to the pattern that emerges repeatedly in non-Western reincarnation cases. She would only say that she was forced to leave her previous parents and wanted to return to them. But she could never recall the family's name, which would have helped the Morgans trace them—if they would have taken the time in the first place. Since they were practising Christians, the couple had little tolerance for Roberta's incessant talk and Mrs Morgan even began punishing her daughter when she continued to talk about her past life.

Roberta stopped speaking of her previous incarnation when she was four years old, which was several years before Dr Stevenson was brought into the case. Mrs Morgan eventually became engrossed with investigating her daughter's recollections, but by the time the psychiatrist was contacted such a goal was practically impossible.

The case of Susan Eastland

Dr Stevenson's investigation of the Susan Eastland case in Idaho dates from 1968, three years before the Roberta Morgan case surfaced. This report seems to represent an interfamily rebirth, since the girl claimed to be the reincarnation of her older sister.

The incidents leading to the case took place in 1961 when Winnie Eastland was killed by a passing car. Mrs Eastland longed for the girl's return, but she was unfamiliar with the reincarnation doctrine. Six months later, however, the girl's sister (Sharon) dreamed that Winnie was returning to them. When Mrs Eastland became pregnant two years later, even her husband began to sense that their deceased daughter was soon to be reborn. His conviction stemmed from an incident in which he 'heard' a subjective voice proclaiming his deceased daughter's imminent rebirth. These bizarre and possibly significant events set the stage, so to speak, for the emergence of little Susan Eastland's early revivifications of her previous life.

Susan began referring (in her parent's opinion) to her past life when she was two years old. When she was asked to give her age, she would consistently respond that she was six years old—i.e. Winnie's chronological age when she was killed. Susan often seemed to behave like the sister she never knew and took an inexplicable interest in two photographs of Winnie in her mother's possession. She invariably claimed that the photographs depicted herself and not her dead sister. She never actually referred to herself by Winnie's name, but when she first began to write, she successfully scribbled the name. Mrs Eastland also explained to Dr Stevenson that Susan sometimes seemed to possess paranormal information linking her to her dead sister.

It seems that, during Winnie's short lifetime, Mrs Eastland possessed a cookie jar with a sculptured cat on the lid. When the children wanted some cookies, they played a game by requesting them—in Mrs Eastland's presence—from the cat. Mrs Eastland would reply in a high-pitched voice (personifying the feline) the number of cookies they were permitted to take. Mrs Eastland packed up the cookie jar when Winnie was killed. But when she unpacked it several years later, she discovered that Susan was familiar with the ritual—even successfully imitating the cat's 'voice' previously used by her mother. While this is perhaps not a strong instance of possible paranormal knowledge, Dr Stevenson points out that it is 'nevertheless harmonious . . . with the interpretation that Susan somehow had access to Winnie's memories'. Whether she picked up the information from her mother's mind or based it on her reincarnation recollections is impossible to say, however.

Susan later surprised her mother by reporting several other events from Winnie's life which she couldn't normally have known. She even knew the nickname of a little boy with whom Winnie liked to play. Mrs Eastland often specifically asked her daughter about episodes from Winnie's life, which sometimes especially prompted the girl's paranormal memories. Such a procedure might suggest that the parent was (perhaps inadvertently) feeding information to her daughter, but Dr Stevenson is sceptical of this explanation for the case. He points out in his report that such a process could perhaps 'encourage an identification with the dead person that would not have happened otherwise. Nevertheless, such questioning, if conducted by a person as vigilant as Mrs Eastland seemed to be, may arouse additional memories without lowering safeguards against normal communication.'

Dr Stevenson kept track of this case for close to a decade, and Susan's final memories of her deceased sister apparently surfaced in 1977, when the psychiatrist was rechecking their details. While talking with her mother in light of a letter from the psychiatrist, Susan recalled a final incident from her previous life. She remembered visiting a bowling alley with her mother and running between the lanes and the food machines. A boy happened to be there and kissed her. This incident was perfectly true, and Mrs Eastland particularly remembered it since her husband became annoyed when informed of the episode.

A final possible paranormal aspect of the case was a small birth-mark on Susan's hip. This mark corresponded in position to an injury suffered by Winnie when she was killed.

The case of Erin Jackson
Erin Jackson lived in a small town in Indiana, where she had been born in 1969. She started talking of a previous life when she was three years old. Dr Stevenson first met the family several years later in 1980, when he visited them.

The child only spoke of her previous incarnation for a year but frequently told her parents that she had been a boy named John. She had lived with her brother James, who liked to dress in black, and with her stepmother, who treated her nicely. While she never offered her past-life family name nor her place of residence, it was clear that she had once lived in a rural location. Erin's identification with her previous life influenced her memories *and* her behaviour, for she evolved into something of a tomboy. She preferred to dress in boy's clothing and felt humiliated when forced into a dress. Even when her conscious memories ceased, the girl still preferred masculine attire. She expressed a desire to learn baseball and become a Cub Scout. Dr Stevenson claims in his report that 'she seemed to know how to read at the age of three, before anyone had taught her. She had a gift for drawing that I judged—after looking at some sketches she had made—unusual for a child of her age. She also composed poems that a much older person might have felt pleased to have written.'

When the psychiatrist finally met her, however, Erin had ceased referring to her previous existence, but her overtly masculine behaviour continued for several more years. Only when she became a teenager did she begin leading a conventional 'feminine' lifestyle.

Both of the girl's parents were Protestants and had no interest in reincarnation. When her daughter began displaying her unusual behaviour, however, Mrs Jackson began reading up on the subject. Though she eventually became tolerant of her daughter's claims, she never encouraged the girls revivications, even though she eventually became a reluctant believer in reincarnation.

A test case reported from Georgia

None of the cases discussed by Dr Stevenson in his *Children Who Remember Previous Lives* is strong from an evidential standpoint. The children had usually finished speaking of their past lives by the time the psychiatrist learned of them. Whether paranormal information was revealed by the children rests on the claims offered by the parents, who were hardly unbiased witnesses. But every so often more evidential cases come to light. The following case, for instance, was reported in 1985 by W. G. Roll and Jeannie Lagle Stewart, a clinical psychologist then working in conjunction with the Psychical Research Foundation in Carrollton, Georgia.

The primary focus of the report was Ginger Waldorf (a pseudonym chosen by the researchers), who was born in a small Ohio town in 1948. The little girl was put up for adoption when she was four, and eventually came to live with a childless couple from a nearby town. By this time, the girl had been neglected and mistreated in a series of foster homes. Ginger eventually evolved into a strongly religious child and began reporting psychic experiences when she was 18 years old, which included a post-mortem visitation from her deceased grandmother's ghost. Her reincarnation memories, however, didn't emerge until she married in 1968. She and her husband were living in another Ohio community when she began suffering from dizzy spells, which she naturally attributed to her pregnancy. But the spells continued even after her child's birth and seemed to reflect a psychiatric/neurophysiological problem.

Ginger's strange symptoms continued over the years 1970-7 while she was trying to re-establish contact with her biological parents. She was living in Texas at this time and the name 'Marietta' kept surfacing in her thoughts. She presumed that this referred to her original first name, but soon learned that nobody familiar with her early life recollected it.

These were frustrating times for Ginger, since her adoptive parents resisted her search for her real parents and her neurological symptoms continued to plague her. She finally decided to undergo hypnotic regression in order to recall her childhood and sought out a clinical psychologist to implement the procedure. It was during this session that the entranced subject explained that Marietta was a town in Ohio, not the name of a person. This revelation led Ginger to visit the city and she seemed immediately familiar with it. She didn't consider this sense of familiarity strange, since she still believed her memories stemmed from her early childhood. The bizarre nature of these early recollections only surfaced in 1980 when she was finally able to establish contact with her real mother and sisters. They failed to corroborate the early memories retrieved under hypnosis, nor were they familar with Marietta. This surprising information led Ginger to think in terms of reincarnation, and she was finally directly to Dr Lendell Braud—a clinical psychologist in Houston extremely familiar with parapsychology. She, in turn, suggested that Ginger contact the Psychical Research Foundation and report her case to them.

The investigation into the case by Jeannie Lagle Stewart and W. G. Roll began in 1984. Roll has long been in charge of the Foundation, and he became primarily interested in verifying the information Ginger could recall, while Jeannie Stewart worked with her therapeutically to help her integrate her past-life recollections.

Roll soon discovered that Ginger recalled a storehouse of information concerning her previous life. She remembered her name (Sarah Jean Jenkins), the name of the street where she had lived, described stores and other sites in historical Marietta, and recollected her death. She also vividly recalled several of her relatives' proper names.

To help facilitate the case, Roll and Stewart conducted a further hypnotic session with their subject on 14 September 1984. She slipped easily into her past existence and 'Sarah Jean Jenkins' communicated with them directly. She described the town near where she lived, spoke of her relatives, and offered several street names. Probably her most specific memory was riding on a paddle-boat, the *Gordon C. Greene*, with its captain (whom she named). She further described her suicide by drowning. Additional details from the Sarah Jean Jenkins lifetime emerged when Ginger was regressed a second time on 27 September.

W. G. Roll and Jeannie Lagle Stewart spent considerable time investigating their subject's recollections. They spoke with several of Ginger's relatives, consulted the Office of Vital Statistics in Marietta (whom Ginger had contacted earlier), and checked with the first psychologist who hypnotically regressed her. The results of their investigation led to their discovery that Ginger's recollections were historically correct, sometimes even down to small details. The street and store names she recalled were eventually traced, and even the existence of the *Gordon C. Greene* was established.

Despite the outcome of the investigation, the reincarnation ordeal was hardly pleasant for Ginger. She was plagued by constant doubts when exploring her past life. Jeannie Stewart and W. G. Roll state in their report:

> Although talkative, Ginger expressed difficulty in finding the right words to describe her experiences. From time to time she would ask if something she had said was 'stupid' or if she was 'bonkers' for having these experiences. In general Ginger appeared to be experiencing anxiety along with the occurrences and needed reassurance and understanding from us. She had reported a period of depression and confusion during her initial search for her biological parents and during her search for events that would match her seeming memories, becoming 'almost obsessed' with the search at times. Ginger's adoptive father and her husband also report Ginger's search at this time as being very disturbing for the family as it was against their wishes. Many of Ginger's questions and comments during the interviews centered on her relationship with her adopted family and her religious views and belief in God.
>
> During the hypnotic regression sessions, Ginger's voice and personality changed noticeably. While assuming the previous personality, her voice became childlike and her personality independent and flippant. Sarah Jean acted with the confidence and security Ginger 'wishes I could be like'.
>
> Ginger reports a phobia of crossing water, although she has had no traumatic experience with water. This aspect would be related to the mode of death of the previous personality . . .

Patterns in American reincarnation cases

The case of Ginger Waldorf is unusual in several respects, since she didn't recall her previous incarnation during her childhood. Her recollections partially emerged spontaneously, but were subsequently elicited (or enhanced) primarily through hypnotic probing. The reincarnation cases reported by Dr Ian Stevenson in his *Children Who Remember Previous Lives* are probably more typical, even though it is impossible to determine the number of children in the United States who recollect past lives.

The fullest statistics parapsychologists have for American rebirth cases were only published in 1983, when Dr Stevenson issued a report on 79 cases from his vast University of Virginia case collection. These reports were not published in the form of case studies. Instead Dr Stevenson published a statistical analysis of the cases by comparing them with the typical pattern of childhood reincarnation cases reported from India, where such cases tend to be more frequently reported. (It is not clear, though, whether childhood cases in India occur more frequently or are just more frequently reported in the press.) This pioneering paper was issued under the title 'American Children Who Claim to Remember Previous Lives' in the *Journal of Nervous and Mental Disease* (Vol. 171, No. 12), which is surely an unusual place for a report on reincarnation!

Most of the cases included in Dr Stevenson's fascinating paper were reported to him by people who were passingly familiar with his work. Some of the other incidents were referrals from interested colleagues. When the psychiatrist looked closely into the backgrounds of these cases, he found the following:

(1) In 16 per cent of the cases, the principal informant (usually a relative) entertained prior beliefs in reincarnation.
(2) In an additional 37 per cent of the cases, Dr Stevenson's primary contact had some interest in the doctrine.
(3) Twenty per cent of the contacts had some general interest in parapsychology.
(4) But 27 per cent of the contacts had little or negligible interest in reincarnation when their cases came to light.

For the remaining 29 per cent of the data base, Dr Stevenson could not determine the family's prior interest in or knowledge of reincarnation.

While the patterns that guide childhood reincarnation cases in both the United States and India are similar, the psychiatrist discovered several subtle differences when these reports were critically examined. It seems that children in contemporary Western culture rarely mention specific people they recall from their previous lives, including their own proper names. Rarely is enough information given in Western cases, in fact, for the child's past-life personality to be historically traced. This problem is compounded by the fact that children in the United States stop speaking about their previous existences sooner than Indian children. (American children stop the references when they are about five years old, while Indian children generally continue talking of reincarnation until they pass six.)

Particularly interesting, too, is the difference in the children's recollections of their previous deaths. Most children in India focus on this traumatic phase of their past lives, with 75 per cent of them spontaneously mentioning the cause of death. But this feature crops up in less than 50 per cent of the American cases. Phobias (such as a fear of water/drowning) usually related to the violent deaths they purportedly suffered in their previous incarnations were evident in both sets of children.

The mystery of cross-gender reincarnation plays an interesting role in childhood reincarnation cases, too. While this phenomenon is exceedingly uncommon in India (representing only 3 per cent of Dr Stevenson's cases), this pattern emerged in 15 per cent of the American reports.

But do these contemporary reports from the United States point to literal reincarnation? Even though their evidential features tend to be weak, Dr Stevenson personally feels that they possibly do point to reincarnation:

> In some Indian cases, the child has made verified statements about a previous life in a family remote geographically from his own. Although most of these cases were not investigated until after the families concerned had met, many were studied within a few weeks or months of their meeting, and in a small number a written record of what the child has said about the previous life had been made before his statements were verified. In many such cases the normal transmission of information has been excluded, or seems improbable, and so it is possible that these Indian children have had genuine memories of a previous life. In view of the similarity of the American cases to the Indian ones in several of their main features, it also seems arguable that some American subjects have had memories of previous lives, but ones that, on the whole, are less abundant and less precise than those occurring among many Indian children.

Dr Stevenson emphasizes that few of these cases seem to result from pure fantasy, but points to the slim possibility:

> It is also possible that only some of the American cases derive from real

memories of previous lives whereas others are fantasies. Many of them have been expressed against the wishes of the child's parents and have frequently involved the child in conflict with his parents. It is also not easy to discern a wish-fulfilling motive in the particular details of most of the previous lives spoken about by these children. As mentioned above, these lives are usually commonplace ones, sometimes lived in less comfortable circumstances than those of the child's family.

While it is clear that reincarnation-type cases sometimes emerge from contemporary culture, it is a shame that the evidence behind them isn't better. The primary problem, as pointed out earlier, is that scientific investigators have rarely been called in to promising cases soon enough by the parents of the children involved.

But metaphysical doctrines such as reincarnation seem to be becoming incredibly popular in the 1980s. The emergence of wide-spread cultural belief in reincarnation might represent a boon for parapsychologists and other scientists or scholars interested in the subject. Cases of children who spontaneously recall their previous lives might be reported by the press more frequently in light of the growing preoccupation with popular metaphysics. Such cases might come to the notice of researchers such as Dr Stevenson sooner. But what the field really needs is *more* researchers interested in reincarnation, and field workers willing to investigate them right on the spot. When these fresh investigations are reported, perhaps the evidence for reincarnation will be strengthened or readily disproved.

Only time will let us know for sure.

PART III
Extradimensional Realities

8

Janice Leslie's UFO Odyssey

I first learned about Mrs Janice Leslie and her strange UFO saga towards the end of 1978. That was during a time when I was growing more and more interested in UFOs and their possible parapsychological significance.

The story of my personal odyssey from conventional parapsychology to exploring the strange byways of the UFO mystery is a complex one. It began when I started looking into the backgrounds of people who report close encounters with UFOs. This project was meant to be a brief diversion from the more formal experimental work in extrasensory perception I was conducting in Los Angeles and New York. I soon discovered that many of these people report previous psychic experiences, and some even claim that poltergeists erupted in their homes soon after their UFO encounters. The possibility that there exists some sort of link between the human psyche and the UFO intelligence couldn't be dismissed. Such observations led me in the late 1970s to begin collecting evidence that perhaps UFOs are literally *created* by the power of the mind. Perhaps at some archetypal level the human race needs to believe in saviours from the sky, which leads us to create the UFO mystery by 'drawing' it from some psychic realm. This general theory was not really original, since several experts on the UFO mystery had previously suggested versions of it, including the great Swiss psychiatrist C. G. Jung. But I was more interested in collecting empirical evidence for the theory than merely raising its possibility.

Some of this evidence came to light when I began investigating UFO abduction cases in 1978—long before the subject became so popular! I had previously been critical of these cases when I wrote on the subject in my book *The Haunted Universe* two years previously (see Chapter 1). In most of the cases reported in the literature before 1980, the witness merely saw a UFO and then suffered a mysterious time-lapse, waking up or regaining consciousness a few hours later. My initial feeling was that these people probably suffered a traumatic black-out when they saw the UFOs and later confabulated (fanta- sized) a 'kidnapping' scenario when hypnotized and regressed back to the scene. I was forced to change my viewpoint, however, when I was invited by a well-known UFO investigator in Los Angeles to work with a few time-lapse witnesses myself. Even though I was careful not to lead these subjects, by using hypnosis I uncovered the same kinds of kidnapping scenarios other investigators had discovered.

But the more I worked with these people, the more uncomfortable I became with the extraterrestrial hypothesis—i.e. that the UFOs they encountered came from some place in outer space. I often found symbolic references in their scenarios that seemed to link their experiences with unconscious conflicts, even though their experi- ences seemed to be obviously real.*

Suffice it to say that by 1979, I was exploring any line of evidence suggesting that UFOs were psychic phenomena generated—perhaps psychokinetically—by or through the mind. This basic approach to the UFO enigma led me to San Francisco to meet with Jeffrey Mishlove, then a doctoral candidate in parapsychology at the Uni- versity of California, Berkeley. Mishlove had been working on a related project, and I travelled to the Bay area to take charge of his files. During our discussions on the UFO problem, my colleague first told me about Mrs Janice Leslie, who had (purportedly) been trained by a psychic in Washington State to make contact with UFOs! She could also predict when and where they would materialize and even summon them from the sky to a limited degree. These claims were difficult to swallow, but they were still fascinating. I found the case especially intriguing because Mrs Leslie's claims closely resembled those of a lady in Massachusetts, who apparently possessed similar powers.†

Some months later I wrote to Mrs Leslie, who lived in a small town in Washington State. I didn't know what to expect, but she turned out to be a competent and extremely intelligent witness who was pre- pared to document her claims. She was an investigator's dream! Luckily for me, she had kept a diary of her experiences, which she

* These cases and my work with UFO abduction witnesses will be chronicled in the following chapter.
† The fascinating case of Mrs Stella Lansing is reported and documented by Dr Berthold Schwarz, a psychiatrist in New Jersey, in the second volume of his *UFO Dynamics* (Moore Haven, Fla.: Rainbow Books, 1983). See also pages 113-16 in my book *The Haunted Universe* (New York: New American Library, 1977).

had turned over to Jeffrey Mishlove in 1978. The documents of the case included complete statements from several witnesses ready to back up her claims. It was in light of these papers that I realized her case represented an important contribution to the UFO mystery. The following events are primarily based on this diary and on related statements which Mrs Leslie kindly permitted me to publish in 1979.

The beginning of the odyssey

Mrs Leslie's story starts on a sad note, since her UFO adventures and encounters began shortly after the death of her husband in 1978. A month later she was taking a vacation in order to enjoy a respite from her home and children. She felt the trip would help her work through her bereavement, and she was staying at a hotel in Portland, Oregon. (Portland is a large but cold city located near the border with Washington State.) One day while having breakfast she saw a notice which Ted Owens, a local psychic and UFO 'contactee', had placed in a local newspaper, offering personal psychic readings, psychic development courses, and related services. Included in these services was a training programme on establishing contact with UFOs and their occupants. Even though Mrs Leslie had never visited a psychic before, she decided to call on him at his home outside Vancouver, Washington, a few miles north of Portland across the state line, where he then lived with his wife and children. She was strangely impressed by the psychic (even though she didn't particularly like him personally) and decided to take his UFO training programme, which he claims puts his students in contact with the SIs—short for 'Space Intelligences'—who he feels control his powers.

Why Mrs Leslie made this decision is something of a puzzle, though it was probably related to some conventional UFO sightings she experienced in childhood.

But just who was this Ted Owens, who came to play such a key role in Mrs Leslie's later UFO contacts? Before chronicling her story further, some discussion should be devoted to this matter.

Mr Owens represents something of an enigma himself. I had known him for several years, and even spent a few days with him in Washington State in 1979 to explore his considerable claims. I never could come to any specific conclusions regarding them, but I found him to be a sincere but complicated man. His early life and career were not particularly impressive or unusual. The self-proclaimed psychic was born in Bedford, Indiana, in 1920 and served his country in the navy during the Second World War. He had experienced psychic encounters since childhood, and he eventually made contact with Dr J. B. Rhine, who in the 1940s was still pioneering his experiments in extrasensory perception and psychokinesis at Duke University in North Carolina. Dr Rhine was impressed with the sincerity of his correspondent and invited him to Duke to help with his secretarial work. It was during this time that Ted Owens began systematically experimenting with his own psychokinetic powers, even though Dr Rhine never experimented or worked with him.

It was only in the 1960s, however, that Ted began taking an interest in UFOs. This was long after he left Duke in order to return home to take care of a sick relative. Early in 1965 the psychic was living in Fort Worth, Texas. He was driving in the country outside of town with his daughter when they saw a strange object in a field by the road. 'The device emitted red, blue, green and white colors that were vivid and very brilliant,' he later reported. 'We watched the device approach our car. Suddenly it vanished instantly as if a light had been turned out.' Later that night, back home in the city, the baffled witness began receiving subjective 'inner messages' inside his mind from the UFO intelligences, which led him to believe that they were responsible for his powers. The truth or possible delusion of this claim is hard to evaluate, but in 1977 Jeffrey Mishlove published a monograph documenting some of Mr Owens's psychic feats.

Over the years, Mr Owens's psychic claims grew more and more grandiose. But even back in the 1960s he claimed the power to influence the weather, sporting play-offs, and world events.

But now let's return to Mrs Leslie's story.

Mrs Leslie's serious training in contacting the UFOs began on 27 August 1978 when she spent two days with Ted Owens, staying in a motel during the nights and spending the days with him. She was accompanied on her visit by her sister-in-law, Jade, since she was frightened of the hypnosis which played a prominent part in her training. Both ladies eventually took the course, and upon completing it Mr Owens predicted that the SIs would begin spontaneously appearing in the sky for them to see. Mrs Leslie didn't have long to wait. As she detailed in the material she turned over to Mishlove:

We left Ted's around 11 p.m. to return to Vancouver. We were driving slowly down a dark curvy road, in an isolated area, between Silverton and Woodburn. As we approached a curve in the road I looked out the window and saw several beautiful beams of light coming from the heavens down to the earth above a maize field. The sky in this area was a beautiful pale blue, the light beams bright, but soothing, while the rest of the sky around was very dark in comparison. Jade pulled over and we jumped out of the car, excitedly watching in awe. We had no idea what we were watching. To the right of the beams was a beautiful, large, supernaturally bright object (a 'low-hanging' star?). The object moved slowly, then stopped, then moved again. The movement was *no optical illusion*!

Mrs Leslie was overcome by the beauty of the scene, but its splendour was interrupted by the inopportune arrival of a policeman who, seeing her car by the side of the road, stopped to see if she needed help. He, too, saw the beams of light and was baffled by them, but eventually suggested that they could be reflections caused by some nearby city lights. Mrs Leslie and her sister-in-law decided to explore this possibility by driving down the road to a point where they could obtain a clear view of the horizon. Perhaps, they felt, this location would give them a better position from which to view the lights of the surrounding towns. The plan didn't pan out, so they ultimately returned to the curve in the road where they had originally stopped:

We returned to the spot in the curve of the road, got out, raised our hands and the beams brightened enormously. My sister-in-law turned her head to comment on how dark the sky was behind us (toward Silver Creek Falls) when a low-flying light came moving slowly, silently from that direction. As the ball of light came over us we heard no noise but watched with mouths open as the craft gave off a beautiful yellow aura. The object disappeared as quietly and quickly as it had come.

The night's psychic adventures still weren't completely over. When the women entered Portland they sighted a red light manoeuvring in the sky over a downtown building. As they watched, the ball seemed to grow larger and it quickly darted along a horizontal path across the sky. It grew even larger before bursting in a brilliant flash of light.

Up to the time the witnesses returned to their home town the beams of light could still be seen in the sky. Now, though, they seemed to draw together to form an arc. A cloud-like form detached itself from the configuration, according to Mrs Leslie's report, and travelled in the direction of her house before suddenly vanishing.

Mrs Leslie had her second strange encounter with the UFOs on 29 August. Ever since the first incident two days before, she had seen an unusual 'low-hanging star' in the sky, which she felt might really be an extraterrestrial vehicle. That night she took her two children outside and showed them the star and tried to establish telepathic contact with it. 'Within 15 minutes,' she claims in her report, 'several darting lights began shooting around the star. My daughter was convinced that I possessed some sort of power. About 10 minutes later we spotted a red ball of light falling straight down.'

In order to confirm her powers, Mrs Leslie decided to give a similar demonstration to her father-in-law by returning to the scene of her previous encounter outside town with him.

I invited my father-in-law, a skeptic of almost anything supernatural, to ride in the country with us. We stopped, I telepathed, nothing happened. My daughter insisted that we'd chosen the wrong road and should return to the area in which we'd called the night before. She was correct. Within five minutes after I telepathed (with the help of my daughter), a bright, white, darting object shot from the lower southern horizon across the sky to the northern horizon, forming a perfect arc. This was not a shooting star, much larger. The speed at which this craft travelled was incredible!

When we arrived home and got out of the car my daughter commented on the cloud formation above the house. The sky around us was perfectly clear, yet just above us was, in her words, 'a hand' of red clouds. I thought little about it actually but glanced up and saw two white lights (tiny, for they were at a very high altitude) shoot enormously fast through the clouds. We call these fast-darting craft 'zippers.' They definitely are not shooting stars. A few of these had appeared at Silver Creek Falls.

By this time Mrs Leslie was convinced that she hadn't deluded herself, but that somehow, through her training, she was making contact with the UFOs.

The odyssey continues

Similar UFO visitations and sightings lasted throughout the first week of September, during which time the entire Leslie family continually saw UFOs darting in the skies near their home. Some would look like bright 'stars' that mysteriously dimmed when a plane came too close to them, while others would glow brilliantly in the sky—only to recede into the distance until they looked just like other stars in the heavens. Like so many close-encounter witnesses, the Leslies also found their domestic life disturbed during this time by poltergeistic displays in their home. These incidents lasted until 10 September, when the first climax in the case took place.

That night Mrs Leslie decided to take a friend of hers, Irene, out into the country to show her some UFOs and to demonstrate her newly discovered powers. The women drove to a desolate river outside

Vancouver. It was a glorious, clear night and the UFOs weren't shy:

> We first saw 'zippers,' then across the horizon, between two hills, moved
> a beautiful white beam of light. It moved slowly, steadily, too close to the
> earth to be led by a jet, and too silent. The trail of light remained for about
> 15 minutes, never losing its perfect linear form. Then, the top of one of
> the hills lit up in white. I thought a craft had landed. Suddenly we heard
> a definite rustle in the trees, not like the rustle of an animal but more
> like a wind-force moving only in one area and moving towards us. A
> clanking noise accompanied the rustle. The car's antenna began to
> vibrate. I was a little frightened, as was Irene, but sat quietly, willing to
> 'make contact' if the unknown force chose to appear. Suddenly we
> couldn't hold our heads up. We were almost knocked out—or maybe we
> were totally. Neither of us had been sleepy before. I think we were
> hypnotized, perhaps our minds were being 'trained' as future receiving
> stations. Who knows? Time passed quickly.
>
> As we left, an enormous full orange moon rose slowly from behind the
> hill.

Encounters of this type lasted through September and finally evolved
further on 30 September, when Mrs Leslie made mental contact with
the UFO intelligences themselves. Mrs Leslie had been at a birthday
party that evening when, some time near two o'clock in the morning,
she received a telepathic message telling her to drive out into the
countryside by herself. In response to this surprising message she
obediently drove to her usual UFO 'viewing spot' outside Vancouver.
There she waited, and a silent blinking red light passed over her car
while a faint arc of light formed in the sky. Once again she felt that
she was receiving a psychic message. This one instructed her to go to
an even more isolated location up the river in the mountains.

Mrs Leslie was too frightened to obey the message, but just as she
was ready to drive home, suddenly—and quite unexpectedly—she
saw two friends of hers, Terry and Bill, walking up the road. Mrs Leslie
was relieved when Terry said that he, too, had seen a large ball of light
accompanying her car. Mrs Leslie grew a little more confident in light
of her friend's remark, so the three witnesses drove into the mountains in response to Mrs Leslie's psychic intuition.

The group arrived at their destination 45 minutes later in Terry's car.
The contact point turned out to be a tree-studded spot near a
waterfall:

> The wind was strong. Terry and I got out, leading the way, and Bill quietly
> followed. I telepathed, waited. Nothing. We looked around for our
> leading star. It was gone. Suddenly the blue became dark, filled with mist.

Because we were at a fairly high elevation, this seemed normal. We waited a while and began to think we'd see nothing. After all, there were no stars visible in the sky. Then I spotted a beam of pure white light rise over the hill just to our left. I was getting excited when Bill said, 'It's probably just a truck.' But where it came from we couldn't figure out.

However, as the object moved farther over the hill at least four white beams shot out. We had no flashlight so couldn't decipher the shape, but from the positions of the beams I would say it was round or close to it. It made no noise. Terry and I walked towards the hill. The craft began to move, as though on wheels of some sort, down the hill through the trees, moving to our right so that it was directly in front of us. A couple of faint beams seemed to shoot up into the air. Then it turned off all its lights. Total silence.

The witnesses waited for a second display, but it seemed that the UFOs were becoming gun-shy. Even though the UFOs were being capricious, however, the witnesses could sense an invisible 'presence' accompanying them in the forest. This uneasy feeling was so intense that they decided to return to their car.

Secure in the comfort of their automobile, the trio decided to drive around the mountains to see if the UFO they had spotted would follow them. They weren't disappointed:

Half an hour later we spotted two large brilliant globes of light on a hillside. Terry remembered that he had binoculars in the car. We all got out and took turns looking. The globes were yellowish-orange and sparkled like crystal in sunlight. At times they didn't appear as globes, but seemed concave. Then again they may have been V-shaped. Because of the sparkling effect it was impossible to tell exactly what the shape was, and we couldn't tell what they were attached to. The object looked something like a concave saucer with two sparkling headlights. But we couldn't be sure because we had no flashlight. We watched a while, then drove around and headed home. We returned to the spot where I had met Terry and Bill, and as I talked with Bill, Terry began to yell, 'Look, look!' I turned too late. Terry said a glowing orange object like a pole with an arrowhead came closely towards him and suddenly darted backwards and disappeared.

Some corroboration of Mrs Leslie's report

Mrs Leslie's UFO encounters, which seem to be related to her initial contact with Ted Owens, are a continuing saga. But when I last communicated with her, in 1979, she told me that because of her waning interest, her UFO experiences were becoming less frequent.

Luckily, though, Mrs Leslie has long appreciated the value of keeping corroborative evidence from the several witnesses to her psychic demonstrations. During the late 1970s she supplied Jeffrey Mishlove with signed affidavits from several of the people who shared in these adventures. Her claim that she has established contacts with the UFOs does not, therefore, rest solely on her own personal word. The following summarized report, for example, is from a friend of Mrs Leslie's who witnessed one of her demonstrations.

The witness, whom we'll just call Betty M. here, took part in a display offered by Mrs Leslie on 15 September 1979. The occasion came when Mrs Leslie invited her to go UFO-hunting near the Washington/Oregon border. Betty accompanied her friend willingly, although she states in her report on the incident, 'I didn't really know what to look for at the time,' and 'I was not really sure of what I thought Janice might be seeing.' Accompanying them on the trip was her 13-year-old daughter and a school friend. Mrs Leslie's two children also decided to take part in the escapade.

After driving out into the country, near some fields and pastures, the group saw several unusual stars which would blink when they waved to them. 'I didn't talk hardly at all,' writes Betty in her signed statement, 'mostly because I just wanted to see more. All of a sudden the animals, dogs and horses [in the fields] all became agitated and the horses across the road were running around in a type of frenzy. We all looked around and to the east behind us a bright beam of light shot up like an aeroplane but there was no noise. Then it went up . . . I could see it was shaped round and had what appeared to be porthole windows.' The object shot over the road and then flew into the sky, where it took on the appearance of a star.

While driving home after their impressive sighting the UFO-hunters stopped by a mist-filled field. Betty explains in her report that she watched Mrs Leslie walk into the field and hold her hands in the air towards the sky. The mist rose and then shaped itself into an arc. This eerie episode so frightened the children that Mrs Leslie stopped the demonstration and the group drove home.

Some conclusions on the case

If the perplexing case of Janice Leslie was completely unique, perhaps we could dismiss it. But it isn't. Several times during the course of ufological history, gifted people have emerged who share her power to 'summon' mysterious lights from the sky. Earlier in this chapter, for example, I pointed out the similarity between Mrs Leslie and Stella Lansing, a Massachusetts housewife who shares this bizarre capacity—though the UFOs that materialize in her presence seem to be more spontaneous and less 'planned'. A third provocative case has been reported in some depth by Jerome Clark and Loren Coleman (two knowledgeable students of the subject) in their book *The Unidentified*. One chapter in this volume chronicles the career of the mysterious Paul Solem, who in 1948 saw a UFO near his ranch in Idaho. His wife shared in the sighting, which prompted the rancher to experience 'inner voices' through which he began communicating with the 'space people'.

The story of Solem's strange adventure is too complicated to relate in detail, so interested readers should consult the book by Clark and Coleman. It is a story complete with psychic phenomena, bizarre UFO materializations, and political intrigue. The following summary represents only the bare essentials of the saga.

After establishing mental contact with the 'extraterrestrials' subsequent to his sighting, Paul Solem travelled to Arizona and became involved with the Hopi Indians, whose elderly chief was extremely impressed by the space prophet. It was his belief that Solem was in touch with the traditional gods, or *kachinas*, of the Hopi. The contactee's charisma received a boost in 1970 when a UFO flap seemingly followed him when he moved to Prescott, Arizona, to spread his spiritual message to the Indians. The upshot of this mission came that summer when Solem offered the local press and the Hopi reservation demonstrations in which he called forth the UFOs from the sky. These demonstrations took place in open countryside or fields, and unusual skyborne lights invariably materialized in response. (News reports on the success of these demonstrations were published in the *Prescott Courier* throughout early August.) The case came to its predictable end eight months later, when Solem predicted a UFO materialization in a field outside Prescott. Many of the faithful gathered to greet the celestial ambassadors, but the UFOs failed to appear. This humiliating failure for the space prophet capped considerable political in-fighting within the Hopi community, and Paul Solem disappeared from the scene, never to emerge again.

Looking back at the Solem case in retrospect, few people ever believed that he was a charlatan, though it is likely he suffered from serious delusions. Nothing more was heard of the enigmatic UFO prophet for several years. Late in 1978, however, I received a curious letter from a couple in Alaska reporting the following strange incident. While driving by a snow-covered field, they spotted a parked car on the road and, in the distance, they could see a lone figure. The person had his arms raised to the sky. The couple thought that the car had broken down, so they stopped and walked into the field to offer the man a ride. He introduced himself as Paul Solem, casually explained that he was summoning UFOs from the sky, and invited them to stay. They didn't! While they observed some curious darting lights in the sky, they didn't think any more about the incidents until they read something on UFOs that I had written.

Whatever the true nature of such experiences, it is clear that Stella Lansing, Paul Solem, and Janice Leslie *possess the exact same power*. It is therefore unlikely that Mrs Leslie's weekend training with Ted Owens was entirely critical to her later UFO contacts. So where did her powers come from?

It is more than likely that her session with the psychic somehow focused her inner psychic capabilities to *produce* this phenomenon psychokinetically, and that the lights she saw had little connection with visitors from outer space. When I looked into the precise procedures Mr Owens used in training her, in fact, I found nothing extraordinary in them. They consisted chiefly of visualization exercises, procedures for learning self-hypnosis, suggestions for developing extrasensory perception, and so forth. It is important to note that specific suggestions to 'see' or 'experience' UFOs play no role in the training. Such sightings take place, claims Mr Owens, as a spontaneous result of his two-day workshop and are not focused on during the exercises included in the training. So the curious experiences of Janice Leslie strongly suggest that some elements of the UFO mystery are linked to the subconscious and not to some civilization in space.

But were the lights Mrs Leslie and her friends saw really UFOs in the conventional sense?

The generic and sometimes misused term UFO stands simply for 'unidentified flying object', but the general public often thinks in terms of extraterrestrial craft—i.e. spaceships in the conventional science-fiction sense. There is little evidence to link the lights seen or produced by Mrs Leslie, Paul Solem, and others with such vehicles *per se*. What they saw—or more correctly what they created—were simply strange lights in the sky of mysterious origin and composition. Nobody could tell if they were spacecraft in the traditional sense, and they probably were something similar to 'thought-forms' or poltergeist displays on a cosmic level.

Because of this fact, it isn't technically correct to suggest that the strange experiences of Mrs Janice Leslie prove that the entire UFO mystery is linked to the creative potential of the human psyche. Students of UFO lore must still deal with people who see landed and obviously metallic spacecraft and their occupants. The reports of people being purportedly kidnapped by these beings must also be seriously considered. In order to solve the UFO mystery, these cases and encounters must play a crucial role in any explanation we might posit. So they will serve as the subject for the next three chapters in our quest to understand the UFO controversy.

9

The Secret Language
of UFO Abductions

Reports of people being 'kidnapped' by UFOs and their occupants have become frighteningly frequent over the last few years. These cases oftentimes read surprisingly alike. The witness(es) will be driving on a deserted road late at night when the UFO first materializes, usually in the sky or by the roadside. The witness then momentarily 'blacks out'. Regaining consciousness only a 'moment' or so later, he or she will discover that up to several hours have elapsed. Later the perplexed victim will report the experience to a UFO investigator, who will request that the subject undergo hypnotic regression in order to retrace the sighting. While reliving the original encounter, the witness will often remember that his/her car stalled and that strange beings left the UFO and took him/her back into the craft. Many UFO abductees explain that they were given medical examinations or some sort of message before being returned to their cars, usually with the command to forget the experience.

The explanation for these bizarre encounters seems obvious: UFOs are vehicles from outer space and their occupants carry out these kidnappings in order to study our species. This conceptual model has been traditionally called the extraterrestrial hypothesis and has been widely adopted by experts in the field.

As a result of my own research and investigations into several UFO spacenappings, however, I have gradually come to a radically different theory concerning the basis of these experiences.

Revisiting the interrupted journey
I first began to entertain serious doubts about the extraterrestrial hypothesis when I read the celebrated case of Betty and Barney Hill, which was recounted in John Fuller's *The Interrupted Journey*. The case is so well known that only a brief summary will be offered in this chapter.

The date of the UFO encounter was 19 September 1961 during a time when the civil rights movement in the United States was in its infancy and marriages between whites and blacks were rare. Neither were such mixed marriages socially sanctioned. Betty and Barney Hill, a couple from New Hampshire (he black and she white), were driving home from Canada through the White Mountains when they first spotted a mysterious light in the sky. The object gradually descended and seemed to be observing them, so Barney stopped the car, got out, and examined the craft through binoculars. By this time the object was hovering by the side of the road. When Barney saw living beings inside the craft he panicked, ran back to Betty and his car, and sped off. The next thing the Hills noticed was a beeping sound which faded as they drove on. They were driving farther down the road, but only later calculated that their trip back home had taken longer than it should have.

Some days later, Betty began suffering from strange nightmares concerning a more elaborate UFO encounter, in which she was taken aboard a flying saucer. Barney was obviously suffering from some sort of related stress since his ulcer started acting up. With no relief in sight, the couple sought out Dr Benjamin Simon, a psychiatrist in Boston who specializes in hypnotherapy. While exploring their time-lapse through hypnotic regression, Betty and Barney gradually recalled that during their flight from the UFO, their car was stopped by mysterious figures who stood in the road. The beings weren't hostile, but took them to their craft, separated them, and tested Betty for pregnancy by inserting a needle into her stomach. Meanwhile they placed some sort of cup over Barney's groin. The couple were taken back to their car when these operations were completed, but only after being instructed to forget the whole episode.

When I first read *The Interrupted Journey*, several years after its publication, I was left unimpressed by the transcripts of the hypnotic sessions conducted by Dr Simon. What struck me was the obvious symbolism contained within their revivified memories. These symbols seemed to relate concisely with conflicts possibly plaguing the Hills at that time. Barney, a black postal employee, was married to a socially prominent white woman in an era when racial strife in the United States was becoming the most serious social issue of the day. Surely the couple must have been harbouring some deep—though not consciously recognized—conflicts over their interracial marriage, especially since such unions were rare and socially frowned upon in staid New England. It struck me that these *same* understandable conflicts cropped up in their abduction scenario: the couple are separated by hostile and mysterious beings, who check to make sure Betty isn't pregnant and then symbolically castrate Barney. Only then are the couple released to continue on their way!

This scenario seemed to encapsulate the couple's emerging concern with the way society viewed their marriage.* Betty and Barney Hill's abduction report sounded to me like a dream in which the couple's social fears were translated into a symbolic drama.

When I first realized the symbolic nature of their experience, I rejected the notion that Betty and Barney Hill had been kidnapped by creatures from outer space. I felt that their recollections, which were point-by-point recapitulations of Betty's previous nightmares, were little more than fantasies. The couple probably did encounter a UFO while driving from Canada, but the time-lapse was most likely a blackout they suffered from the trauma of seeing such an unconventional object—similar perhaps to the short-lived fugue that Dave Ostovich suffered when he tried to escape from the ghost he saw in my Reseda home (see Chapter 3).

New light on the UFO abduction syndrome

As more and more was learned about UFO spacenappings, I found that I had to revise my opinions. During the 1970s two sensational cases came to light which placed the UFO abduction syndrome on a different footing.

The first of these occurred in Pascagoula, Mississippi, on 11 October 1973, when Charles Hickson and Calvin Parker were spacenapped while fishing late one night on a dock by the Pascagoula River. This case was important because Charles Hickson consciously remembered the encounter, in which he and his young friend were caught by robot-like creatures and taken to a UFO, which had landed near the dock. Even though Calvin Parker blacked out when he saw the robots and never recalled the kidnapping itself, there was no need to use hypnosis to retrieve Hickson's vivid recollections of his terrible ordeal. So here, finally, was a clear-cut case in which the abduction scenario obviously wasn't a fantasy produced by hypnosis. Subsequent research even documented that UFO sightings were rife in the Pascagoula vicinity that night.

The second important UFO abduction case during this period took place near Snowflake, Arizona, on 5 November 1975. While clearing

---

* In a classic experiment conducted by psychologists some years ago, white subjects were instructed to give shocks to black volunteers. The researchers found that the subjects consistently gave more powerful shocks to the blacks who they (the subjects) believed were dating white women.

some trees in a forest region outside town, Travis Walton and several
of his co-workers experienced a close encounter with a UFO. When
the curious (and brave!) tree-remover ran directly under the vehicle,
a beam of light shot him, which so frightened his friends that they fled
the scene in their car. Walton disappeared for several days, and when
he later found himself wandering along a road and phoned for help,
he reported a typical UFO kidnapping.

With cases such as these in the literature, there could be no doubt
but that such spacenappings were *physical events*. The logical implication, of course, was that the 1961 encounter recalled under hypnosis by Betty and Barney Hill was also a genuine spacenapping.

But why, I began to think, should the scenario of the couple's
experience be so rich in symbols relating to their social, psychological,
and perhaps sexual concerns?

Contacts in the Tujunga Canyons

The primary case which offered me the clues to the UFO abduction
mystery was brought to my attention in 1978 by Ann Druffel, a
Southern California UFO investigator with some 20 years' experience
behind her. Ann was still investigating the purported spacenapping of
two women from the Tujunga canyons on 22 March 1953, which
involved several psychic elements. These canyons, situated fairly close
to my own suburban home, are beautiful but relatively unpopulated
regions on the outskirts of Los Angeles. The key players in the case
were Sara Shaw and Jan Whitley, two young women who were sharing
a single-bedroom cabin in the area when the episode occurred. The
fascinating story behind the case had only gradually come to light.

When Sara Shaw first sought out Mrs Druffel, she couldn't remember many details of her frightening experience. She explained only
that she and Jan were roused in the dead of night when a curious light
flashed through their bedroom window. At the same time a deep and
disquieting silence came over the canyon. Both she and Jan had risen
from the bed to find the cause of the light, she went on, when they
found themselves suddenly paralysed. When they recovered a
moment later, they realized that over two hours had been stolen from
their lives.

Sara eventually moved away from the canyons and from her roommate, developed a strange compulsion to study medicine, and later
experienced a 'flash' of insight in which she was given a cure for
cancer. She did not, however, relate these inexplicable developments
in her life to her 1953 experience. She only began to think in terms
of a possible UFO connection 20 years later, when she saw a tele-

vision programme on the subject. Mrs Druffel was intrigued enough with Sara's story to schedule her for hypnotic regression, and three sessions were conducted (by three different clinicians) between 1975 and 1978. These sessions threw new light on her original 1953 experience. I was brought into the case to help unravel the psychological experiences that Sara went through (such as her 'flash' of enlightenment) as a result of her previous ordeal.

As might be expected from the original report, a typical UFO spacenapping scenario came to light during the regressions. During each session Sara began by recalling the strange light in the window and getting up from the bed. But then she recalled that a group of skinny, black-garbed beings teleported into the cabin through a closed window. Even though they didn't seem to be particularly hostile, they took Jan and Sara captive and floated them outside to their craft, which was (apparently) hidden in the canyon. Jan fought the mysterious intruders, but Sara reported that she was curiously indifferent to the goings on. She found the UFO occupants friendly and even thought the experience was, to use her own phrase, 'sort of fun'. The two captives were separated and Sara was given a physical examination by the male entities, who carefully undressed her while the female beings stood by passively. She was then taken to a conference room where she was given a 'cure' for cancer. The two women were finally returned to their home, only to 'wake' from their paralysis with no memory of their previous adventure.

The case could have been stronger had Jan been able to corroborate her friend's story under hypnosis, but unfortunately she could never be successfully regressed. She remained traumatized by the incident for several years, however, often reliving the nightmarish ordeal of the paralysis and the pain she felt when it occurred.

The spacenapping report Sara Shaw gave us under hypnosis gave me the opportunity I had been waiting for since first becoming interested in the UFO mystery. It offered me the chance to make a detailed psychological study of a UFO kidnapping victim. Previous UFO investigators focused their reports primarily on the specific events reported by their witnesses, but never explored their psychological backgrounds in any depth. I hoped to rectify this situation by examining the Shaw case in considerable detail. I began by studying Sara's present feelings and thoughts concerning her 1953 encounter. During several subsequent interviews we explored her childhood and I took a complete sexual history, since sexual elements often play a conspicuous role in abduction reports—the pregnancy test reported by Betty Hill serves as a case in point.

It was during this process that I discovered that Sara's UFO experience, far from being an extraterrestrial kidnapping, seemed to reflect several conflicts which were plaguing her while she was living with Jan.

While talking with Sara and repeatedly going over her encounter, it soon became apparent that she came from a rather disturbed family background. She had been taught by her mother to retreat from contact with men and had been imbued with highly misleading views regarding relations with them. This faulty and damaging upbringing so profoundly influenced Sara that she finally decided, in a subconscious bid to please her mother, to isolate herself from the opposite sex completely. Becoming a roommate with someone like Jan Whitley was certainly logical, since Jan was a strong-minded woman who considered independence a virtue and had gone 'off to the wilds' to live a hermit-like existence isolated from men and from society in general. Sara ended up living with Jan for two years before realizing that her life was not fulfilling. After receiving some professional counselling, she lost her distrust of the opposite sex and eventually entered into two (unsuccessful) marriages.

Sara's UFO abduction experience makes considerable sense when it is reinterpreted in light of her psychological background, since her scenario contains clear symbolic references to the conflicts which led her to seek counselling. During the hypnotic regressions she remembers that strange overpowering figures entered into her *bedroom*, kidnapped her, and *separated her from Jan*. Despite the frightening nature of the episode, Sara found the adventure *fun* and realized that her captors were friendly. The *male entities took off her clothes and examined her* while the *female entities looked on passively*. It doesn't take a psychoanalytically-trained Sherlock Holmes to see that these experiences were messages from Sara's own subconscious, which sought to inform her that her living situation was unsatisfactory. She would only find fulfilment if she could break away from Jan and enter into social and sexual relationships with men. Sara's abduction scenario reads, in fact, like some sort of rape fantasy which left her with a curious sense of fulfilment and satisfaction.*

* I am certainly not saying that rape is ever fulfilling or satisfying. It is the curious contradiction between the 'rape' and Sara's odd paradoxical reaction to it that is so noteworthy. It is also interesting that being overpowered by masked impersonal intruders is a fairly common female sexual fantasy. Finally, nothing in the analysis of the Shaw case is meant to suggest that counter-culture lifestyles of any kind are psychologically suspect. I am only positing that they were not right for Sara at this point in her life.

This interpretation of her experience makes even more sense when we look at Sara's life subsequent to her UFO encounter. She and Jan moved from the canyons shortly after the incident and Sara gradually grew away from Jan, both socially and psychologically. She eventually lost contact with her completely. During the time that she had no contact with Sara, Jan developed breast cancer and required surgery, just when *Sara was becoming inexplicably obsessed with medicine and cancer cures.*

Now the sceptical reader might suggest, as I originally did in the case of Betty and Barney Hill, that Sara never really experienced a UFO spacenapping at all. Maybe she simply blacked out when she saw the light in her window and later confabulated the kidnapping story when she was hypnotized years later. I could never buy that interpretation of the case, however, for one simple reason: even though we could never successfully hypnotize Jan, she spent many years traumatized by the experience which occurred that night. She often relived in frightening detail the paralysis she experienced, the intense pain she felt tightening in her head before her blackout, and the mysterious time stolen from her life. It was obvious to both Mrs Druffel and me that *something* frightening took place that March night which she was successfully blocking. But what?

Reconceptualizing the abduction mystery: a new hypothesis

My collaborative research with Ann Druffel on the Sara Shaw case led me to reject the popular theory that UFO spacenappings are orchestrated by extraterrestrial beings. I began to toy with the theory that we ourselves have somehow created the UFO mystery and are unleashing it into our relatively secure three-dimensional world. Later I began thinking that perhaps some X intelligence exists in the Universe, symbiotically linked to life on this planet and to our minds, which is sending the UFO phenomenon to us. A corollary to this hypothesis would be that UFO abductions do not represent random events, but occur to special people at special times in their lives. My germinal theory was that a person harbouring strong unconscious conflicts somehow invites a UFO spacenapping experience. Somehow his or her concerns and charged emotions serve as a beacon that attracts the UFO experience. The intelligence behind the UFO phenomenon (whatever its true nature) may then create a UFO encounter for the witness by modelling it upon those same conflicts.

Simply speaking, my original theory was that a UFO kidnapping represents an encapsulated dramatization of the witness's own mental conflicts. The goal of the experience—like a dream—would be to bring this conflict and its solution to conscious recognition. But why then do most people forget their close-encounter experiences when they return to their homes or cars? Because the information revealed within the UFO abduction scenario is basically threatening to the person, either his/her conscious mind or the intelligence behind the UFO experience programmes its repression. The information emerges only when the subject is capable of dealing with it.

Now let me say that this theory does not posit that these close encounters are subjective or otherwise imaginary. They really do take place in the physical world, but they tend to be ignited by a purely mental process.

Searching for evidence in support of the new conceptualization
After developing this radical theory to explain UFO abductions, I naturally began looking for evidence to support it. The obvious first step was to study the experiences of other spacenapping victims and delve into their psychological lives—i.e. in order to find connections between their experiences and possible conflicts buried in their minds. It didn't take much analysing before several such cases came to light. The most pertinent was probably the famous 1967 ordeal of Mrs Betty Andreasson. This formidable and impressive case has been thoroughly documented and described by Raymond Fowler in his book *The Andreasson Affair*, so once again only a general synopsis of its key features will be offered here.

The scene of this nightmarish experience was the rural home in Massachusetts where Mrs Betty Andreasson lived with her seven children. The date of the incident was the cold night of 25 January 1967. These were troubled times for the housewife, since her husband was recuperating in the hospital from a serious car crash. Her chief support during these trying weeks was her oldest daughter, Becky, who was helping to take care of the other children. The other witness to the events that fateful night was Mrs Andreasson's father, Waino Aho, who was visiting them. Most of the family members were watching television when the extradimensional drama unfolded.

The first intimation that something unusual was taking place came when the lights in the house began to flicker and everything became eerily silent outside. The electricity finally went out completely and a weird pink light began glowing through a kitchen window. Curiosity finally got the better of Mr Aho, who proceeded to look outside for the source of the light. What he saw was alarming. Later he would tell investigators that he saw strange creatures 'wearing headdresses' literally hopping through the backyard. It struck him that they looked like 'freaks' dressed up for Hallowe'en. But before he could observe anything further, the elderly man was placed in suspended animation with the rest of the family. When they emerged from this state some- time later, they discovered that considerable time had elapsed.

During the next few months, both Becky and Mrs Andreasson slowly began to recall more details of their experience, and they came to the conclusion that there was more to their encounter than met the eye. Becky even dimly recalled slipping from the trance during the time-lapse and seeing strange beings in the house with the family. What she saw matched the description of the 'freaks' seen by her grandfather. Betty Andreasson eventually began contacting UFO researchers throughout the country in the hope of better dealing with her encounter. Her search finally led her to Raymond Fowler, a seasoned and careful researcher living in Massachusetts, who sched- uled her for a series of hypnotic regressions. By this time it was 1977.

During the hypnotic sessions Betty recalled how the 'freaks' entered her house by materializing right through a closed door. She described them as grey in colour, short, and without hair. They had large heads, huge slanted eyes, and slit-like mouths. The subject's next recollec- tions were rather bizarre, for her response to the intruders was to enquire whether they wanted some food, to which they responded cryptically. The creatures lost little time in taking their captive outside, and floated her to their UFO, where she underwent a series of physical and spiritual rituals. She was first taken to a bubble-shaped room, and afterwards escorted to a second chamber, placed on a platform, and bathed in a cleansing white light. Next she was given the obligatory physical examination, which included the insertion of a needle into her abdomen similar to the procedure reported by Betty Hill in 1961. But the needle ritual did not conclude Betty Andreasson's experi- ences. When she was released from the table, the diminutive crea- tures took her to some alien realm seemingly beyond the earth. There she was placed in a tube which was filled with liquid before she was guided down a dark tunnel to a different location where she was confronted by a dazzling light. This light was so intense that she thought she would be incinerated by it. The light was gradually transformed into a vision of the mythical Phoenix being consumed and reborn as a worm. When this richly symbolic scene was con- cluded, the little beings told her to forget what she had seen and she was returned to her home.

The 1967 spacenapping of Mrs Betty Andreasson is particularly evidential since, unlike so many similar cases, there was more than one witness to the incident. Before his death, Mr Aho talked openly of the aliens he had seen in the backyard, while Becky gradually recalled the moment when she slipped out of her state of suspended animation.

My personal interest in the incident primarily concerns the strange nature of the visionary experiences Mrs Andreasson witnessed during the kidnapping. It seems obvious to me that these related to her intense religious beliefs. So let's retrace this case from a religious/psychological perspective.

By her own confession (no pun intended), Mrs Andreasson is a deeply religious Christian and has long believed that her experience had nothing to do with beings from outer space. She prefers to believe that it represented some form of angelic visitation. The sympathetic reader of *The Andreasson Affair* should be able to appreciate this viewpoint since her experiences within the UFO were filled with religious symbolism. (It is reported, in fact, that she has become even more religious as a result of her encounter.) This information leads me to suspect that her abduction experience was linked to some spiritual crisis she was undergoing at the time. Remember that her husband was in a serious condition in the hospital, which had saddled her with enormous domestic and emotional responsibilities. Both her financial and emotional future were up in the air, since it wasn't certain her husband would survive. Now many people—especially those who hold deep religious convictions—will reappraise their beliefs in the face of such severe psychological and emotional stress. The unexpected death of a close relative (or threat of death) can even turn a person from his/her convictions if the crisis seems meaningless.

The possibility that Mrs Andreasson's religious concerns prompted her close encounter even shows up in the spacenapping scenario itself.

The concept of spiritual death and rebirth is certainly one of the central themes within Christian belief, best epitomized by the ritual of baptism. This same basic concept can be found in the Masonic tradition of the initiation by fire and water, over which the spiritual candidate must triumph to reach spiritual perfection. Note that these rites represent the same themes that crop up in Mrs Andreasson's story. Remember she was placed in a tube filled with water and was then reborn by gliding down a dark tunnel—where she was purified by a glowing light which threatened to consume her. She then witnessed the similar immolation and rebirth of the legendary Phoenix, a widely acknowledged symbol of spiritual rebirth and transformation. Mrs Andreasson's entire UFO ordeal strikes me as an objectified but symbolic journey, in which the intelligence behind the UFO tried to help the troubled woman reconfirm her Christian faith.

It is also obvious to me that the UFO occupants even told Mrs Andreasson that they had come to offer her spiritual enlightenment. This message was contained in an interchange which took place at the beginning of her spacenapping.

When the creatures first materialized in her home, Mrs Andreasson's first response was to offer to cook them some food. Her otherworldly guests replied that they could only eat burned food, thereby making a cryptic reference to the 'burnt offerings' mentioned in the Bible. In response to this strange information, Mrs Andreasson began to prepare some meat for her visitors, but they informed her they couldn't eat that kind of food. They explained that their nourishment came from food 'tried by fire' and was 'knowledge tried by fire'. The UFO occupants asked her it she could provide them with that kind of nourishment, and the housewife fetched a Bible for her guests. The aliens offered her a small book in return—which mysteriously vanished some time subsequent to the encounter, although Becky remembered seeing it.

Now for what purpose would beings from some distant solar system engage in such a meaningless, if not ridiculous conversation? This episode can only be explained by the theory that the creatures came specifically (or were specifically programmed) to offer their captive some sort of spiritual revelation. Perhaps they were trying to make this mission known to her the best way they could. The logical implication is that whatever intelligence created the UFO that materialized at Mrs Andreasson's rural home knew what conflicts were brewing deep within her mind.

More evidence for the new conceptualization

This interpretation of the Betty Andreasson case suggests that UFO close encounters can be triggered by specific events in the witness's life. In this case, the UFO sighting and kidnapping were probably prompted by spiritual concerns brought on by her husband's brush with death. Sometimes, however, these UFO-triggered events can be more subtle. This may sound like a strange claim, but any psychiatrist knows that even seemingly inconsequential events in a person's life can have lasting and far-reaching effects. It could have been such a subconscious conflict that resulted in a famous spacenapping reported from Wyoming in 1974.

The case was reported in the press on 29 October 1974 when the Rawlings (Wyoming) *Daily Times* published a story on Carl Higdon's elaborate spacenapping. The chief investigator on the case was Dr Leo Sprinkle, a psychiatrist from the University of Wyoming, who is interested in UFO studies. Dr Sprinkle travelled to Rawlings a few days later to look into the matter and eventually prepared a lengthy report on his findings, which he passed on to APRO (Aerial Phenomena Research Organization) in Tucson, Arizona. Unlike many people who experience these personal invasions, Carl Higdon consciously remembered much of his kidnapping. Dr Sprinkle used regressive hypnosis merely to retrace his subject's experience and fill in a few gaps. The following is a summary of the story in its final, pieced-together form.

Carl Higdon—then a 40-year-old driller—decided to go hunting in the Medicine Bow National Forest on 25 October. This preserve is some 49 miles south of Rawlings. Sometime near four o'clock in the afternoon, the driller spotted a small group of elk and fired his rifle, only to see the bullet travel 50 feet before falling to the ground. That was when he noticed an eerie silence coming over the forest. The perplexed hunter walked over to retrieve the bullet, but was startled when he heard a twig snap behind him. When he turned to find the source of the noise, he saw a strange-looking man wearing a black outfit. The figure was relatively tall and his hair stood straight up. He offered Higdon some pills, which he swallowed without hesitation. The figure then beckoned the hunter to follow him. Before the driller could comply with the request, the strange being pointed some sort of implement at him and Higdon found himself sitting inside a cubicle with a helmet covering his head. The strange man was there with him. Levers on the cubicle's console started to move up and down upon command and the craft took off, shooting to some distant location, where it landed.

When the cubicle had landed at its destination, Higdon left it and found himself standing next to a tower. A group of people consisting of a middle-aged man and four children (between 11 and 17 years old) were talking nearby, but they paid little attention to the visitor. The UFO occupant then took his charge up the tower, where he was briefly examined and then told that he 'wasn't what they needed'. With that diagnosis completed, Higdon was returned to the cubicle and back to earth.

What actually took place next has remained a little confusing. We only know that Higdon found himself back in the forest totally disoriented. Eventually he was found wandering by a roadside by a passing motorist, who took him to a local hospital. The driller was in such a confused state that he didn't even recognize his wife. Even more bizarre was the fate of his truck, which was found three days later in a part of the forest inaccessible by road! The only memorabilia Higdon had from his encounter was the flattened bullet, still in his pocket, which he had retrieved before the strange man showed up.

The story of the unusual abduction of Carl Higdon was first published by Coral and Jim Lorenzen of APRO in 1977 as a chapter in their book *Abducted!* It wasn't until 1979 that Dr Sprinkle issued his full 133-page report on the incident.

But what trauma could have produced such a bizarre sequence of UFO-related events?

During the course of his conversations with Dr Sprinkle, Higdon brought up the fact that, some years before his close encounter, he had undergone a vasectomy. He openly wondered whether this operation had something to do with his experience and his rejection by his kidnappers. 'I had a vasectomy,' he told the psychiatrist, 'and I was wondering if that was the reason that I wasn't any good.'

Before proceeding further, please reread the specific self-derogatory manner in which the driller refers to his operation. Notice that he specifically degrades himself by remarking that he 'wasn't any good', which is a far cry from what his kidnappers told him. They said only that he wasn't needed. My opinion—and I think any competent psychiatrist would concur—is that Mr Higdon was experiencing some residual conflicts over his operation. If this remark had been made during a psychotherapeutic session with a psychiatrist and not during a UFO investigation, I am sure the clinician would have been eager to explore its significance. It is clear, for some reason, that Carl Higdon considered himself useless because of the operation and was pro-jecting his feelings on to his captors—or that his captors were reflecting his concerns back to him.

The reader may think I'm stretching with this interpretation, but I don't think I am.

Few people realize that a vasectomy can be extremely traumatic in Western culture, where it is sometimes seen as legal castration. Even though it is a simple procedure, some men—brought up to conform to Western culture's overblown macho stereotype—suffer severe psychological reactions to the operation. (Women sometimes display similar conflicts over their femininity in the wake of hysterectomies.) This is the reason, in fact, why many men irrationally resist the operation even though it doesn't impair sexual functioning. Some-times vasectomized men experience clinical depression when they realize that they can no longer engender children.

It is perfectly logical to believe that Carl Higdon was suffering from an unconscious or only partially conscious conflict over his surgery when his UFO experience took place. This conflict even seems to be dramatized in his ordeal. Remember that the encounter began when the driller *shot* a bullet at an elk, but found that it had *lost its potency.* The overt sexual symbolism displayed by the ineffective bullet needn't be belaboured! It is certainly interesting that Higdon was subsequently taken to a distant location, where he was shown a family consisting of four children—especially since Higdon himself had four children of the same relative ages. Only after seeing this representation of himself and his children was the captive told he wasn't needed. The symbolism in this scenario strikes me as rather obvious. The scenario of the spacenapping reflected Carl Higdon's fear that he was worthless because of his operation, which had robbed him of his masculinity—symbolized by his inability to further expand his family.

Like the scenarios embedded in the Shaw, Andreasson, and Hill cases, this spacenapping story resembles a dream Higdon could have had during this time.

Some conclusions concerning the nature of UFO abductions

It is highly likely that most UFO abductions contain similar hidden messages and symbols directly relating to conflicts buried deep within the witnesses' minds. Trying to understand the secret language of the UFO abduction syndrome is not, however, an easy matter. Very few published reports provide the type of personal information we need to uncover the triggers to these encounters. It could be that, in some complex cases, only detailed psychological explorations into the personality structure of the close-encounter witness could ever 'solve' them.

Despite the formidable difficulties in searching for the basis of many such spacenapping incidents, I don't think it takes a psychiatrist to recognize the conflicts that gave rise to Sara Shaw's or Mrs Andreasson's encounters. The relationship between their inner conflicts and their UFO scenarios was rather blatant. The fact that sexual and spiritual concerns oftentimes prompt spacenapping episodes is extremely evidential, since these concerns represent the same topics which repeatedly occur in dreaming.

Before concluding this chapter, though, let me again emphasize that UFO spacenappings *represent real encounters with physical objects and beings.* What I don't believe is that these craft and their occupants come from a distant galaxy. Rather they come from some dimension closer to Earth linked directly to our minds.

10

Birth Traumas
from Outer Space?

During the same time that I was developing my 'objectified dream' or life crisis theory to explain UFO abduction cases, other researchers were similarly growing disenchanted with the extraterrestrial hypothesis. Some of them began focusing on paraphysical explanations for UFOs, linking these objects to some psychokinetic potential connected to the human mind. Probably most surprising was when two veteran British UFO researchers, Jenny Randles and Paul Whetnall, reached conclusions on the nature of these bizarre spacenappings that were nearly identical to my own, and presented them in their book *UFOs: A British Viewpoint* in 1979.

While these ufologists were toying with parapsychologically-based models for close-encounter cases, other researchers were falling back on the concept that UFO abduction cases were purely hallucinatory. It was this theory that took the field of UFO studies by storm when a researcher in California began publishing papers on the hallucinatory nature of UFO kidnappings. This general theory, and the research behind it, led to the later development of 'birth trauma' theories to account for UFO abductions—i.e. that when a person encounters a UFO or thinks he/she does, for some inexplicable reason the experience prompts the witness to undergo a vivid hallucination. This hallucination is archetypal in nature and is broadly based on the witness's own birth memories. The birth memory/hallucination theory soon caught on and had a brief but popular life. It is still cited with obvious relish by some commentators on the UFO scene, so in this chapter we will be examining it in some depth. Let's begin by tracing it back to its embryological (pun definitely intended) beginnings.

Research on reports of 'imaginary' abduction
For those UFO researchers who believe in the physical reality of the

spacenapping syndrome, no challenge seemed greater than the one posed by a series of reports written by Dr Alvin Lawson in 1977. In that year Dr Lawson—a professor of English at California State University, Long Beach—undertook a curious project. Working in collaboration with Dr William McCall, a noted southland physician and hypnotist, he recruited several volunteer subjects, hypnotized them, and then requested them to 'pretend' they were being kidnapped by a UFO. The sessions were highly structured since each subject responded to a series of specific questions, which guided the reports:

1 Imagine you are in your favourite place, relaxed and comfortable, when you suddenly see a UFO. Describe what you see.
2 Imagine you are aboard that UFO. How do you get aboard?
3 Imagine you are inside that UFO. Describe what you see there.
4 Imagine you are seeing some entities or beings on board that UFO. Describe them as completely as you can.
5 You are undergoing some kind of physical examination. Describe what is happening to you.
6 You are given some sort of message by the occupants of that UFO. What does the message say, and how was it made known to you?
7 You are returned safely to where you were before you sighted the UFO. How did you get there, and how do you feel?
8 Imagine it has been some time since you have had the UFO encounter. Is there anything which indicates that your personality or your physiological and/or psychological functions have been affected in any way by your UFO experience?

This interesting project involved the services of 16 subjects, and Dr Lawson later compared their reports to selected 'genuine' spacenapping cases from the UFO literature. The researcher could find no substantial differences between the two sets of reports, which led him to conclude that real-life and imaginary spacenapping scenarios represent the outcome of the same subjective process—in other words, that both types of reports are psychological experiences and not physical kidnappings.

This was a bold conclusion to reach, but Dr Lawson certainly had enough faith in his findings to present them to the UFO community that same year. First he delivered a paper on his research to the 1977 MUFON UFO Symposium held in Scottsdale, Arizona. He reported them again the subsequent year to the American Psychological Association which was meeting in Toronto, Canada. His research gained considerably more prestige in February 1978 when a report on his project was featured in *Science News*. Even the news media fell in love with Dr Lawson's concept, since it promised to 'explain' some troublesome UFO reports without recourse to belief in flying saucers or little green men from Mars. The California researcher so endeared himself to the sceptics that he became the *bête noire* of the extra-terrestrial enthusiasts, for his elaborate research caused many researchers to reconsider their explanations for UFO abduction reports.

What was the psychological basis for these purportedly halluci-natory episodes which time and time again conformed to similar patterns? This was an important issue, and Dr Lawson soon began exploring it. He first began toying with the theory that they resulted from information previously contained within our own memories back in 1977. He reached this conclusion when he realized that many of his experimental subjects reported experiences obviously taken from their own life travails. (Many of the subjects, for example, based the descriptions of their physical examinations on operations or treatments they had once undergone.) These observations eventually led Dr Lawson to compare the experiences of UFO abductees to the human encounter with birth. By looking back over his imaginary abductee reports, he found what he considered to be 'birth imagery' in several of them. Many of his subjects described journeying down a tunnel or floating in fluid while a captive on the UFO. The embryonic shape of so many aliens was notable in the accounts, while the subjects often talked of entering into a brightly lit area afterwards.

Dr Lawson was not merely interested in making such striking observations, he also realized that he was obligated to test his theory experimentally. In order to implement such a project, he relied upon a revised version of his original 'imaginary' abduction protocol. This time, however, he compared the reports offered by subjects born conventionally with those of several people delivered by Caesarean section. Dr Lawson found considerable tunnel imagery in the first group, but relatively little in the second. This research finally prompted him to propose formally that UFO abduction experiences represent disguised birth memories which, at crucial times, take on hallucinatory forms so real that even the witness doesn't realize they aren't real. Dr Lawson has argued that encountering a UFO, coming close to death, or taking a hallucinogenic drug could prompt the emergence of such symbolic journeys.

Looking back at this research a decade later, I am still puzzled as to why this theory caught on so pervasively within the UFO estab-lishment. My feeling is that many UFO researchers, while eager to

collect and explore reports of strange lights in the sky, felt uncomfortable with close-encounter cases. Dr Lawson's work let these
researchers continue with their fascination for some aspects of the
UFO mystery, while giving them grounds for rejecting UFO spacenapping incidents. For example, the British UFO expert John Rimmer
relied upon the Lawson birth trauma research several times in his
book *The Evidence for Alien Abductions*. In the personal conclusions
which close the book, he writes that UFO spacenappings seem to be
a phenomenon somewhat independent of the UFO mystery in
general. He also points out several strong objections to the extraterrestrial hypothesis. These factors led him to posit:

> All these considerations lead me to conclude that the abduction
> experience is almost totally psychological in origin, and individual cases
> can be explained without recourse to extraterrestrial intervention. The
> original stimulus that triggers off the psychological process in many
> cases seems to be some form of personal crisis, and the abduction is a
> symptom, rather than the cause, of a change in attitude or lifestyle. In
> some cases there may be a physical stimulus that initiates the psycho-
> logical process—direct stimulation of the cerebral cortex by a natural
> electrical phenomenon has been suggested; but although this is
> possible, I do not believe it to be an essential part of the phenomenon.
>   The Birth Trauma Hypothesis presents one of the most potentially
> fruitful lines for future research. Even if it does not provide a definitive
> answer, it is important for opening up the question of the nature of the
> hypnotic evidence.

Problems with the research on 'imaginary abductions'

The summary offered in the previous pages traces the evolution of Dr
Lawson's theory from 1977 through 1984. I have outlined it in some
depth since his work eventually became extremely popular within
the field of UFO studies, typified by the way it was used by Mr
Rimmer in his book on close-encounter cases. I, however, was never
impressed either by Dr Lawson's research or by the implications he
drew from it. My own position is that Dr Lawson's evidence is based
on crucially flawed research and that his evaluations were contaminated by several sources of bias and experimental error. Furthermore,
it is my feeling that there currently exists no objective evidence
supporting his birth trauma theory. To understand why I reached this
conclusion, it is necessary to understand the precise way in which Dr
Lawson conducted his research. There are several cardinal rules by
which scientific research must be conducted, and the simple fact
remains that—despite his interesting results—Dr Lawson and his

collaborators violated every one of them.

The first thing the critical reader of Dr Lawson's research should appreciate is that his imaginary spacenapping scenarios were elicited by posing a series of *deliberate* episodes to his subjects. This procedure virtually programmed the subjects to relate stories conforming to the type usually given by real-life spacenapping victims. Such a procedure literally ensured that a certain degree of similar information would show up in their reports by chance. This problem was compounded by the fact that Dr Lawson's subjects—even though they were screened concerning their knowledge of UFOs—were probably familiar with certain basic information concerning flying saucers and their occupants. This information could have been picked up through the newspapers, science-fiction movies and TV shows, and from several other sources. Perhaps this was an unavoidable problem which no experimenter could have completely surmounted, since the UFO mystery has been pounded into our minds by the news media for years. But the more the critical reader studies Dr Lawson's papers, the more evident it becomes that other sources of bias could have contaminated his research even further.

One major source of bias cropped up when Dr Lawson decided to ask Dr W. C. McCall to conduct the hypnosis sessions. Dr Lawson made his choice because in the past Dr McCall had worked with several people claiming to have undergone time-lapse spacenapping experiences. Even though it was a logical decision to employ Dr McCall's services, he was not really a good choice. Remember that Dr McCall was completely familiar with the patterns and contents of typical UFO abduction stories. So it is highly probable that, through cues or leading questions, he programmed his subjects to make the type of responses he expected or hoped for. Let me say, however, that this source of contamination is only a possibility. Dr Lawson never published complete transcripts of his imaginary abduction sessions. In this respect, it would be rather illuminating to see exactly what Dr McCall said while taking his subjects through their UFO odysseys. But by any proper experimental criterion, Dr Lawson should have used a clinician less familiar with UFO literature to conduct these sessions.

This was only the beginning of Dr Lawson's continual use of improper experimental procedures! His second experimental blunder came when, upon completing his experiment, he evaluated his data. By this time the researcher already firmly believed that his imaginary scenarios matched the patterns of 'real-life' UFO spacenappings—even down to the smallest details. So to prove his point, he chose four purportedly genuine spacenappings from the literature (*post hoc*) and proceeded to point out the considerable coincidences between them and his 'imaginary' hypnotically induced reports. The simple fact is that considerable bias—both conscious and unconscious—probably went into Dr Lawson's selection of these four critical cases. He offers his readers no evidence that these 'control' reports were chosen in such a way as to minimize his own bias. He could easily have chosen these specific cases (perhaps unconsciously) simply *because* they matched the information contained within his imaginary reports. In order for Dr Lawson's comparison to be valid, the control cases should have been chosen randomly by a researcher unfamiliar with the specific hypothesis Dr Lawson was testing. This second researcher should have been unaware of what the experimental subjects had reported. That 'real' and imaginary UFO kidnapping reports are indistinguishable is crucial to Dr Lawson's position; but the sad fact remains that he never really substantiated this hypothesis objectively. His highly psychological conclusions were little more than *post hoc* findings, based on nothing other than his own subjective evaluations.

But the indefatigable Dr Lawson didn't stop with these methodological errors. To compound them he tried to show in his written reports that highly specific details commonly crop up between his imaginary and purportedly real close-encounter reports. But once again, Dr Lawson's procedure was only minimally scientific and highly selective.

The real tragedy was that Dr Lawson could easily have properly tested his experimental hypothesis that real and imaginary UFO kidnapping stories seem to be indistinguishable. Experimental psychology has come up with several techniques by which two sets of selected data can be objectively compared. Dr Lawson should have created a series of 'imaginary' abduction stories by carefully editing his transcripts and removing any suggestion that they were hypnotically programmed. These bogus reports could have been randomly shuffled in with a similar set of ostensibly genuine reports from the UFO literature. This collection of reports would then be turned over to an independent (blind) judge familiar with UFO literature. His task would be to read over the entire set of transcripts and try to differentiate between the imaginary reports and the 'real' stories solely by their contents. Special statistical tests exist that can show whether the judge's guesses were correct beyond chance expectation. (Dr Lawson would be betting, of course, that the judge would be incapable of making this determination.) This procedure is, in fact, the only way Dr Lawson's theory could possibly be objectively tested to the satisfaction of the psychological and scientific communities. Despite the fact that it has now been several years since Dr Lawson collected his data, this simple experiment has never been conducted—even though I specifically suggested it to him in 1977.

What the Lawson research cannot explain

The readers of Dr Lawson's several reports will note, of course, that the similarities said to exist between real and hypnotically programmed spacenappings were taken completely out of context. So while Dr Lawson might reasonably posit that his hypnotically programmed scenarios seem to parallel real-life UFO kidnapping cases in a general and global way, certainly he cannot say that his reports conform to the precise patterns of real-life cases. For example, his research fails to explain the fact that two different time-lapse spacenapping captives will sometimes recall literally identical experiences when hypnotically regressed. Sometimes these similarities will be so complex that they seem to be copied from each other. Take a look at the following chart, for instance, in which I have compared two separate spacenapping cases from the considerable literature on the subject. Note the surprising and consistent similarities between them. For the present let's call the witnesses Mrs X and Miss Z. Both were abducted in the evening or at night from their rural homes:

Time factor/event	Mrs X	Miss Z
Landing of the UFO and prelude to the abduction	Saw a light in a window and felt that a strange vacuum had engulfed the house.	Saw a light through a window and noted an oppressive silence coming over the house.
Entry of the UFO occupants	Teleported into the house through a closed door.	Teleported into the house through a closed window.
Size of the beings	Noted two sizes since a few of the occupants were taller than the others.	Noted two sizes, since some of the occupants were several inches taller than the others.
Nature of the UFO abductors	Noted a sense of friendliness, but felt so in their power that she was incapable of reacting against their wishes or defying them.	Was curiously unafraid of them and considered them friendly, but also noted that—as soon as they entered—they were in complete control of the situation and she could not rebel.
Journey back to the UFO	Floated to the UFO by the aliens.	Floated along a beam of light to the UFO.

Ordeals aboard the UFO	Hovered over a table and was given a medical examination.	Hovered over a table and was given a medical examination.
Communication with the aliens	Telepathic	Telepathic
Reaction to the aliens and the examination	Felt pain at one point, but one of the UFO occupants relieved it by touching her head.	Felt alarmed when seeing the aliens, but they vanquished her fears by petting her.
Aftermath of the abduction	Several more UFO-like visitations and fleeting memories of an abduction.	Developed unusual obsessions and an extraordinary desire to study medicine.

Any critical reader can appreciate the great similarities between these two reports. The account I have taken from Mrs X, as the reader might have figured out by now, is based on the story Betty Andreasson told to Raymond Fowler while hypnotically regressed. Her elaborate UFO kidnapping in 1967 from her home in Massachusetts was unearthed in 1977 and was published two years later. On the other hand, the lady I call Miss Z is really Sara Shaw, whose abduction took place in 1953 from a desolate canyon near Los Angeles. The report was originally unearthed through hypnosis in 1975 and published in 1980. (Both of these cases were briefly summarized in the previous chapter.) Even though they read like carbon copies, these two cases occurred on opposite sides of the continent and were separated in time by 14 years. Nothing was known concerning the Betty Andreasson report when our subject, Sara Shaw, was regressed. Nor had anything been published on the Shaw case at the time Betty Andreasson finally remembered her experience.

So in conclusion, what is the scientific status of Dr Lawson's theory that there exist no substantial differences between real and imaginary UFO kidnapping reports? My feeling is that the Southern California researcher has offered the UFO community some interesting observations, but that his data certainly cannot be considered documented findings. The manner in which he collected them broke too many rules of scientific methodology and could have been contaminated by several sources of bias.

Birth traumas revisited

By this time it should be clear to the reader that Dr Lawson is not in a position to suggest *any* theoretical model for UFO abduction experiences based on such spurious findings! But as I pointed out earlier, one far-reaching result of his research was the evolution of the birth trauma/memory model in ufology. This conceptual model posits that UFO abductions are birth memories that are re-experienced later in life for some as yet unknown reason, perhaps stimulated by a real UFO or pseudo-UFO encounter. Dr Lawson bases this theory on his feeling that birth imagery regularly crops up in UFO abduction reports. It is his further belief that the birth memory theory can be experimentally tested in a number of ways—such as by examining UFO abduction reports previously placed in the literature for birth imagery. The California researcher even suggests that UFO 'kidnapping' victims will report specific types of alien encounters based on the type of birth they experienced. Dr Lawson has relied on both these lines of evidence to support his views.

(1) Dr Lawson believes that birth imagery is self-evident in most abduction accounts. Writing in the March 1987 issue of *Fate* magazine, where he formally presented his controversial theory, he points to the Betty Andreasson report of 1979 as a representative example. Dr Lawson writes as follows:

> Betty's abductors were typical fetal humanoids: short and frail with grayish skin, oversized heads and eyes and underdeveloped facial features. The richest birthlike event occurred in what Betty called the Cylindrical Room where she was enclosed in a clear plastic chair with a fitted cover which her captors filled with gray fluid. For a time she breathed through clear tubes which fit into her nostrils and mouth. She reported that she could taste a pleasant substance and she felt relaxed and happy.
>
> The Cylindrical Room scene, only one of several such echoes in Betty's narrative, is obviously a return to the womb. The transparent chair in which she floated in fetal position suggests the amniotic sac; the gray fluid is the amniotic medium; the breathing and feeding tubes are the umbilical cord. Swallowing fluid is a common fetal event and pleasant and unpleasant taste sensations have been well documented.

Dr Lawson proceeds to point out that Betty spent much of her time during her UFO captivity floating through tunnels, elevators, and other 'birth canal' passageways. These props led her (in his mind) to symbolic representations of amniotic chambers by way of cervical-type doorways.

The researcher has also posited that every UFO report will include similar birth imagery.

(2) Dr Lawson feels that experimental subjects born by Caesarean section report abduction scenarios suspiciously lacking in critical

birth imagery. To prove his theory, he (again working in collaboration with physician/hypnotist W. D. McCall) conducted several more imaginary UFO abduction sessions with eight Caesarean-born subjects. They found that seven of these subjects reported no tunnel imagery, while their eighth subject offered a single but debatable reference. Two additional subjects with whom they worked (who had had conventional births) reported specific tunnel imagery. Dr Lawson used these findings to claim in his *Fate* report that he could therefore point to 'statistical' evidence to support his theory.

Flaws in the Lawson birth trauma theory

Before I proceed any further, let me say that there are five serious problems with Dr Lawson's birth memory theory, not to mention problems in the evidence he has collected in support of it. Some of these problems are primarily theoretical, while the others are empirically based. Each will be covered only briefly.

(a) *The birth memory model is not consistent with the UFO evidence in general.* No serious researcher doubts that the UFO phenomenon sometimes displays a technological side. The evidence that some UFOs are physical craft is overwhelming, and an excellent reference guide to the evidence can be found in Jenny Randles's book *UFO Reality: A Critical Look at the Physical Evidence.* A second equally excellent source of nuts-and-bolts UFO cases can be found in Richard Hall's *Uninvited Guests.* Since the UFO abduction phenomenon is part and parcel of the UFO mystery in general, it is rather short-sighted to posit an explanation for them that cannot equally subsume all aspects of the problem.

(b) *The birth memory theory cannot explain several features of the abduction mystery.* Cases of mutual or even multiple UFO kidnappings occasionally crop up in the UFO literature. Dr Lawson tries to skirt this issue, arguing that the witnesses in these cases usually report 'separate subjective experiences', but not truly concordant ones. This is not necessarily correct, for some cases containing mutually corroborating features can be found by checking the literature. (See, for instance, Jerome Clark's chapter 'The Ultimate Alien Encounter' in my anthology *UFO Abductions* published in 1980, and reprinted in 1989. In this strange case, two witnesses driving to Utah described insect-like UFO occupants even though they had never discussed their time-lapse episode with each other.)* But more important, Dr

* The famous case of Betty and Barney Hill could provisionally be cited, but the corroborating links in this case are extremely weak. Betty's abduction experiences were first revealed to her in a series of dreams, which she recounted to Barney before they both decided to seek psychiatric help.

Lawson's theory totally fails to explain the psychological factors that could cause two or even three people to experience 'birth memory' hallucinations at exactly the same time. This would be tantamount to two people suddenly experiencing a rare form of psychotic episode precisely at the same time and for the same length of time. Such a phenomenon has never been reported in psychiatry.

(c) *The birth memory theory is inconsistent with the cases upon which Dr Lawson draws.* Special reference should be made to the way Dr Lawson presented the Betty Andreasson case to support his views. He placed great significance in the fact that the aliens she saw looked like embryos—clear evidence, to his mind, of birth imagery! But anyone familiar with the case will recall that these same creatures were seen by a second witness before the spacenapping took place. The father of the primary victim saw them hopping over the front lawn before his own blackout. Certainly this must have been a mighty strange birth image!

(d) *The birth memory theory is inconsistent with basic embryology.* Embryologists today have a good working knowledge of exactly what an infant experiences during the birth process. In no sense does the baby glide down a tunnel-like canal into the hands of welcoming figures. The infant would experience little more than a very unpleasant crushing, suffocating sensation while leaving the womb's totally dark environment before entering a lighted room. The baby's head actually rests close to the opening of the cervix, and the infant never would experience anything like a tunnel. The process of birth could be compared more to emerging from a tight cocoon than to slipping down a slide. Nor would the neonate have much conception of its personal form, since it takes some time for the baby to develop his/her body or ego-boundaries. It could not even see much in these early days, for a baby's sight isn't developed enough to differentiate figures from a foreground.

(e) *Dr Lawson's theory is inconsistent with the psychology of anomalous experience.* If birth memory hallucinations really rest at the core of the UFO abduction experience, then we would expect to find a similar syndrome occurring within other psychological contexts. But it doesn't. The type of psychological syndrome Dr Lawson is positing is unheard of in psychology or psychiatry. Nor does this theory explain *why* the sighting of a UFO or flying object would be integral to such a bizarre hallucinatory experience in the first place.

Frankly speaking, the birth trauma/memory theory for UFO spacenappings cannot surmount any of these five theoretical/empirical objections. But what is even worse, the critical and experimental evidence Dr Lawson has collected to support his theory is next to useless; for it is based on the same kind of subjective processes that destroyed his work with imaginary abduction reports. To begin with, the California professor never formally proposed what would or would *not* be considered birth imagery before he undertook his examination of the UFO literature. He merely began reading through several spacenapping reports specifically looking for such imagery and then reported—completely out of context—anything that struck him as suspicious. This was hardly a valid procedure, since just about anything could be considered a birth image according to Dr Lawson's unspecified criteria. Critics of psychology like to make fun of the way psychoanalysts find sexual imagery in every dream report they read, and Dr Lawson can be criticized on similar grounds. The only thing that he has proved is that, if you search long and hard enough, you will eventually find what you are looking for.

The test Dr Lawson later designed to prove his theory was also built on a series of dubious premises. His experiment relied on the existence of critical differences between the hypnotically elicited reports of subjects who experienced conventional vs Caesarean births. While it is his position that the differences between these two sets of reports represent 'statistical evidence' favouring his theory, this is not the case. Remember that there really is no evidence that imaginary spacenapping reports resemble true-life UFO abduction cases. So the fact that two groups of experimental subjects—both hypnotically programmed to report UFO kidnappings—represent different types of experiences is meaningless. Such a finding would simply have no bearing on the nature of true-life UFO abduction narratives. But what is more important is that Dr Lawson based his findings on a ridiculously small sample size. His conclusions rely on the reports of 10 subjects, which he broke down into sub-groups of 8 Caesarean subjects and 2 people born more conventionally. There is no mathematical test known to experimental psychology by which such tiny sub-groups can be evaluated that would result in statistically significant findings. So there is no way really to show objective differences between Dr Lawson's subject populations.

There also exists a second serious problem that confounded Dr Lawson. The basic validity of his experiment rests on whether 'tunnel' imagery is related to birth in the first place. Earlier in this chapter I showed that this opinion is based on fallacies and is inconsistent with embryology.

It seems fairly obvious, in light of these factors, that little evidence has ever been collected to support Dr Lawson's birth memory theory for UFO abduction cases. While he has perhaps collected enough observations to propose such an experimental hypothesis, neither he nor anybody else has tested it in a convincing way.

I pointed out earlier that many of Dr Lawson's views and theories tend to be inconsistent with many abduction cases. This fact became even more apparent in 1981 when Budd Hopkins, a New York-based investigator, began publishing the results of his research. Mr Hopkins first came into prominence when he issued his exciting book *Missing Time*, in which several cases that he had personally investigated were reported. In many of them the witnesses bore either scars or unusual marks on their skin which resulted from the UFO-related ordeals. These cases came to light when the Lawson research was still receiving plenty of publicity and was challenging the UFO community to re-evaluate UFO spacenapping reports. Hopkins soon became an important and insightful critic of both Lawson and his research on the basis of his own investigations. Hallucinatory episodes don't leave scars in their wake!

Since I never took the Lawson material on the birth trauma theory seriously, I never felt obligated to search out cases inconsistent with it. One evening in 1987, however, I received a surprising telephone call from a casual acquaintance. This call reawakened my interest in UFO abduction cases since 'physical' evidence was a prime ingredient in the case.

11

A UFO Abduction in Suburbia

'Hello, Scott? This is Sammy. Do you know anyone who can hypnotize me?'

It was a strange request, especially coming from someone like Sammy. I had known Sammy Desmond (pseudonym) for five years, though only casually because we occasionally played pool at the same neighbourhood billiards establishment. I got to know him better when I saw him hitchhiking late one summer night and gave him a lift to his house, which was close to my own home in Northridge, California. Sammy lived in Reseda (a neighbouring area), where his parents raised horses on a large lot set conspicuously in the midst of several modern post-Second-World-War tract homes.

Sammy knew that I was interested in the paranormal, and often told me that he wanted to share some of his unusual experiences with me. I never encouraged him since, after 20 years in the parapsychology business, listening to somebody recite a list of personal psychic experiences doesn't exactly excite me. But I was curious as to why he wanted to be hypnotized when he phoned me early in 1987. Sammy was 33 years old, but because of his extremely delicate features could easily pass for 10 years younger. Besides his work stripping wallpaper, his primary pursuits consisted in occasionally enjoying recreational drugs, often pursuing recreational sex, and attending rock 'n' roll concerts. An interest in hypnosis struck me as unusual for someone whose pursuits were primarily hedonistic rather than scientific.

When I finally asked Sammy *why* he wanted to be hypnotized, he said something that so piqued my interest that I eventually spent six months investigating what seemed to be some sort of UFO encounter. Because Sammy's story is so complicated, I'll have to start from the time when this man of mixed-Hispanic heritage was just a lad.

Sammy's childhood experiences

Sammy was born in Los Angeles in 1953 and has spent his entire life in the San Fernando Valley, a large suburban section of Los Angeles. Like many people who later become UFO victims, his bizarre encounters date back to his early childhood. When he was six years old, Sammy was living with his parents in the suburb of Canoga Park. He was sleeping in a guest house in the rear of the property, and he woke up that critical morning with the sensation that somebody was staring at him. He opened his eyes and saw what he described as a 'silhouette' of a tall man standing by his bed.

'I touched my eyes right away,' he later told me. 'I thought I was dreaming.'

Typically for a youngster that age, he dived under the covers until he thought the figure would be gone. But when he peeked over the bedclothes, the figure was even closer.

'It had moved right next to me, so I got a close-up look at it,' Sammy explained. 'Instead of at the head of the bed, it was right at the left side of my bed. It was just sort of looking down at me, and I began to freak out. It was a silhouette, but I could see that it was like it was [made of] thick fog.'

The figure seemed to be six feet tall, but Sammy admitted that it was difficult to judge.

'When it noticed that I was getting scared, it moved away,' he continued. 'When it moved it didn't seem to have legs. It sort of floated to the other end of the bed, really slow. I was freaking out and it stayed there for about an hour. I was so scared since I had never seen anything like that before. I hid under my covers until my parents came looking for me.'

This bedroom visitor never returned, but the episode was the precursor of even more unusual adventures. These new incidents began in 1965 when Sammy and his family moved to another house in the same general vicinity. He would often wake up feeling as if somebody were 'poking' him with a finger. Each time this occurred, Sammy would see a brownish cloud in his room, often hovering near the ceiling. Sometimes the frightened teenager would even watch the cloud come down to the bed and start poking him. His reaction was (predictably enough) once again to hide under the covers! These bizarre experiences occurred sporadically for several years and Sammy could never figure out what they represented. He often spoke to his parents about these unusual experiences and shared them with his friends; but they told him *not* to tell anyone else about them, fearing they'd think he was going crazy.

These experiences—whatever their true nature—eventually stopped, but the next phase of Sammy's ordeal began during the late 1960s. By this time the young man was working for his father's construction company and started suffering from attacks of what he considered 'nervousness'. These would sometimes cause him to hyperventilate. Bizarrely, metal objects he was handling would suddenly break during these unusual episodes. This phenomenon especially focused on house and car keys. He would insert them into the locks and they would suddenly break in half, just as if they were brittle or chemically treated. These incidents occurred so often that he went through dozens of keys in a period of six months. But if he tried specifically to demonstrate the phenomenon for anybody, nothing would happen! Eventually all sorts of metal objects would break when he touched them.

What is so interesting is that these occurrences, so similar to what later became known as the 'Geller effect', took place before the Israeli psychic/entertainer became known in the United States.

By this time, the Desmond family—consisting of Sammy, his parents, and his two sisters—were living in a house in Reseda. This area is a predominantly residential part of Los Angeles that was originally farmland and orange groves before being developed into a dormitory suburb. (The story of the San Fernando Valley is told within a fictional setting in Roman Polanski's brilliant film *Chinatown*.) It was in this typical California stucco dwelling that Sammy's most important experiences took place. The strange brown clouds returned to plague him, though on these occasions they rarely touched. It might be significant that during this phase of his life, the youth—finally taking on the full responsibilities of the world—was constantly plagued by depression. Sammy has long believed that this period of depression and insomnia had a bearing on his subsequent experiences.

Invasion by the lights

The events that led to Sammy's most dramatic encounters didn't occur until he was 30 or 31 years old. He was still living with his parents in Reseda and his father was gradually succumbing to cancer. From what he could recall, the events recounted below probably took place during the winter of 1984.

Sammy was sleeping in the living room since his parents were using separate bedrooms, thus cramping the family's living quarters. He was still plagued with insomnia, and it was during these restless nights that 'the lights' came.

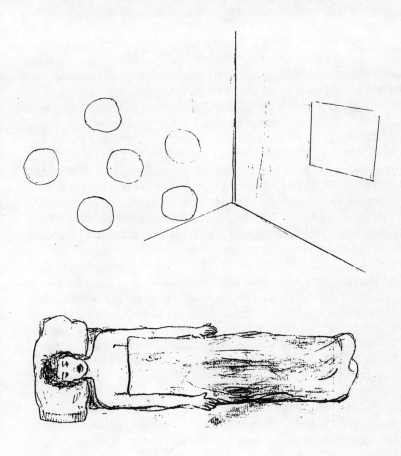

Sammy's drawing of the lights that heralded his abduction.

'I was lying in bed [in the living room] staring at the ceiling and I noticed a large ball of light, like maybe an egg-shaped light with maybe four or five or six smaller ones—perfectly round—circling around the big oval one,' he explained to me. 'It was circling over my head.'

From what I could discover from the description, the larger light was about the size and shape of a football, while the other lights were slightly smaller. The lights gradually faded and disappeared and the incident was relatively innocuous.

Sammy was perplexed by the lights, so when he retired the next night, he began to wonder whether the event was part of a dream. But then the lights appeared for a second time and again circled near the ceiling.

By this time, too, Sammy was telling his parents and family about these nocturnal incidents. His parents tended to dismiss them, but his sisters were more receptive. Sammy's sisters—whom I'll call Sarah and Cathy—were more concerned with their brother's experiences since Cathy (the younger of the two) had also seen the lights in her room. She said they pulled the covers over her head and poked her, which had terrified her. She was willing to tell Sammy about the incident, but had refrained from telling her parents, fearing they would think she was taking drugs. It should also be remembered that during this period, Mr Desmond was slowly dying of cancer and the family had more on their minds than strange lights in the house!

The denouement to these episodes came perhaps a month later. Sleep was difficult for Sammy since his bed consisted of only a sleeping bag placed on the living room floor. Mr Desmond was in such pain because of his illness that he often paced the house at night, which also prevented Sammy from getting to sleep.

One night during these difficult weeks, while his father was pacing in the adjoining kitchen, Sammy casually looked up to the ceiling only to see the familiar circling lights. His first reaction was to call to his father to come into the living room and see the lights. The young man began to call out, but the lights immediately responded by descending and shielding his body. Sammy suddenly found himself paralysed and totally incapable of speech.

'My eyes were wide open,' he told me, 'and I could see my Dad pacing in the kitchen. I was trying to call him to help me and this thing held me down and I couldn't move. I managed to open my mouth, but when I tried to talk, nothing came out. It [the lights] was holding me down so hard that I started to pass out. I didn't though. I fought it and I could feel my whole body vibrating like I was ready to pass out. I fought it and fought it, and finally it let go.'

Sammy's response to the event was predictable. 'I jumped up and woke the whole household and told them,' he said. 'And they told me to go back to sleep and that I had a nightmare.'

The bizarre lights returned the next night and the same sequence of events took place. The lights suddenly appeared, descended, and paralysed Sammy so that he couldn't move or scream. He began to perspire and felt himself passing out. He was so afraid of losing consciousness that he finally broke the spell cast upon him by the lights and woke the entire household with his screams.

The final and most dramatic encounter with the mysterious lights took place the third night of the invasion. Sammy was still sleeping in the living room, but because of his previous experiences he was very restless and couldn't sleep. He merely lay awake watching television and thinking over what was happening to him. It was about two-thirty in the morning when the circulating lights appeared again.

'By this time I was very scared of the lights,' Sammy admitted to me. 'They had held me down and I was afraid of passing out. I thought that I'd die or something if I passed out.'

But for some reason, Sammy had become used to the lights—even intrigued by them. So he was psychologically prepared for them when they reappeared this night. They kept their distance when they materialized for this encounter, and remained in the house only briefly before disappearing and then reappearing outside in the Desmonds' backyard. So Sammy did something which, in retrospect, struck me as rather strange. He got up from his sleeping bag and opened the back door of the living room that led directly to the property's back lot. He then 'invoked' the lights and actually invited them back into the house. He was wearing only his underwear when he made this invocation, a point which will become of some importance later in the case. He then returned to his sleeping bag and waited to see what would happen.

Just why Sammy took this course of action has always piqued my curiosity. By this time it should have been clear that the lights could gain entry into the house without the necessity of a door or window. Sammy didn't seem to appreciate this fact and even recalled that he was feeling in a 'weird mood' when he opened the door. Could it be that he—like many other possible UFO witnesses—was under some sort of mind control? (During these puzzling episodes, the subject will carry out strange or inexplicable commands without realizing the inappropriateness of his or her behaviour—similar to the way a good hypnotic subject will respond to the suggestions offered to him by a facilitator.)

'I went back to bed and sort of waited to see if anything was going to happen,' continued Sammy during our talk. 'And it did. The lights came down to the window* like it was checking out the situation. I was lying there and, all of a sudden, the lights appeared again above me. This time they held me down again and this time I couldn't fight it and I passed out.'

---

* This window is located at the back of the living room close to the back door.

So far Sammy's story was certainly unusual and seemed only peripherally linked to UFOs. The lights appeared to come under the category playfully (and perhaps erotically) called 'bedroom visitors' by Fortean researchers. Sometimes these unwelcome visitations seem linked to UFO occupants, and sometimes they seem totally inexplicable. But when Sammy proceeded with the rest of his story, an X-factor seemed suddenly to complicate it.

When Sammy regained consciousness after his blackout, it was daylight. It was now approximately 7.30 or 8 o'clock in the morning, and it was clear to him that he had lost several hours of time. He woke to the sound of three incredibly loud clanging sounds, like two pieces of metal being banged together. From the corner of his eye he also saw a light flash out of the house through the opened back door. Then he realized that he was no longer wearing his underwear, though he *knew* he had been wearing it when he opened the door to the backyard the previous night. Sammy tried to figure out a normal explanation for the sounds and the lights, but decided instead to take a shower. That's when the next surprise hit him.

'I was taking a shower and my belly button started hurting,' he explained. 'It had hurt when I woke up. Not badly so I didn't look. It just felt like it hurt. It was a strange place to have a pain. So while in the shower I looked at it and I saw a hole—like a syringe hole—like someone had lit a big nail and stuck it in my navel and it looked like it had burned the skin around it. And I could tell it was something like a cylinder or something that burned the skin around it. I got out of the shower; I kept examining it wondering if I could have scratched it in my sleep. Then I noticed that my belly button was *leaking* a clear, gooey fluid. That really freaked me out.'

Then Sammy realized that dirt peppered his feet, even though he had not ventured outside when he invoked the lights to come back into the house.

His first reaction was to tell his parents about the fluid, but they thought it was some sort of residue from his shower. Sammy knew their explanation wasn't cogent because the thick consistency of the fluid wasn't consonant with water residue.

Over the course of the next three days, Sammy told several of his friends about the strange incident. His navel continued to ooze and the puncture mark was still clearly visible. Several of his friends and his older sister saw the mark and/or the oozing, and Sammy considered consulting a physician. He was actually ready to make the appointment when, suddenly and inexplicably, the oozing stopped and the puncture mark vanished without a trace.

Sammy first told me this story in February 1987 and repeated it several times over the next few weeks when I plied him for more details. The more he told me about his crazy experience with the lights, the more the story gradually made sense to me. Seeing mysterious nocturnal lights and experiencing a subsequent 'time-lapse' of several hours is typical of the UFO abduction syndrome. I was impressed, though, by the fact that *never during our talks did Sammy ever link his experiences to a UFO or UFO abduction.* He simply didn't know what to make of his experiences, which was why he was turning to me for help in the first place. He desperately wanted to know what had occurred during those lost hours. When I deliberately asked him what he felt the cause of the incidents could possibly be, he could only guess that something demonic was responsible.

I was naturally excited by Sammy's response, since it was clear that the case hadn't been contaminated by any possible bias towards a ufological explanation on Sammy's part. That some sort of UFO connection was evident was obvious to me from the strange puncture in the youth's stomach: the insertion of some sort of syringe or tube into the navel is certainly well known in the UFO literature. Such a procedure played a conspicuous role in the celebrated UFO abduction of Betty and Barney Hill recounted by John Fuller in his 1966 book *The Interrupted Journey.* I also knew that Budd Hopkins, who is America's leading expert on UFO abductions, was soon bringing out his book *Intruders.* Budd had been discovering several 'needle injection' abduction cases, and I suspected that several such reports would be included in his book.

Even though these thoughts were uppermost in my mind, I carefully refrained from mentioning them to Sammy. I wanted to take pains *not* to influence his recollections should he undergo hypnotic regression in the future. What I wasn't ready for was the fact that his experiences did not stop after the time-lapse episode. His story grew even stranger! Sammy later told me that he deliberately withheld the following story from me when we first spoke, fearing I would think that he was crazy because of what he witnessed.

The backyard invasion

Several weeks after the periodic visits of the circling lights, Sammy was sleeping in the living room as usual. His younger sister had just come home from a date. Sammy's curiosity was aroused when he heard the horses, corralled behind the house, whinnying restlessly. The family's dogs were barking and Sammy thought that perhaps an intruder was sneaking around the property, so to see what the problem was the

Sammy's drawing of the 'twinkling beings' he saw in his backyard.

brave young man peeked through the back door.

'I couldn't believe what I saw,' he told me. 'I walked out into the backyard and I saw these lights. I was too nervous to go out [beyond the porch]. And I saw these little twinkling lights coming closer and closer to our gate which separated our horses' yard from our grass backyard.'

Sammy called to his sister to join him but she refused. She was still spooked from her own experiences with the lights, and jumped into bed to hide, thereby probably missing the experience of a lifetime.

Sammy began to become unnerved by what he was observing and went back into the house.

'I peeked out the door,' he said, 'and I saw what they were. This is really weird, but they were about eight really tiny "things" about the shape of little kids.'

When I questioned him further, it became obvious that these beings were about three or four feet tall.

'They had helmet-type heads and puffy bodies sort of like space-suits,' he continued. 'I know this sounds ridiculous, but they were black with little twinkling lights all over except for the faces. They seemed to have visors; there was no sparkling around the face.'

While the amazed witness watched, the beings began climbing the fence separating the corral from the rest of the yard.

'They were climbing over the fence,' Sammy told me, 'and they were having a difficult time climbing over it since they were so little and it was kind of a tall gate. I was peeking out the back door. I tried to tell my sister to look, but she was afraid to look. There were six to eight of them and I'm watching them and they're moving around. It was pitch black out there. I turned on the [outside] lights at one point, but I couldn't see them as well, so I turned the lights back off because they [the beings] glowed in the dark.'

The creatures—or at least the first of them—finally managed to scale the fence and ran to the side of the house by his sister's window.

'That's when I slammed the door shut, because I thought they were going to come into the house.'

Sammy responded in his usual manner by shouting and waking up everybody in the house. He told them what he'd seen, and his parents quickly grabbed a flashlight and searched the property. But by this time the twinkling beings had disappeared.

These experiences with the strange invaders did not end with this bizarre incident. Sammy's father eventually died from cancer, and his mother sold their property and moved into a mobile home. Sammy began moving from apartment to apartment, often being plagued by the nocturnal lights in his consecutive residences. His only response to these incidents was to draw upon his childhood Catholic back-ground and pray, which often caused the lights to depart—sometimes with a loud screeching sound.

The lights stopped bothering Sammy by 1987, but his curiosity about the incidents never ceased. For three years he had been obsessed with discovering what occurred during his time-lapse experience. He still didn't relate his experiences to anything ufological, but he eventually met an amateur hypnotist and told him the entire

The rear of the property, showing the corrals and the fence over which the 'twinkling beings' tried to climb.

story. The gentleman offered to regress him back to the time of the incident, and Sammy was interested in the prospect. But remembering my own interest in the paranormal, he decided to hold off until talking with me. It was this initial contact in January 1987 that opened this report. I proceeded to ask Sammy about his friend's professional qualifications, and as I suspected, the contact was a lay hypnotist with little background in clinical psychology. I was reluctant to recommend that Sammy pursue hypnosis with this particular gentleman, since recalling a UFO abduction (which I figured had probably occurred) might be traumatic. I was far from sure that a lay hypnotist would be prepared to handle a subject freaking out while reliving a possibly traumatic incident. I was also reluctant to conduct the regression myself, since I had already developed some preconceived notions about the meaning of Sammy's experiences.

I discussed the use and misuse of hypnosis with Sammy for an extended period of time over the course of several conversations. I finally told him that if he really wanted to be regressed, I would see to it that a competent psychologist would conduct the session. I also explained that I wanted to talk with his family and friends to verify his story.

Sammy readily agreed to my plan of action, and my first instinct was to call Dr Thelma Moss, a former UCLA psychologist with an expertise in hypnotherapy. When I spoke with Dr Moss I told her relatively little about the case other than that it dealt with a memory-lapse incident. I didn't want to fill her in with too many details concerning the case. Dr Moss—who is an old friend and colleague of mine—was intrigued with the information I gave her, and we immediately scheduled the first session to regress Sammy for 7 April at the psychologist's bright and cheerful new home in Los Angeles. The goal we were striving for was simply to see if Sammy would make a good hypnotic subject.

The first regression

While driving to Dr Moss's house, I tried to prepare Sammy for the upcoming session. He was nervous since he didn't know Dr Moss and constantly urged me to conduct the regression myself, but I reassured him that I would be in the room with him during the entire session. I also took the opportunity of asking him whether he had experienced any unusual dreams during the weeks immediately after the time-lapse episode. My hunch was that elements of whatever happened during that night might have partially emerged during Sammy's sleep. His memory was jolted by the suggestion, and he recounted a recurring dream that *did* seem to coincide with the strange visitations. During the dreams he would find himself in a large factory-like room wearing a red jumpsuit and half-immersed in water. He could never figure out the meaning of the dream, since it was totally unlike any he'd experienced before.

As we drove from Sammy's bachelor apartment to Dr Moss's residence, I warned him to tell the psychologist as little as possible about his unusual experience. I didn't really want her to know we were dealing with a possible UFO abduction case, and I didn't want to bias her expectations about the session. (Of course, these were my secret motivations, and I still refrained from mentioning anything concerning UFOs to Sammy.) Dr Moss knew of my concerns and graciously agreed to work under these somewhat unusual restrictions.

That warning turned out to be a total waste of time! Sammy has a terrible memory and is nothing if not talkative. When we finally arrived at Dr Moss's impeccably decorated house and sat down for the session, Sammy immediately told her about most of his bizarre experiences—the figure by the bed, the circling lights, the liquid oozing from his navel, and so forth. Dr Moss took the whole thing in her stride, but before beginning the regression session probed a bit by asking Sammy to 'imagine' what *could* have occurred during the time-lapse period. Sammy continued to deny any knowledge of the lost time, but felt that 'somebody' had experimented with him and had probably placed something in or withdrawn something from his stomach. He refused to speculate any further, which was fine with me.

Dr Moss is a seasoned professional when it comes to hypnotic regression, so she asked Sammy to lie down on the couch in her study and smoothly guided him into hypnosis. She used a very gentle form of induction in which she assured the subject that *he* was in charge of the session and could enter trance as deeply as he desired. Despite these constant reassurances from Dr Moss, Sammy was still nervous with the regression and what he might be forced to recall. His body began twitching and perspiring—and perhaps significantly—he placed his hands (protectively?) over his navel. He also said that his body felt itchy, which Dr Moss felt was merely a ploy his subconscious was using to resist the hypnosis.

It was clear, however, that Sammy was gradually succumbing and entering into hypnosis. He 'drifted off' into some foreign room in which he found himself being poked unpleasantly. He also felt a peculiar pressure on his chest which he couldn't explain. Some sort of white light was shining and illuminating his body, and finally Sammy saw that he was lying on a narrow trolley, with eight or so beings (in silhouette) grouped around him.

Sammy complained that all these images were scrambled and confusing to him, so Dr Moss decided to spend the rest of the session exploring his emotional reactions to the experience. It was evident, however, that whatever happened was not too traumatic for the subject. Even though he continued to perspire during the session, Sammy never reacted with any pain or panic to his emerging memories. It was for that reason that, when the session concluded, Dr Moss agreed that there was no reason why I shouldn't continue with the hypnotic sessions myself. She didn't feel that Sammy's response would be violent or would call for professional intervention, and she thought the subject might feel more relaxed with me. Since I have used hypnosis with UFO abductees in the past, the suggestion didn't strike me as untenable.

The entire session lasted for about 45 minutes and Dr Moss was a bit puzzled by it. Sammy had not specifically mentioned a UFO, but Dr Moss whispered to me while Sammy was gone from the room, 'This sounds kind of UFOish to me.'

The dematerializing tape-recording

More surprises were in store for me when Sammy and I drove back to his apartment, which is close to my own home. He told me that several images had come to mind that he refused to reveal to Dr Moss while undergoing the regression. The silhouetted beings, he said, had been especially interested in examining his genitals—but he was reluctant to report their curiosity to the female psychologist. He also experienced a mental image of a truly frightening device. He watched briefly during the regression while a long (two or three foot) metal syringe-like object was inserted into his navel at an angle. These images and experiences convinced me more and more that we were probably dealing with an almost classic UFO abduction.

My own personal surprise came later that night, long after Sammy was safely home. Because Dr Moss invariably tape-records her regression sessions, I had carefully checked out her equipment and recorded Sammy's regression. But when I sat down to transcribe the tape, I discovered that it was completely blank! I knew I hadn't screwed up the recorder since I had checked and even voice-tested the device right before the session began. The fact that the tape was totally blank was stupefying, so I decided to place the tape in a special file I was keeping on the case. I figured that I'd have a recording engineer examine the tape to see if it could have been defective. But when I returned the next day to retrieve it from my files, it was gone! It had simply vanished, and to this day it has never reappeared.

I had read of other UFO researchers confronting similar strange shenanigans, but this was the first time it had ever happened to me personally. It was positively spooky.

Since I was certain that we were dealing with a UFO abduction case, my immediate goal was to get some funding for a complete investigation. I wanted to procure a complete medical and psychological evaluation of Sammy, and also to gather some funds to pay for some further regression work with my subject. My first plan of action was to establish contact with Dr Bruce Maccabee, who controls the Fund for UFO research in Mt Rainier, Maryland. The Fund has supported research on UFO abduction cases in the past, and I was hopeful that they would find this case of interest—especially since Sammy was *still* not associating his experiences with UFOs. The case was still 'clean'. Dr Maccabee wrote back immediately to say that the Fund would be interested, and sent me the necessary forms to complete. What was disheartening was that Dr Maccabee warned me that it would take several months to get the grant evaluated. This information caused me to panic for several reasons. By now it was getting towards the middle of April. I knew that Whitley Strieber's book *Communion* and Budd Hopkins's *Intruders* were soon to be published. Both books would deal with UFO abductions and would generate a great deal of TV and radio exposure, especially since Strieber was a best-selling author. His book deals with his personal UFO abduction, and I knew he'd be soon working the TV talk-show circuit. If Sammy saw or heard any programme interviewing either Strieber or Hopkins, their stories and research could significantly influence my subject—whom I wanted to keep in the dark as much as possible about UFOs.

Things were beginning to develop significantly with Sammy, too. He phoned me on 14 April to say that some specific memories of his experiences were spontaneously emerging:

1 He now knew that the fluid oozing from his navel had not been taken from his stomach, but that something had been *injected* into him. This information had come to him in some way intuitively.
2 He also kept having visions of standing outside his house and then 'zooming' upwards, where he would find himself in a room partially submerged in water.

Sammy also complained of a recurrent depression, but it wasn't clear to me whether this was due to his emerging memories or to some other, extraneous factor. During the period of our work together, Sammy became involved in some personal problems which weren't working out too well. Despite these problems, however, he wanted to continue with the regressions, so I chalked up his mental problem to psychological factors. My assessment was probably correct, for when I stopped by to see him a few days later he told me that even more memories were beginning to emerge. He explained that while lying down to sleep each night, he was practising a form of self-hypnosis based on the suggestions Dr Moss had used during their prior regression session. The results were promising, and he was beginning to get a much better mental picture of the syringe penetrating his abdomen. It contained a tube of some dark substance, encased at the top of the needle, which was subsequently fed into his stomach. But what was even more surprising was that, after this operation, Sammy felt that he was forced to watch a screen on which he saw himself engaged in explicit sexual activities. Sammy told me that this was so embarrassing that he refused to watch. But it was an additional clue that his entire abduction was overlaid with sexual meanings. Sammy guessed that whatever beings had abducted him might have been interested in his sexual life, and at some point had partially immersed him in water.

This last memory seemed to link directly to the recurrent dream Sammy experienced soon after the incident with the lights, and which he recounted to me before his meeting with Dr Moss.

The hypnotic work continues
With all these pieces of the puzzle coming forth so rapidly, I decided it was time to proceed with more hypnotic work. Even though I had

not heard from the Fund, I simply couldn't wait any longer before pursuing the case. My plan was to use a more direct form of hypnosis with Sammy and trace his time-lapse experience step by step from the time the circling lights appeared. The first of my sessions with Sammy took place on 6 May 1987, during which he recited a typical UFO abduction story. I conducted a follow-up on 18 May to see if he would come up with the same scenario first communicated to me on the 6th.* By this time he was becoming somewhat belligerent towards me, complaining that I still hadn't explained the *meaning* of his experiences to him. I replied that my only promise was to help him *remember* what occurred during his time-lapse, not to offer him a formal explanation for his frightening ordeal.

Sammy and I met for the last regression on the evening of 9 June. I wanted to check again whether he would repeat the same story he revealed during the sessions of 6 and 18 May, or would elaborate upon his earlier impressions. He didn't, but properly intertwined his previous impressions into a typical and completely consistent UFO abduction scenario.

In order to hypnotize Sammy, I used what is called an Ericksonian hypnotic induction, which is a form of conversational induction in which the subject is 'tricked' into trance. This procedure works well with subjects who resist entering hypnosis, and Sammy was a particularly resistant subject. Because I wanted to be very careful with the session, it took me well over 30 minutes before I even began regressing him back to the circling lights that paralysed him. (For more information on this procedure, the reader might wish to consult *Hypnotic Realities* by Milton Erickson, Ernest Rossi and Sheila Rossi.)

Sammy began the session by easily recalling being in his living room, turning off the TV set, and getting ready for sleep. Next he recalled seeing the curious lights circling the ceiling—the same lights he'd previously described to me and Dr Moss. When he described them as paralysing him and making him black out, I became very firm with my hypnotic suggestions. I told him that even though his conscious mind had blanked out, his subconscious mind knew exactly what had transpired, and that I was talking *directly* to his subconscious. Sammy responded to the suggestion immediately and perfectly.

'I decided to let the lights do whatever they wanted to do,' he began by saying.

---

* ABC-TV's news programme *20/20* featured a story on UFO abductions on 14 May, but Sammy didn't watch it and didn't even know about it.

When I asked him what happened next, he responded, 'They started coming closer and closer and came on top of me. They were all over my body and I felt like—like I was blanking out.'

Sammy paused at this point in the story, so I gave him more explicit suggestions to remember what happened.

'My whole body started tingling,' he replied. 'I just felt like I wasn't lying on the floor any more.'

Sammy next found himself floating upwards, obviously being taken somewhere outside the house and into the sky. He couldn't see much because he was surrounded by the lights, which were levitating him. Sammy was keeping his eyes closed during the experience, but he realized he was outside since it was so cold. He could feel his stomach churning, but he was still too frightened to open his eyes even though he knew he was travelling somewhere. Finally his journey came to its end.

'I was inside a room,' Sammy recalled. 'It was a small room, all white, light-coloured and round. There was a table in the middle and there were wall lights and things all over. The only thing I remember in the room besides the table was a huge white bright light in my face.'

When I asked Sammy where he was positioned, he replied—as I suspected—that he was lying on the trolley.

'It was a hospital-type skinny table,' the subject continued. There were some alien creatures in the room with him. Sammy had a difficult time seeing them because of the light in his face and could only see them in silhouette.

'There's six, seven, maybe eight people looking down at me,' he continued. 'I could see the shapes of their heads and clothes. I couldn't see their faces very well because of the light, which was blinding me.'

I naturally asked Sammy what they looked like so far as he *could* see.

'They look small-boned and little,' he replied in an instant. 'They're medium-sized, four and a half feet or five feet tall. They weren't real little, but they weren't big. They had bald, pointy-type heads.'

I was puzzled by this description, so I pressed Sammy for more information.

'Their heads weren't oval or round,' he replied. 'They were more egg-shaped and I could see that they were all bald-looking.'

Sammy explained further that the beings were examining him. They had implements or clamps in their hands, and they were poking him, and next performing some sort of operation on his chest. One of the beings placed a round, brown, rubbery weight on his upper chest, and Sammy could see that a metallic silver bar protruded from its side.

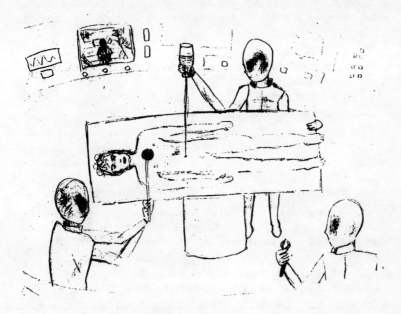

Sammy's drawing of the examination he was given during his
abduction.

The object felt warm, and throughout the procedure the beings kept
talking among themselves. The aliens apparently never spoke or
otherwise communicated directly with Sammy, who couldn't understand what they were saying. He could only describe their speech as
sounding like a bunch of 'mumbled up words'. Of course, this
description matches the typical 'gibberish' so many other UFO
abductees often report. Sammy also reported hearing what sounded
like radio static in the background. Most notable, though, was that the
procedure with the weight somehow made Sammy feel more calm
and he began to relax.

This off-the-cuff remark sparked my personal interest, since many
UFO abductees describe injections or procedures which suddenly
caused them to relax. I had previously encountered a similar
phenomenon while researching an old 1950s case, which Ann
Druffel and I reported in our book *The Tujunga Canyon Contacts*.
Roughly similar was the way the extraterrestrials comforted Betty Hill,
which is fully described by John Fuller in *The Interrupted Journey*.

It was fortunate that Sammy was calmed by the beings, since what
happened next wasn't exactly pleasant.

'I looked up,' Sammy reported, 'and they were putting this needle in my stomach. It was really long, maybe two feet long and it looked too fat to put into me. As it went in, I started to panic.'

When I asked more specific questions about this particular incident, Sammy confirmed that the needle was inserted directly into his navel. A dark fluid in the top of the syringe was slowly injected into him. Sammy started to panic, and for the first time during the ordeal it seemed as if the extraterrestrial beings were communicating with him.

'They looked my way and said, and this is how it sounded in English, something like, "Calm down, it's OK, it's not going to hurt." And it didn't hurt. It just felt like pressure.'

I asked Sammy what he was doing during the operation, other than merely lying paralysed on the trolley. Sammy admitted that his curiosity was getting the better of him.

'At first I didn't want to look,' he confided to me. 'I looked away because it looked like it was going to hurt bad. So I turned my head a little and to the left of the room, and it looked like me on TV.'

It was at this point that the most obvious sexual element of the abduction scenario occurred. What happened next was so threatening to Sammy that he wouldn't reveal what he saw even under hypnosis. It was only later that he was willing to share this information with me, more as a friend than as a researcher exploring his experiences. It turned out that some sort of screen was positioned to the side of the trolley upon which images could be projected. Sammy was certainly startled by what he saw. He was suddenly watching some sort of screening of his past sexual encounters. He was so embarrassed by these scenes that he turned his face and refused to look any longer. He turned his attention back to the syringe and saw a great deal of dark fluid still being pumped into his abdomen.

When this rather unpleasant procedure was completed, Sammy simply remained lying on the trolley for a considerable length of time. He found himself still paralysed, and the beings were still examining him when they spotted a small bruise near the base of his genitals. The beings then manoeuvred the trolley (with Sammy still lying on it paralysed) into a partially upright position, simultaneously immersing their subject in a bubbling tub of water.

It immediately struck me, of course, that this part of the scenario probably related to the strange dream Sammy experienced shortly after his original time-lapse in 1984.

Sammy's physical examination came to its conclusion when he was bathed, and the beings communicated to him that he could leave. Two of the little figures escorted their charge from the room, which gave Sammy his first real opportunity to examine his captors.

He described them to me in some detail. 'They had flat faces,' he said. 'They had white jacket-sort of outfits, sort of like hospital uniforms. I could just see a side view of their faces. They had flat faces and long heads, bald heads. They had hardly any noses.'

Unfortunately, Sammy's ordeal still wasn't completely ended. The two bald-headed beings escorted him to the end of the small examination room, where he was met by two different creatures. These beings were rather amorphous in form though humanoid in shape. They seemed to be composed of fog, perhaps similar to the being Sammy saw by his bed when he was a small child. These fog-like beings took him from the chamber into an adjoining room, a huge room with transparent metal floors which enabled Sammy to see that the environment was composed of several storeys. Since poor Sammy suffers from a fear of heights, he panicked and started to run from his captors—only to realize that he didn't have any place to hide! The two fog-like beings subsequently approached him and stood on either side of him, and Sammy once again found himself becoming inexplicably calm.

Sammy's recollections became confused at this point in the story. He recalled leaving the room by some unknown means and floating back to his home through the darkness, surrounded by the same lights that originally captured him. What so amazed the young man was that, even though the back door to the house was still open, he entered it by teleporting directly *through* the ceiling or walls. He then regained consciousness and realized that it was daylight. Before he even knew what was happening, he heard three metallic clangs and saw a light dart from the house and back into the sky. It was probably at that point that Sammy forgot most of the previous night's adventures. He merely hopped from his sleeping bag, puzzled that he was not wearing his underwear—which he later found elsewhere in the living room. It was seven-thirty in the morning and he decided to take a shower. That's when he discovered the syringe mark in his abdomen and noticed dirt powdering his feet. When he finished showering he was still upset and told his family what little he could recall.

Anyone familiar with UFO abduction problems will appreciate the obvious parallels between Sammy's story and many others in the literature. The insertion of the syringe into his abdomen, the time-lapse, and the sexual components of the story—these are all part and parcel of the UFO abduction syndrome. What is so impressive is that Sammy knew nothing about UFOs or related matters when we began working together. He only associated his experiences with the UFO phenomenon the first time when he watched an Oprah Winfrey show in late May, in which Budd Hopkins discussed his celebrated research. Luckily, by this time the essentials of Sammy's story had already emerged from our first regression sessions.

I was especially intrigued by the syringe that was purportedly stuck into Sammy's abdomen. The first time such an operation was reported was, as I mentioned earlier, in the Betty and Barney Hill case of 1961. Since that time, several other cases dealing with female abductees have been researched by Budd Hopkins, who includes them in his block-buster *Intruders*. It has been Hopkins's theory that these operations probably entail the removal of an ovum from the subjects, perhaps for some kind of genetic experimentation. Mr Hopkins states in his book that he later played tapes of his subjects' recollections for a gynaecologist, who felt the stories sounded like a surgical procedure used to remove an unfertilized egg through the abdomen with the help of fibre optics. But in Sammy's case we have what appears to be the same operation performed on a male! So it may be that Hopkins's theory is wrong, or that possibly the UFOnauts have been studying Sammy for years—growing increasingly puzzled by his sexual activities.

But can we really believe Sammy's story?

Corroborative evidence from Sammy's family
Luckily, there is no lack of witnesses to Sammy's story, since he constantly informed his family of his strange experiences. When I first began to work with Sammy, I continually pressed him to let me talk to his sisters and to his mother. My chance finally came when Sammy called me on 10 July 1987 to say that his relatives were in town. It seems that his sister Sarah and her husband were fixing up a house they were buying, and Mrs Desmond was helping with the painting. I lost little time in picking up Sammy and driving to the house that same evening.

When we met later that night, I found both Sarah and Sammy's mother to be cordial and considerate people more than willing to talk to me about Sammy's disturbing experiences. Sarah explained that Sammy had been telling her of his experiences for years, but she hadn't paid much attention to them. There were simply too many to recall, she said with a pixyish grin. But she did clearly recall the incident in which their younger sister, Cathy, was attacked by the fog-being, perhaps the same creature Sammy saw when he was six. Sarah said that she was sharing her bedroom with her sister when the younger girl screamed that a fog-like cloud was in the room. Sarah told me that she turned on the bedroom light immediately and, to her horror, saw her sister choking and being forced—seemingly against her will—down on to the bed. Sarah was so frightened that she ran to get her parents. Mrs Desmond rushed to her daughter and shook the girl until she emerged from her trance.

Mrs Desmond also recalled Sammy telling her of the tiny sparkling beings he saw at the side of the house. She didn't know what to make of the story.

I wasn't able to speak to Cathy concerning her own experiences, which was disappointing since she also experienced the lights that plagued Sammy. She was pretty freaked out by the incident and didn't want to talk with me. Despite this minor setback, both Sarah and Mrs Desmond told me that Cathy often reported the lights to *them*.

Mrs Desmond turned out to be my main source of information, though, and she confirmed several of the episodes in which Sammy screamed out during the night. She also recalled that he often complained of the lights that so often bothered him, though she herself never encountered them. She also recalled perfectly the fateful night of Sammy's purported abduction. Much to my surprise, I learned from Mrs Desmond that Sammy *did* recall what happened to him during his time-lapse for a short period of time when he first returned home. Only later did he presumably lose his recollections of the (understandably) traumatic episode.

Without any prompting from me, Mrs Desmond said that Sammy told her—immediately after emerging from his shower—that he had been 'taken someplace'. Mrs Desmond explained that Sammy was obviously still terrified by the events.

'Sammy said that he had been taken somewhere else,' she said, 'into a big room where everything was white with lots of light and they had him on a bed or table or somewhere and that they had put a needle in his stomach and taken something out.'

Mrs Desmond continued by saying that Sammy wanted to show her the incision mark in his abdomen, but that she didn't want to see.

Sarah—who was always sceptical of her brother's stories—also heard this tale while he was confiding in their mother, and she was more willing to challenge her brother's experience.

'I never really paid attention to his stories,' she told me, chuckling good-naturedly. 'I figured this experience was just a bad dream. So I said I wanted to see and he lifted up his shirt and he pressed [his navel] and it all squirted out.'

Sarah's face wore a look of disgust when she described the incident.

When I asked her for more details, she said the fluid 'looked like clear fluid or pus'. Her only reaction was to tell her brother that it was gross, and to see a doctor.

End note
My investigation of Sammy Desmond's experiences is still not concluded. I am still hoping to talk with his other sister to learn of her experiences, while Sammy is helping me to locate some of his friends who examined the incision in his abdomen. So far I have been in contact with a second witness to Sammy's experience, an ex-TV executive and long-time friend of Sammy's. He saw the mark on his friend's abdomen when Sammy told him of his experience the day after it occurred. He also saw the oozing liquid and was perplexed by it. I am also hoping to consult a physician (if possible, an obstetrician) to see whether a soft-tissue X-ray might reveal the remnants of any scarring where Sammy's abdomen was punctured, though that seems unlikely according to the physician I have already consulted.

What is probably most intriguing, though, is that Sammy has suffered from bouts of depression for most of his life. Sometimes—even when he was a child—he would look towards the sky asking for somebody to take him away from the drudgery of his earthly life. Sammy has repeatedly told me that his preternatural experiences usually tend to coincide with these episodes. Could it be that when Sammy beckons to the sky, somebody—or something—responds?

PART IV
Miraculous Realities

12

Psychic Phenomena
and the Communion

One of the most sacred moments in the life of any Roman Catholic comes when he or she receives Holy Communion. There, kneeling before the altar, a small wafer (called the Host) is placed on the tongue of the supplicant, who swallows it with a sip of wine. These symbolize the body and blood of Christ. The ritual is enveloped in a sense of the supernatural since, according to Catholic teaching, the Host and the wine physically transubstantiate into the flesh and blood of Christ at that moment.

The fact that partaking of the Eucharist (the bread and wine) is particularly sacred is emphasized by the elaborate preparations the Catholic makes for it. In order to receive the Sacrament, the supplicant must be in a state of grace, free of mortal sin, so must confess his or her sins and be absolved before the ritual. To receive Communion while in a state of sin is sacrilege itself, a teaching first declared in the Bible in the eleventh chapter of I Corinthians. It is also traditional for the person to fast briefly before taking part in the service. Abstaining from food and drink (except for water) for one to three hours is suggested. Some Catholics will also recite the Mass in order to better prepare themselves for Communion. Holy Communion is to be received a minimum of once a year between the first Sunday of Lent and the eighth Sunday after Easter, though it can be taken more frequently.

Because Communion is primarily a mystical ritual, it is not surprising that outbreaks of the paranormal occur when it takes place. Tales have been told of the Host suddenly bleeding real blood or turning into physical flesh. Other stories report strange lights emanating from the Communion wafers. So many of these tales have been placed on record that Joan Carroll Cruz, a Catholic writer in the United States, collected and published them in 1987 in a lengthy book entitled *Eucharistic Miracles*. In this chapter, however, we will be focusing on a single paranormal aspect of the Communion service.

The ritual of Holy Communion is practised daily throughout the Catholic world and has been regarded with special reverence by the saints and mystics of the Catholic Church. Many of them would enter a state of ecstasy or even levitate while partaking in it. Some mystics even claim that they feel physical pain if the Eucharist is withheld from them. Many of the great saints and mystics of the past purportedly lived for years without any nourishment *except* for the Sacrament. This miracle—called divine *inedia*—was thoroughly documented in the life of Thérèse Neumann of Konnersreuth, Germany, who died in 1962 having refused food for years. (We will be returning to the strange case of Therese Neumann later in this chapter.) The most remarkable supernatural aspect of Communion, however, is a very rare miracle—mentioned only passingly in the Catholic Church's hagiographic records—called 'Miraculous Communion'. During this miracle the recipient receives Communion not from a priest, but with the purported help of a supernatural being such as an angel. The miracle occurs in several different forms. Sometimes the Host will levitate out of the priest's hand when the ritual begins and literally floats into the recipient's mouth. On other occasions it will spontaneously materialize in the mouth of a saint or mystic waiting to take Communion. Several such reports were collected earlier in this century by Father Herbert Thurston, a Jesuit priest and a keen student of the paranormal. He placed them in his posthumously published book *The Physical Phenomena of Mysticism*, from which some of the following reports have been summarized.

Some historical examples of Miraculous Communion

A fairly modern example of this latter miracle is given by Dr A. Imbert-Gourbeyre, a French physician who spent years studying reports of miracles, in his book *Les Stigmatisées*. This volume includes a 200-page report on Palma Matarelli (1825-88), an Italian housewife from the town of Oria. Palma turned to religion in 1853 upon the death of her husband. The first sign of her supernatural gifts came in 1857 when she was impressed with the wounds of the stigmata. (These strange bleeding wounds materialize on the hands and feet and correspond to the traditional marks of the Crucifixion on Christ's body. Sometimes a wound in the side or a bleeding 'crown of thorns' will open simultaneously.) Even though the case was investigated by the Church, their official representatives never determined to their satisfaction whether Palma's displays were divine or diabolical in nature. But the stigmata was only one example of this simple woman's gifts.

Dr Imbert-Gourbeyre, who literally lived with Palma while investigating her purported gifts, witnessed her miraculous Communions on several occasions, since Palma sometimes produced the miracle two or even three times a day. On one occasion Dr Imbert-Gourbeyre and a friend, the Canon de Angeles, were visiting Palma when it took place.

'I was sitting sidewise to Palma talking to the Canon', writes the investigator, 'when I felt her hand gently tap me on the forearm. At the same instant the Canon fell to his knees. I turned to look at Palma, and I saw her eyes shut, her hands joined, her mouth wide open, and on her tongue I perceived a Host. I kneel down at once, I adore, and I watch her. Palma put out her tongue still further as if she was bent on making me see the Host clearly, then she swallows it . . .'

Since Palma had no obvious resources for obtaining the Host beforehand, the physician considered the incident miraculous. Readers of the French scholar's work today may not be so impressed, however.

Even his contemporaries considered Dr Imbert-Gourbeyre somewhat credulous, so we should read his report on Palma Matarelli sceptically. It doesn't appear that the physician ever seriously considered that Palma could have stolen the Host, perhaps while taking an earlier Communion from her priest. She could have secreted the wafer in her mouth but not swallowed it. She could then have produced it later in a 'miraculous' way to impress Dr Imbert-Gourbeyre and his illustrious friend. While this *modus operandi* for the miracle cannot be totally dismissed, the suggestion is offset by the frequency with which she produced the miracle. Remember that these supernatural Communions often occurred twice a day. If they had been fraudulently produced, Palma would have needed a huge number of Hosts to continue with the fakery. This was a possibility that Dr Imbert-Gourbeyre summarily rejected.

The French doctor was not as lucky as the many priests who have directly observed the spontaneous materialization, dematerialization, or related strange behaviour of the Host during the miracle. These reports read more impressively than those contributed by Dr Imbert-Gourbeyre, even though many of them are rather dated testimonials.

Several priests testified to Church officials in Italy, for example, that miraculous communions were frequently bestowed upon St Catherine of Siena (1347-80), a Dominican nun who felt the pain of the stigmata on her body. Catherine was a lively and physically becoming girl who resisted marriage and entered the sisterhood in 1367, even though she continued to live with her parents for some time. She was devoted to prayer, and her many ecstasies and raptures led to stigmatic pain in her limbs, although full-blown lesions never opened. (This phenomenon is called the 'invisible' stigmata and was frequently reported by the saints.) Catherine was anything but reclusive and was, for her day, a remarkable social activist. She tried to mediate between opposing factions in the city of Florence's battles with the Papal government and even met with the Pope over the disputes.

During the official ecclesiastic investigation which led to her canonization, several priests testified that they had personally witnessed Catherine taking miraculous Communion when they themselves were preparing to offer her the Sacrament. Father Bartholomew Dominic, who had often given Communion to the nun, reported to the committee that sometimes the Host would become agitated in his hand—as if it was a living creature trying to escape his grasp.

'This at first troubled me,' he testified to the officers, 'for I feared lest the Sacred Host should fall to the ground; but it seemed to fly into her [St Catherine's] mouth. Several persons told me that the like had happened to them when giving her Holy Communion.'

One of these witnesses was Francesco Malevolti, who told the same commission that once 'when the priest was about to give her the Body of our Lord, before he had drawn more than a palm's length near her, the Sacred Host would depart out of his hand and like an arrow shoot into the mouth of the holy virgin'.

A very different version of the miracle is recorded by St Catherine's confessor, Raymond of Capua, who was himself beatified in 1899. Raymond of Capua testified that, one day in church, he had finished consecrating a Host and was ready to break it in half when it snapped into three parts. One particle fell on to the altar and instantly vanished. Raymond explained that he searched fruitlessly for the particle. Later he discovered St Catherine kneeling at the back of the church. She told him that the particle had been brought to her by a supernatural force so that she could enjoy Communion without disturbing the priest.

A very similar miracle is recorded in the life of Blessed Elisabeth von Reute, a mystic who lived in Upper Swabia and died in 1420. Her biography was written by her confessor, Father Konrad Kügelin, soon after her death. He reported in the book that he once gave Elisabeth Communion in her cell since she was too sick to come to the church for it. He was carrying the Host on a plate when he suddenly discovered that it was gone. His first thought was that the wafer had fallen from the plate, so he retraced his steps but still could not find it. He prepared to explain the situation to Elisabeth, since he could no longer give her Communion, but to his surprise he found the nun in high spirits when he approached her cell.

'You laugh,' he told her, 'while I am in deep distress.' He refrained from explaining *why* he was so upset, but he really didn't have to elaborate.

'Do not be troubled any more,' she responded as she began to describe a vision she had just experienced. 'Our Lord has already revealed to me that you have lost the Sacred Host. You have not lost it. I must tell you that Jesus Christ, my beloved Spouse, came to me in human form, preceded by an angel magnificently clad, and that He gave me the Blessed Sacrament with his own Hand.'

A more recent account of a teleporting Host is given by Father Bernard Laviosa in his book *Vita di S. Maria Francesca della Cinque Piaghe*, a biography of an Italian nun who died in 1791. Father Laviosa personally gave Communion to Sister Maria on several occasions. He reported in his book that on one occasion during Mass, the nun complained of its length and her insatiable yearning for Communion. 'Accordingly I made my preparations at once and to gratify her I hastened my Mass as much as I could,' he writes. 'When, however, I came to the point of giving her Communion, hardly had I turned round and pronounced the words *Ecce Agnus Dei* when I perceived that the Host was no longer between my fingers. I was terribly upset . . . but she [Sister Maria] signed to me that she already had the host upon her tongue, and I on seeing this was able to set my mind at rest.'

The miracle was also witnessed by a server at the Mass, who saw the Host spontaneously materialize on Sister Maria's tongue.

The puzzling case of Thérèse Neumann

Evidence documenting the existence of this rare miracle does not rest solely on antiquated reports sometimes dating back several centuries, for it has also occurred several times in recent years.

The life story, visions, and miracles of Thérèse Neumann represent one of the most fascinating controversies in the history of the Catholic Church. She lived her entire life (1898-1962) in Konnersreuth, a small town in Bavaria near the Czech border. She had a basically happy childhood and performed domestic and farm work to supplement her family's meagre income. This situation changed dramatically in 1918 when she began suffering from a series of medical problems. These conditions began in March when she was fighting a fire in the town, injured her back and was forced to stay in bed. She fell down a flight of stairs and injured her head a month later, which resulted in severe convulsions and some internal injuries.

After this unfortunate mishap, Thérèse's medical problems became progressively more serious. Her eyesight began to fail, and she eventually became a blind, bedridden invalid. Her convulsions were sometimes so severe that she would be thrown from bed. Nor could she keep down any solid food.

Reading this case history today, it certainly looks as if these later symptoms were more psychosomatic than medical. The list of her problems seems consistent with *hysteria*, a syndrome common in her day but relatively rare in modern times. Sufferers of classical hysteria convert subconscious conflicts into dramatic physical symptoms— including difficulty with eating, convulsions, bouts of inexplicable paralysis, and loss of sight. That Thérèse's problems were primarily psychological seems obvious, too, from the spontaneous 'cures' she experienced in subsequent years. One by one, beginning in 1925, her illnesses disappeared, to the surprise of her family and friends.

Despite this more psychologically sophisticated evaluation of Thérèse Neumann's condition, to the simple people of Konnersreuth it was clear that their fellow villager had received healings from God. They became even more awestruck when Thérèse began exhibiting a wide range of supernatural powers. Stigmatic wounds were impressed on her side one night when Christ appeared to her in a wondrous vision. The full stigmata soon manifested, and between the 1930s and her death in 1962 hundreds of visitors to the village observed her ecstasies and spontaneous bleedings. Tours were even scheduled through her house and into her room when the stigmata erupted. (Despite this seeming commercialism, these tours were religious in nature and conducted with dignity and solemnity for the many pilgrims who came to Konnersreuth.) Sometimes the stigmata even glowed.

The wounds of the stigmata represented merely one side of Thérèse Neumann's considerable spiritual propensities. She often experienced bilocations, strange episodes in which she would be seen in two different places at the same time. She refused to eat, and during the terrible years of the Second World War even donated her ration card to others. She apparently could heal the sick and exhibited other mystical wonders—including Miraculous Communion.

Many priests testified, for example, that at times Thérèse would fall to her knees while they were giving her Communion in her room, whereupon a Host would suddenly materialize on her tongue. Later, when they returned to their churches, they would find that Hosts had mysteriously disappeared from their stock!

A different form of Miraculous Communion was recorded in 1929 by Dr Fritz Gerlich, a life-long friend and biographer of the mystic. In his book *Thérèse Neumann von Konnersreuth*, he offers his readers an eyewitness report on a spontaneously disappearing Host. Dr Gerlich was kneeling directly in front of Thérèse while she was receiving Communion from her priest. When the priest placed an unbroken Host on her outstretched tongue, 'Suddenly the Host disappeared. Her mouth was wide open. She had not closed it since first opening it. From the first moment she opened her mouth, she did not make any motion of swallowing.'

It was Dr Gerlich's opinion that the Host had supernaturally merged with her body.

The American Catholic writer Paul Schimberg reports a similar story concerning Thérèse's Miraculous Communions in his book *The Story of Thérèse Neumann*. One day she was visiting the home of a dying woman for whom she was caring. Suddenly she fell to her knees, opened her mouth, and placed her hands on her breast as though receiving Communion. The family of the elderly woman ran to their home's chapel and discovered that a Host, which had been left there earlier in the day, had disappeared. It had been placed there by a priest who intended to give it to Thérèse when she took Communion later in the day.

On permanent record also is the testimony of Thérèse's life-long friend and confessor, Father Naber, who was the village priest of Konnersreuth. He told ecclesiastical officials that, on one memorable occasion, a Host detached itself from his hand while he was giving Communion to Thérèse and floated into her mouth. This incident, dating from 1929, took place in public and was witnessed by several of the townsfolk. It was also purportedly photographed.

In light of these reports, so meticulously documented by the witnesses, it seems unlikely that Miraculous Communion is merely a legend. It undoubtedly represents a remarkable form of psychic phenomenon linked to the Communion ritual. I will have more to say on the explanation for this miracle at the end of this chapter. For the present, however, I would like to examine two fairly recent reports of the miracle. Both of these events took place in public and were witnessed by dozens of onlookers. They represent a strong rejoinder to those sceptics who might complain that the evidence for Communion miracles rests solely on the reports of priests and other (perhaps biased) partisans of the supernatural.

Two recent examples of Miraculous Communion

The first of these took place in the little Spanish town of San Sebastian de Garabandal, and served as the climax to a complicated series of events dating from 1961.

The story of the Garabandal miracles began on 18 July 1961 when two local children, Conchita Gonzales and Mary Cruz Gonzales (they were not related), slipped from a town celebration to steal some apples from a nearby orchard. While they were engaging in their petty theft, a vision of an angel appeared to them. This vision kept recurring, and soon two other local children began sharing the experiences. Eventually the figure of the Virgin Mary began appearing to the children, either individually or when they were gathered together, and soon the apparition became the talk of the town. These visionary experiences, which resembled those which took place in 1918 at Fatima (Portugal) continued until 1962. The children would usually be at home when they first received the 'call' to meet with the apparitional figure. They would then suddenly leave their homes and slip outside at appointed times as though supernaturally summoned. Hundreds of villagers and sightseers witnessed the children as they held their spiritual vigils. Probably the most remarkable aspect was the trance the children entered during the vigils, which sometimes took place on a low, shrub-covered hill near town. Lights shined directly into their eyes would be ignored, and the children would remain insensitive to pinpricks and other discomforts. Even more bizarre was the way they would run down the hill during their ecstasies. In a series of films I viewed privately in 1980, the children could be seen rapidly running backwards down the hillside, yet mysteriously manoeuvring through the brush and holes in the ground with stupefying precision! No matter what the cause of the children's visionary experiences, these films were extremely impressive.

On 3 July 1962, Conchita—who had become the unofficial leader of the little band of visionaries—proclaimed that a miracle would take place in 15 days. The exact nature of the miracle was left a mystery but set the stage for her Miraculous Communion.

On the night of 18 July, Conchita awoke from sleep, stumbled from bed, and walked out into the street, where she fell to her knees. Droves of villagers—who had been keeping her under observation while they waited for the promised miracle—instantly lit up the street with flashlights and torches. According to the several eyewitnesses present, Conchita remained still and then opened her mouth and stretched out her tongue. In a flash, a Host materialized on it and was even photographed. Conchita held the wafer outstretched for several moments so that everyone could see it before she swallowed it.

One eyewitness report of this incident has been placed on record by Don Alejandro Damians, a Barcelona resident who had followed Conchita through the street. He was approximately two feet away from the girl when the miracle took place.

The sight of that fantastic mob on the run, shoving and elbowing one another, could not be more terrifying.

I attempted to follow Conchita, but a crowd, fifteen or twenty deep, separated us. I sometimes caught a vague glimpse of her. She turned left along the lane formed by the side of her house and a low wall. She turned left again, and there, right in the middle of the alley, which is fairly wide at that spot, she suddenly fell to her knees.

Her fall was so unexpected that the avalanche of people were carried past on either side of her by the weight of their own numbers. I was fortunate in not being carried past with them, and before I knew it, I unexpectedly found myself to her right, with her face a mere eighteen inches from mine. I staunchly withstood the pushing of those behind me, striving with all my might not to be wrenched from my vantage point. I succeeded.

The shoves gradually ceased and relative calm ensued.

Shortly before midnight, the clouds obscuring the sky had slowly drifted away, and the blue mantle of the heavens had become studded with stars shining about the moon.

In their light, and that of an infinite number of torches in the alley, I could see quite plainly that Conchita's mouth was open and her tongue out in the position customary when going to Communion. She was prettier than ever. Far from causing laughter or looking the slightest bit ridiculous, her expression and attitude had about them an awesome, moving mysticism.

Suddeny, without my knowing quite how, without really realizing it, without Conchita changing her expression in the slightest, the Sacred Host appeared on her tongue. It was totally unexpected. It did not seem to have been deposited there, but might be described rather as having materialized there, faster than the human eye could see.

Other witnesses claimed that the Host only gradually formed on her tongue. But whatever the case, the spectators agreed that the appearance of the Host was clearly supernatural. The Miraculous Communion presaged the end of the Garabandal visions, for they began to decline at that time and ceased entirely by 1965. Conchita today lives in New York, where she is married to a blue-collar worker. She still maintains the authenticity of her previous experiences in Spain and books are still being written on the Garabandal episode.

The most recent case of Miraculous Communion I know of was

reported from the village of Praia do Pedrogao, Portugal in 1970. The recipient of the miracle was Maria Horta, who caused a considerable stir in Portugal's ecclesiastic community. Maria ostensibly developed several supernatural gifts after she was miraculously cured of leukaemia in 1959. Since that time she has been impressed with stigmata-like wounds which manifest on her forehead, religious statues sometimes bleed in her presence, and she has received Miraculous Communion several times. These usually occur when she is in church. Several onlookers have seen her fall to her knees and open her mouth, and have watched Hosts instantly materialize there.

It is highly likely, of course, that many similar miracles are occurring in other predominantly Catholic countries as well, but are never reported by or to Church officials.

Explaining Miraculous Communion

If nothing else, this brief chapter has tried to show that the miracle of Divine Communion can manifest in several ways. It has been repeated in many variations throughout recorded Christian history. But just how can this miracle be explained? What intelligence lies at the heart of these materializations. Answering that puzzle will serve as the theme for this section of *Beyond Reality*.

Some cases of Miraculous Communion no doubt represent instances of deliberate fraud. This simple fact must always be kept in mind while we evaluate these episodes. Magdalena de la Cruz (1487-1560), a Spanish nun who lived shortly before the reign of Philip II, confessed that she had deliberately faked the miracle on several occasions in order to impress her religious superiors with her sanctity. Vittoria Biondi, an Italian 'mystic' who lived during the eighteenth century, also received Miraculous Communions in public—until local Church officials searched her room and found several Hosts hidden there! It is debatable, however, whether such calculated fraud can explain the well-witnessed Miraculous Communions received by mystics such as St Catherine of Siena or, in our own times, by Thérèse Neumann. Catholic Church doctrine proclaims that these miracles are *charismata*—i.e. signs produced by God to inspire the witnesses to seek spiritual enlightenment. My own opinion, however, differs from Catholic dogma.

I began studying the lore and evidence supporting the existence of religious miracles in 1975 from a purely scientific viewpoint. Not being a Catholic by faith, my interest in miracles grew from my professional interest in psychic phenomena in general. It is my feeling that Miraculous Communion has little to do with anything purely spiritual. I believe that it is produced by the *mind* of the recipient. Certain forms of Miraculous Communion, such as when the Host floats out of the hands of the officiating priest, seem to be examples of psychokinesis occurring in a religious setting. Other forms of the miracle—such as the disappearing and rematerializing Hosts that behaved so strangely in the presence of Thérèse Neumann—seem to be little different from the way poltergeists will make household objects disappear and reappear. (Such incidents may represent religious analogues to the type of spontaneous dematerializations covered in Chapter 1.) Since most parapsychologists agree that poltergeist eruptions are produced through the agency of the human subconscious, Miraculous Communions may result from a similar process.

This notion is especially pertinent to the case of Thérèse Neumann. It should be clear that despite her apparent medical problems, her symptoms can be easily explained as hysterical reactions. Each and every one of her problems—her mysterious illnesses, sudden blindness, paralysis, and so forth—were probably conversion reactions (physical but nonorganic conditions) caused by religious conflicts within her own mind. It is precisely this sort of disturbed person who is likely to become the focus of a poltergeist. But in the case of Thérèse Neumann, perhaps the power within her psyche expressed itself within a religious rather than a secular context.

This informal hypothesis is not, however, meant to denigrate the religious or spiritual implications which result from the study of the miraculous. It merely shows that the intelligent layman can believe in the existence of miracles without necessarily adopting any prescribed dogma concerning them. On the other hand, Miraculous Communion is one of the truly great miracles of the Catholic Church. So it may well be proper to ask: can the power of pure religious faith and belief *bring* the miraculous into existence? This will be the subject of this book's final two chapters.

13

Medjugorje

Medjugorje is not some sort of exotic foreign delicacy, but a small community situated in central Yugoslavia. The community (which is pronounced Měd-ū-gōr-̄jee) is located within 100 kilometres of the Adriatic Sea in a region once known as Bosnia. In fact, it lies close to Bosnia's historical border with Croatia, a border somewhat obscured by the creation of modern Yugoslavia after the First World War.

The location of the village is crucial to understanding the events currently taking place there. Even today Yugoslavia is a curious mixture of separate peoples and religions. Most experts doubt, however, that this combination of cultures has been successful. One writer on the subject has stated that rather than a melting-pot, the county is 'a cauldron in which a host of nationalities seethed and bubbled but never managed to coalesce'. Special hostilities have traditionally existed between the Serbs and the Croats. Throughout the history of the region, each has tried to subjugate the other. Whichever culture temporarily subdued the opposition usually engaged in bloody massacres that continued right into the present century.

Apart from the social strife in the country, modern Yugoslavia has had its fair share of religious problems. Different factions within the Catholic Church have been battling for territory as well as souls, while a large Muslim community (left over from the days when the country was part of the Ottoman Empire) still exists in Yugoslavia. It was during this battle within the Catholic community that a miracle came to Medjugorje, when the Blessed Virgin Mary began materializing before a group of awestruck children. Soon she was creating miracles for everyone to see.

The appearance on Earth of a beautiful lady claiming to be the Blessed Virgin Mary is part and parcel of Roman Catholic tradition. Many people in recent centuries have seen this figure, who invariably comes to deliver a message from God. Now visionary experiences tend to be completely subjective. Since they usually take place within the spectator's mind, they can't be verified and the sceptic has every right to reject them. It is certainly possible that most such experiences are the pathological result of religious fervour or some sort of related psychological disturbance. But every so often these visitations break forth from the inner world of the mind and become visible to more than the original witness. On other occasions the figure will deliver prophecies that come true.

During the last two centuries, several of these cases have been documented and some have been declared miraculous by the Roman Catholic Church:

● Beginning on the night of 16 July 1830, a young postulant in Paris named Zoé Catherine Labouré began seeing a vision of the Blessed Virgin Mary. The figure confided a series of messages to her concerning coming calamities to the Church. These prophecies were fulfilled within a few days.

● In 1846, two children in La Salette (a small village in the southeast part of France) began witnessing similar visions. The figure warned them of a terrible famine, which came to pass when the great potato famine struck that year. Other prophecies made by the Blessed Virgin Mary did not come true.

● A more impressive Marian manifestation occurred in France in 1871 when the country was battling the Prussians. The radiant figure of the Blessed Virgin Mary, bedecked with stars, appeared in the sky over Pontmain, where she was described—in the same way—by two separate groups of children.

● A further collective appearance by the Blessed Virgin Mary occurred in Ireland on 21 August 1879, when a 'tableau' depicting her and several other figures spontaneously materialized near a church at Knock. The immobile figures were seen by several of the townspeople.

● Probably the most famous of these visitations was reported from Fatima, Portugal, in 1918, when three children encountered her figure repeatedly in a field near the village. While nobody else could see the figure, many villagers reported seeing orbs of light or hearing strange buzzing sounds when the children spoke to the lady. She predicted that a great miracle would occur in the field on 13 September 1918. On that day some 30,000 people watched while the sun—or a shining orb in the sky—revolved and cast multicoloured lights into the sky. The object then zigzagged towards the ground before returning into the heavens.

- This renowned miracle was repeated in a different manner in the summer of 1961 when a group of children in Garabandal, Spain, repeatedly encountered the Blessed Virgin Mary. Later pilgrims to the city reported seeing the spinning of the sun. The Blessed Virgin predicted a miracle for everyone to see in the future, but it never came to pass.

- Perhaps the most convincing of these miracles took place throughout 1968 in Egypt, in the Cairo suburb of Zeitoun. A silent white figure began pacing the roof of a Coptic Catholic church, whose dome would glow with supernatural light when the figure materialized. The apparition was generally considered to be the Blessed Virgin and was repeatedly photographed.

These brief summaries encapsulate several decades of Marian visitations, and many others could be cited.* In general, though, these miracles can be broken down into two categories. Some of the apparitions appear before large crowds of people, but usually remain silent—for example, such incidents occurred at Knock and Cairo in 1879 and 1968 respectively. But a more prevalent pattern is for the figure to materialize before a small group of children. These children are typically rather young and report a series of related encounters, during which the Blessed Virgin Mary offers a series of predictions or secrets. On rare occasions, people watching the children will share in the encounter by seeing or hearing strange sights and sounds. Something of this sort began to happen in Medjugorje and the neighbouring community of Bijakovići in the summer of 1981, and these events have become the most controversial Marian visitation in recent years.

The coming of the figure

The events leading up to this complicated religious and political controversy date from 24 June 1981, which is the feast day of St John the Baptist. A terrible storm had struck the region the previous night, which had set fire to the local post office and to some pine trees. It looked as if the forces of nature were preparing Medjugorje for a

* For a history of such visitations written from a religious perspective, see Don Sharkey, *The Woman Shall Conquer* (Kenosha, Wis.: Prow Books, 1964). For a more secular look at the same material, see Kevin McClure, *The Evidence for Visions of the Virgin Mary* (Wellingborough, Northants: Aquarian Press, 1983).

religious storm of equal magnitude.

The day after the storm, two teenaged girls (who were visiting relatives in Bijakovići for the summer) were taking a stroll up a hill behind some houses outside the town. Ivanka Ivanković and Mirjana Dragicević were 15 and 16 years old respectively and did not consider themselves particularly religious. Nor were they taking a walk for their health, but to escape the supervision of their relatives in order to smoke some cigarettes! The girls were still climbing the hill when they saw a luminous but opaque figure hovering over the ground in the distance. For some reason which she could never figure out, Ivanka cried out, 'Mirjana, look there, it is the Madonna!' The girl was pale with fright, but her companion dismissed the suggestion—even though she scurried down the hill with Ivanka moments later. It was then that the second phase of the visitation by the Blessed Virgin Mary took place.

When they reached the houses nestled at the bottom of the incline, the girls encountered their friend Milka Pavlović—who, in true bucolic fashion, was rounding up a flock of sheep. The two original witnesses described their encounter to the shepherdess, and she soon joined them in retracing the path up the hill. By this time it was six-fifteen in the evening, and it didn't take the girls long to reach the spot where the form had materialized earlier. Each of the girls distinctly saw a greyish form in the distance holding something in her hand, but they could not see much more than the figure's outline. For some inexplicable reason the witnesses once more had the intuitive sense that the phantom was the Blessed Virgin Mary, even though their emotions represented a curious mixture of fear and excitement. They soon found themselves entranced by the spectral visitor on the hilltop.

Ivanka would later reminisce that 'we didn't know what to do, where to put ourselves. We felt a mixture of joy and fear. So much joy, so much fear, it's impossible to describe it.'

By this time a further potential witness entered the scene. Earlier that day, Ivanka and Mirjana had stopped by to see their friend Vicka Ivanković (no relation to the former) in town. The two girls hoped she would stroll up the hillside with them, but she was sleeping off a rough day spent in a neighbouring community. She finally woke up at the same time that (unbeknownst to her, of course) her friends were descending the hill and—finding a note they had left for her—she decided to search for them. She was scaling the hill when she found her friends immobilized and facing the mysterious figure.

'Look, it's the Madonna,' they cried out to their friend—who was so frightened that she ran back down the hill, where she encountered two youths, 20-year-old Ivan Ivanković (no relation to either of the girls) and 16-year-old Ivan Dragicević.

When they heard what was taking place up the path, they couldn't resist Vicka's entreaties to accompany her back up the hill. This return trip was to be fateful, for the whole group saw the silent white lady. Vicka was the last to see the apparition, since she shaded her face from the spot where the figure was purportedly floating. Curiosity finally got the better of her though, and she too finally looked up and saw it. She later gave the following description to reporters:

> But then, all of a sudden, I looked up and saw her standing there, just as clearly as I can see you now. She wore a grey dress with a white veil, a crown of stars, blue eyes, dark hair and rosy cheeks. And she was floating about this high in the air on a grey cloud, not touching the ground. She had something in her left hand that she kept covering and uncovering—but you couldn't see what it was. She called us to go nearer, but none of us dared to.

Shaken by the experience, the youngsters returned home and immediately told their families what they'd seen earlier. Not surprisingly, they weren't believed. Some of the family members even mocked them. But rumours of the miraculous visitation began to circulate in the small village, where gossip is a more immediate source of information than the telephone or the printed word.

One resident in the community who didn't laugh when he heard the story was Marinko Ivanković (predictably enough, no relation of *any* of the other Ivankovićes in the case), who was a local mechanic. He was strangely impressed when he heard the story from Milka and Mirjana the day after the first materialization. He decided to keep a close watch on the girls, and he didn't have long to wait. For the strange visitation to Medjugorje was to be repeated the next day—i.e. two days after the Blessed Virgin Mary's first appearance.

The day began innocuously enough. Ivanka and Mirjana worked that morning in the tobacco fields near the town, which was their regular summer employment. Even though the events of two days before had frightened them, they felt compelled to return to the scene of the visitation. They discussed the matter between themselves, but before returning to the hill they visited the two Ivans and asked them to take part in the expedition. The young Ivan decided to accompany his friends, but the older youth refused on the grounds that he'd experienced enough. The exact events get a little complicated at this point in the story, but eventually several of the original witnesses returned to the spot of the materialization. On this occasion they were

joined by a young boy named Jakov Cõlo. When the youngest began
the short climb, they once more saw the figure, which seemed to
congeal out of a mist. Mirjana was the first to catch sight of the figure,
which, she later said, wore 'a long grey dress and white veil. I could
see the outline of her face quite clearly, though she was a long way
away at the top of the hill.'

The silent woman seemed to beckon to them, so they ran towards
the spot where she was materializing. They flew up the hill in a couple
of minutes, even though it usually took 12 minutes to scale. They
didn't even bother to follow the path leading up the hill, but ran
without thinking. When they reached the peak of the hill close to the
apparition, they found themselves thrown to their knees.

Now, for the first time, the figure spoke to her young followers,
saying little more than that they should go in peace with God. She also
told them to care for their relatives.

Because of the commotion the incidents had caused, the villagers
mobilized quickly when they learned that the youngsters were
returning to the hilltop. Several townsfolk followed them. While they
couldn't see the apparition, they watched the group's spectacular flight
up the hill. Most of them didn't know what to think and returned to
their homes 15 minutes later when the encounter ended. Marinko
Ivanković (the young mechanic mentioned earlier) was not among
them, however, for he returned from work in a neighbouring
community just at the time the visitation ended. But he realized that
something important had taken place when he encountered the
young witnesses. Some of them were crying and, moved by the
celestial visitations to his community, he decided to inform the local
priest of the miracle.

Roman Catholic officials don't particularly like reports of miracles,
and the events taking place in Medjugorje and Bijakovići immediately
suffered from this traditional incredulity. Even though the existence
of miracles is supported by the Church (though it is not a required
belief), each report is sceptically evaluated before a formal investigation is organized. It takes extraordinary initial evidence to encourage
Church officials to move on a miraculous report, especially sketchy
reports. So it isn't strange that the assistant priest of the local church
dismissed the story when Marinko summarized it for him. But even
though the Church was silent on the matter, the newly materialized
lady was not—a fact proved the following day when she revealed her
mission to the young people.

By this time they were intent on returning to the spot of the original
sighting for a third time, in hopes that the figure would reveal her

identify and purpose. Marinko decided to join the expedition, even though he was taking no chances and carried holy water with him. (This precaution was taken in case the apparition turned out to be demonic.) The supernatural nature of the visitation became apparent that night when the entire town of Bijakovići was illuminated by three flashes of dazzling light. The source of the light was a mystery, since it did not result from lightning strikes. The youngsters had already met at the bottom of the hill when these flashes burst forth, and by their light they could see the Blessed Virgin Mary standing at the top. So they quickly scaled the hill, followed by hundreds of local people eager to share in the miracle. The youngsters fell to their knees when they reached the apparition while Marinko—who could not see her—threw holy water in her direction, commanding her to depart if she were evil.

The pretty lady merely smiled.

The young people now took matters into their own hands by asking her to explain her mission. The radiant being responded by saying, 'I am the Blessed Virgin Mary.' She soon elaborated by explaining, 'I have chosen this place specially, because there are many faithful believers here.'

The young people began to pray, and soon the entire congregation of bystanders joined in. When the prayers were concluded, the young witnesses turned to them and explained that the Blessed Virgin Mary would return the following evening. This second public visitation took place right on schedule, even though the hundreds of onlookers saw nothing but the entranced witnesses staring into space. On this occasion, however, the Blessed Virgin Mary extended her simple message and requested the people to reconcile themselves with God and each other—perhaps a cryptic reference to the perpetual strife between the battling factions that make up Yugoslavia and even her own Catholic community.

The controversy and the Blessed Virgin Mary's message

Because the size of the constant crowds was increasing and producing enormous publicity throughout the country, the police intervened on 27 June. This was a Saturday and constituted the fourth day of the visitations. The police arrived in Bijakovići and took the six young people to Citluk, a nearby town on the Croation border. Here they were interrogated by law enforcement officers who were worried that the 'miracles' were a plot perpetrated by the Catholic Church. When the youngsters steadfastly maintained the reality of the visitations, they were sent to a local physician for medical evaluations. Dr Ante Vuyević was a general practitioner in Citluk and could find nothing wrong with Ivan Dragicević, who was the only witness he examined. The physician wanted to look at the others, but evening was drawing in and they wanted to return to the hill so the physician didn't detain them.

The local parish authorities in Medjugorje were likewise becoming more and more concerned about the purported miracles. The parish priest, 40-year-old Father Jozo Zovko, was not present in the village when the visitations commenced. The dedicated Franciscan priest was relatively new to the parish and had been away on retreat. When he finally returned that weekend, the assistant priest of his church explained the situation and suggested that the youngsters were either taking drugs or were dupes in a Communist plot to discredit the Church. Father Jozo, who was less biased, met with them himself, and it didn't take him long to reject the suggestion that they were using drugs; but he couldn't completely dismiss the suggestion that the incidents were some sort of political manoeuvre by the Communists.

Despite these behind-the-scenes machinations, the youngsters returned to the hill with a mob of curiosity-seekers and religious pilgrims in hot pursuit. Nothing too exciting transpired between the witnesses and the Blessed Virgin that evening, but the case was soon to become even more complicated.

Even though the parish priest had urged his congregation not to follow the youngsters up on to the hill, his words had little influence on the villagers. By five o'clock the following afternoon, large crowds were swarming over the hills. Fifteen thousand spectators eventually congregated. The youngsters took their usual places by running up the hill at breakneck speed, neither stumbling over the bushes nor looking where they were running. During this vigil, however, the Blessed Virgin Mary—still completely invisible to the bystanders—offered a more extended message. She beseeched people to preserve their faith and urged them to believe in her even if they couldn't see her form. The young witnesses responded by asking the lady for a public sign so that the community would know they weren't shamming, but the apparition seemed to ignore the request.

Even though the apparition declined to give a public sign, several such incidents were soon to follow.

The first of these took place the following Monday, which was the feast day of St Peter and St Paul. Since it was obviously an important religious occasion in the parish, Father Jozo once more tried to influence his congregation to ignore the strange visitations. During his morning sermon he proclaimed that there was 'no public revelation' contained in the Virgin's messages. Whatever was taking place up on the hill, he said, was best left private between the young witnesses and the figure. But any attempt to stem the flood of people to the hillside was completely fruitless and the crowds continued to grow.

The local Communist Party chiefs were getting more restless, too, so that day they showed up in the village and rounded up the young witnesses. They were taken to nearby Mostar (a town directly north of Medjugorje) for psychiatric evaluations. The psychiatrist in charge of the undertaking tried to get them to confess, even purportedly holding a pistol to the head of one of them. (Vicka's response to the threat was simply to say, 'The economy's in a bad enough shape without you wasting ammunition like that!') When the psychiatrist found nothing psychiatrically wrong with them, he sent them back to their village. They were followed, however, by Dr Darinka Glamuzina, a woman physician and an outspoken atheist, who still wanted to expose the miracles. There was some suspicion that the local Communist authorities specifically requested that she investigate the miracles, but her exact role in the case remains a little puzzling.

Whatever the case may be, Dr Glamuzina was standing close to the youngsters when they met with the Blessed Virgin Mary that evening on the hill, and she requested permission to touch the figure when it materialized. When the young witnesses gained the consent of the lady, the physician thrust her hand into where the figure was presumably standing. She felt a violent tremor which spread through the length of her arm, which she publicly described to the delighted crowd. The shock of the experience disoriented her, and she stumbled back down the hill and refused to return. She immediately withdrew from the case and never spoke of the incident again.

The sequel to this incident was even more impressive. Somebody in the crowd held out an epileptic and mute boy, and the witnesses asked the Blessed Virgin to cure the poor child. The boy was spontaneously cured later that night and spoke for the first time.

The specific events of the following days and weeks become even more complex, since both the local Communist officials and the Church became deeply embroiled in the Medjugorje miracles. It wouldn't serve much purpose to report all the nightly visitations and the apparition's banal messages, so I will merely summarize the subsequent events.

It was probably inevitable that the political powers in Yugoslavia would try to stop the cult of Medjugorje from spreading. Several manoeuvres were undertaken, and Father Jozo (who eventually became more favourable in his opinion of the visitations) was jailed for several months. This incarceration was doubtless a warning to other priests in the region to play down the case. The young witnesses were eventually banned from the hill, so the location of the daily visitations of the Blessed Virgin Mary was transferred to the small church in the village. The specific messages from the lady also began to change with time. From the simple and devout opening messages they took on a surprisingly ecumenical bent. She began saying that God did not object to people following different creeds and that each person's faith, if sincere, should be respected. She proclaimed that the spiritual power of the Catholic Church still outweighed that of any other faith, but she continued to urge that no religion should be disdained.

Of course, these messages were highly significant since—as I pointed out earlier—this region of Yugoslavia has been filled with religious strife. It was beginning to look as though the 'visitor from the heavens' was responding to the cultural problems besetting the area and was not what she purported to be.

In true and traditional Marian fashion, the lady—repeating the pattern she initiated at La Salette and Fatima—finally gave the young witnesses a series of secrets. These messages have never been publicly revealed.

Nor was the grey-clad apparition opposed to commenting on local ecclesiastic matters, often brusquely criticizing Monsignor Pavao Zanic (the Bishop of Mostar), who presides over the region. These criticisms have led the Bishop to become a long-time opponent of the case and the young witnesses. His feeling is that the Medjugorje visitations represent a plot by some Franciscan priests who opposed his rule. This suggestion has been explicitly rejected by the Blessed Virgin Mary in her messages.

The visitations were not stopped by the opposition of the Communist Party or by certain factions within the Church. So eventually the political opposition died down, and the local officials granted the youngsters free rein to carry on with their public meetings with the apparition. Their banishment to the community church was lifted even though that is where most of the visitations continued to take place.

Although several years have passed since those strange events during the week of 24 June 1981 took place, several of the original witnesses continue to enter their trances and meet with the lady from the sky. Even the government has taken that old-fashioned 'if you can't beat them, join 'em' position on the case. It is currently promoting Medjugorje as a tourist attraction in order to bolster the economy!

Public visions and miracles at Medjugorje

During the first week of the visitations, the youngsters suggested to the mysterious lady that she should produce a public sign to convince the crowd of her reality. The figure offered no response to this request. Despite her indifference, public signs *have* been seen in the village and continue to this day. These wondrous phenomena have been witnessed not only by the villagers, but by level-headed visitors and pilgrims to Medjugorje. Virtually every book written on the case contains some descriptions of these miracles, and the following reports are based on three primary sources: Svetozar Kraljević's *The Apparitions of Our Lady at Medjugorje*, Mary Craig's *Spark from Heaven*, and Lucy Rooney and Robert Faricy's *Mary, Queen of Peace*.

Exactly when public miracles began taking place in Bijakovići and Medjugorje is a little uncertain, even though we know that strange lights were seen over the region during the first week of the Marian visitations. Some of the first miracles followed the pattern set when the little mute epileptic boy was cured on 29 June 1981. It didn't take long before other spectators and pilgrims claimed similar cures. Probably the most dramatic of these occurred on 29 July 1981 when the young people's meeting with the lady was taking place in the church in Medjugorje. One of the pilgrims in the crowd that day was a German paraplegic, Matija Skuban, who felt an electric current flow through his body while praying. This experience was followed by a physical healing, and the pilgrim proceeded to walk to his first Communion in years.

More healings were reported as the cult of Medjugorje spread throughout Europe. It soon appeared as if the entire district was being pervaded by the Blessed Virgin Mary's spiritual presence. That's when the more public marvels began to spread through the region. The most common of these prodigies were radiant lights that sped or floated through the sky overlooking the local townships. The youngsters claimed that they had observed these lights since 14 July, but soon everybody was seeing them. Several pilgrims and other observers even claimed that, later that month, they saw the Croatian word for 'peace' written in the sky over a neighbouring town. But the most miraculous display came with the 'dance of the sun', which has been repeatedly reported from Medjugorje since 1981. (This miracle seems to be some sort of reminder of the great prodigy produced at Fatima in 1918, which was described earlier in this chapter (pages

199–200).

Several reports of this particular miracle were collected by Mary Craig, who came to Medjugorje in 1982 to investigate the case and prepare a documentary for the BBC. She cites several descriptions of the miracle in *Spark from Heaven*, such as the following one:

> I was with a large group of people outside the church [related a taxi-driver], and suddenly I noted the sun doing strange things . . . it began to swing to and fro . . . Finally a ray of light separated itself from the sun and travelled like the rays of a rainbow towards the place where the Virgin had first appeared. It then rested on the church tower, on which a clear image of the Virgin appeared.

An entire community witnessed a similar display in Turcinović (located near Medjugorje) while taking part in a funeral. The procession was leaving the departed woman's house when they suddenly saw the sun spinning. Not only did everybody see the miracle, but they could stare into the sun without their eyes becoming irritated or damaged. This curious phenomenon soon became the hallmark of the Medjugorje solar prodigies.

Some of the witnesses to these miraculous events did not believe in their preternatural nature, but preferred to think that they were normal meteorological effects. This was the opinion, for example, of Father Umberto Lončar—a priest visiting the region—when he saw the spinning sun on Monday, 3 August 1981. Even though he remained sceptical, the priest witnessed a similar phenomenon one cloudless evening that finally converted him:

> At six-twenty exactly I saw a huge red and violet cloud over Cermo. The cloud was massive and was moving in my direction at unusual tremendous speed, then hovered over the hill of Križevac for a minute or two, moved eastward and seemed to sink into the earth. Because of the hills and trees between me and the cloud, I couldn't see what was happening, so I ran to the upper floor of the rectory to get a better view. After the cloud disappeared from sight, I descended to the terrace between the rectory and the church. Precisely at six-forty, the red and violet figure of a magnificent lady arose from the hill of Crnica. The red and violet faded in intensity as she ascended in the sky; then she disappeared. The last thing I saw was a brilliant white scarf that dangled from her feet and swung in the air. The vision . . . lasted about thirty seconds in all.

The conviction and sentencing of the innocent Father Jozo in the middle of the summer did little to stifle the miracles. By this time Medjugorje was becoming the most popular pilgrimage centre in Europe (with the possible exception of Lourdes). Many pilgrims began experiencing visions up on the hill, or even while using binoculars to view the site of the original Marian visitations! It is highly likely, however, that these sightings were purely subjective. Some purported photographs of these 'visions'—such as the Blessed Virgin Mary standing by a cross on the hill—were circulated, but they were probably fraudulent, even though exceptions to this sort of spiritual racketeering could feasibly exist. While conducting her research in Yugoslavia for the BBC, for example, Mary Craig procured the following report from a priest, Father Rudolf Kadlek, who was visiting from Zagreb:

> After Mass on 26th June, just after six in the morning, as we came out of the sacristy door, all the pilgrims (about eighty of us) watched the uncommon manifestations occurring at the cross. A shining white cloud descended on the Križevac hill.* The cross itself disappeared completely. In the cloud, the silhouette of a person in white in a long white garment could be seen. The person could be seen through the transparent shining cloud, but it could not be clearly seen who it was. Suddenly, a completely round white circle, like a large white host, with a small white cross above it, appeared. A woman standing next to me who photographed the spectacle of the white cloud developed a good, sharp photo without the cross. The spectacle was viewed by all the people present on the hill . . . as well as from all the places in the area of the church, the roads and fields of Medjugorje, on 24th, 25th, 26th June from six-thirty in the morning until seven.

Even though the photograph may be disputable, it is interesting that so many people collectively saw the phenomenon. So either the 'cloud' was physically real or the witnesses were sharing some sort of collective hallucination.

The suggestion of a collective hallucination is the only really logical counter-explanation for the public miracles seen in Medjugorje throughout 1981 and 1982. The problem with this explanation, however, is that it really only reclassifies rather than explains the phenomena witnessed there. Let me explain this remark a little.

Collective hallucinations are a subject upon which relatively little has been written or studied in the behavioural sciences. Psychology knows, frankly speaking, virtually nothing concerning its parameters or the phenomenon's limitations. When I was studying abnormal psychology in college, for instance, I was never exposed to *any* information on the subject. Nor did any of my textbooks even refer to such a phenomenon. So it certainly seems likely that, far from being

---

* This is a cross that has been erected to mark the location of the Blessed Virgin Mary's first appearance on the hill.

common, 'collective' hallucinations represent a rare phenomenon. Could such a bizarre psychological effect be occurring in Medjugorje regularly month after month? Despite my own reservations, the sceptic could reasonably posit that the pilgrims to the village (or the villagers themselves) sometimes become so worked up while there that some of them—usually stuck in the crowds that form in the streets by the church—suffer hallucinations. When they report their 'visions' verbally by shouting them out, people nearby may become inclined to see similar wonders. Groups of people subjected to extreme stress and isolation sometimes 'cue' each other in this manner. In this respect, shipwrecked people may see rescue ships in the distance and even share their observations with each other.* Since we know that *this* phenomenon takes place, possibly a similar effect can occur under less severe circumstances—such as during religious services and revival meetings.

Even this solution to the miracles reported from Medjugorje cannot explain every prodigy placed on record, though. It cannot, for example, explain the fact that several people reported staring into the sun in order to follow these solar miracles without damaging their eyes.

The best example of this phenomenon I have read comes from Sister Lucy Rooney, a nun living in Italy who travelled to Yugoslavia in 1981 to investigate the miracles. She eventually saw the spinning sun herself and writes calmly of her experience in her booklet about her visit:

> I myself saw the sun spinning just as Mass was beginning on 25 June 1984, about 7.05 p.m. (6.05 by the sun's time). No one was excited; a few people were pointing to the sun. The phenomenon lasted about five minutes. I could look right into the sun which appeared to be a flat disc, off-white in colour, spinning rapidly. From time to time light pulsed out from behind the disc. I tried to see if my blinking coincided with these pulsations of fire, but it was not so. I found that I could look away without my eyes being dazzled. Afterwards, the sun returned to its normal brilliance, and for the next hour, before it set, I could no longer look at it directly.

Note especially that the witness deliberately *experimented* with the effect by blinking. She was obviously trying to discover whether the effect was real or not.

---

* See, for example, E. W. Anderson, 'Abnormal Mental States in Survivors, with Special Reference to Collective Hallucinations', *Royal Naval Medical Service Journal*, 1943, *28*, 361-77.

While reading Mary Craig's *Spark from Heaven*, I was surprised to learn that she too witnessed the same miracle while collecting information for her documentary. She shared the experience in 1986 with Roger Stott of the BBC crew. The two reporters had returned to Medjugorje after conducting some interviews elsewhere in the region. When the miracle took place, they were outside the church with a crowd of people waiting for some of the original witnesses to appear. When they emerged from the clergy house, a flash of light illuminated the sky and she and Stott looked upwards. Despite her own incredulity, she saw the sun dance. 'I witnessed what so many have called the dance of the sun,' she reports in her book, 'the sun moving back and forth as though on a yo-yo string, its central incandescent white disc surrounded by spinning circles of yellow, green and red light.' She could hear other people in the crowd commenting on the prodigy. Before she realized it, she stared into the sun with no protection for 10 minutes. When she looked away from the sky, she didn't even see spots before her eyes. That's when she called to her colleague to see if he too were experiencing the display. Mr Stott confirmed that he was.

The BBC reporter's response to the miracle was, curiously enough, not exactly religious. She noticed that the other witnesses were on their knees praying, but she felt no similar impulse.

'Why, I don't know,' she writes in *Spark from Heaven*, 'but I had no sense of the numinous, only of the passing strange.' She felt she was observing some sort of strange meteorological phenomenon, but not a religious miracle—though she never could explain why her eyes weren't damaged by staring into the sun. Nor have similar 'meteorological' effects been reported from elsewhere in Yugoslavia.

Today in Medjugorje
A brief up-to-date look at Medjugorje was published in the 15 January 1988 issue of the *National Catholic Reporter*. It was a mildly depressing piece, since one focus of the report is the commercialism that has taken over the village. The illustrations printed with the article include a popularly distributed 'supernatural' photograph showing the Blessed Virgin Mary superimposed on shrubs. Even more disheartening is a photograph of a souvenir stand. Over a dozen of these shops have been erected on the dirt street outside the church in Medjugorje.

It is estimated that seven to eight million people have visited the community over the last six years. That's not surprising since travel bureaux in the United States regularly organize pilgrimages and tours to Medjugorje.

The *Reporter* article was written by Thomas C. Fox, who is a professional journalist. He was disturbed by what he found in Medjugorje. Aside from the commercialism taking over the village, he saw several pilgrims deliberately looking into the sun, obviously hoping to see it dance. Reports have come from Yugoslavia that some of these people have damaged their eyes irreversibly by engaging in this practice. The spiritual focus of Medjugorje is still the original band of witnesses, who have since grown to maturity. They still communicate with the Blessed Virgin Mary daily in the church, and large crowds gather to watch these sacred communions. Thomas Fox reports:

> While in Medjugorje, I was allowed into the choir loft with two visionaries, Marija Pavlović and Ivanka Ivanković, during one of their daily apparitions. The two appeared prayerful and relaxed as they variously sat, knelt and crouched on a heap of old carpets, saying the rosary. At 5.40 p.m., to the minute, Franciscan Father Slavko Barbarić, pointed to his watch and motioned the two to kneel in front of a large crucifix attached to a side wall. Within moments after they had taken their places, the visionaries lifted their heads to the wall, eyes fixed on a common point. Their lips moved occasionally, and after three minutes they began to whisper together in Croatian. Marija later said they were praying the Lord's Prayer—and that Our Lady never prays the Hail Mary with them.
>
> During the apparition period, I prayed with the two visionaries. The notion that Mary was physically standing before me was personally moving. I cannot say those emotions lasted or that the experience somehow changed me.

Many unresolved religious and political issues remain in the case, and they probably won't be settled for some time. Several years ago, a group of Yugoslavian bishops appointed a commission to look into the visitations. Even though the psychiatrists serving on it found nothing wrong with the young witnesses, the bishops never issued their report. Vatican officials finally intervened in 1987 and requested the bishops to organize a second commission. Monsignor Pavao Zanic is still scandalized by the Marian visitations and considers them fraudulent, a view that—in the past—he shared with everyone he could. The latest word on the Medjugorje miracles has come from Archbishop France Franic of Split-Makarska, who recently proclaimed that Church officials should desist from publicly commenting on the case until this second commission is ready to release its findings.

So as with many reports of miracles, the believers will continue to believe, and the sceptics will continue to doubt.

Some personal reflections on Medjugorje

What is really taking place in Medjugorje? Were the youngsters communicating with the Blessed Virgin Mary? Or were they experiencing hallucinations? Or possibly lying?

My opinion is that none of these competing theories is correct, but that they were making contact with a separate reality system.

I said earlier in this chapter that Marian visitations have been reported for decades. Small groups of children will often be the witnesses of these visitations, a pattern that has stretched from La Salette in the last century to Fatima, Garabandal, and Medjugorje. It is important to recognize that these visitations do not take place randomly. Marian materializations tend to break out in predominantly Roman Catholic countries *in times when social, religious, and/or political strife is rampant.* This is an extremely important principle to remember, for it literally guides these manifestations. The reader might like to refer back, at this point, to the summaries of past Marian visitations printed at the beginning of this chapter. Review them carefully and then place them within a cultural/historical context. What does one find? The manifestations that impressed Zoé Catherine Labouré took place during a period when the dominant Catholic regime and the French government were trying to stabilize their power structures. The result was a violent insurrection in Paris that left many dead shortly after the first visitation. Both the visions reported from La Salette and Pontmain, France, occurred in response to possible social calamities—the great potato famine that struck Europe in 1830, and the imminent destruction of Pontmain. (The Prussian troops inexplicably suddenly turned back from the town and spared it, a situation widely believed to be the result of the Blessed Virgin Mary's intervention.)

In our own century, the famous Marian visitations at Fatima took place during a civil war that was pitting the Communist government against the Church in a power struggle. Similar religious strife exists in Egypt between the Coptic Catholics and the Muslim population, which probably set the stage for the Zeitoun miracles.

I think the same situation existed in Yugoslavia in 1981 when the Marian visitations first began there. I pointed out earlier that modern Yugoslavia incorporates many separate cultures and peoples locked in bitter historical enmity. The history of the bloody battles between the Serbs and the Croats is so horrendous that it would be in gratuitously poor taste to recap it in this chapter. The fact that the country was pieced together after the First World War from these diverse racial groups certainly did not suppress the problem. Even more distasteful were the religious territorial battles taking place between different factions within the Church, each trying to gain control of more local prelates. In light of these pressures, something was bound to give—and it did in the form of the Madonna's visit to Medjugorje in 1981.

My provisional theory is that Marian visitations represent thought-forms that break into physical existence—usually in Catholic countries—when they are especially needed. In times of great social and religious strife, the people in these communities probably turn to their deep religious faith for emotional sustenance. Their constant prayers and preoccupations will somehow establish contact between the community and a separate reality system, which responds by 'sending' them a figure from its realms. This heavenly 'messenger' will be programmed by the community to respond to their concerns.

Note that in the Medjugorje case the Blessed Virgin Mary's message specifically spoke of religious tolerance. She urged that everybody's faith and religion should be respected. This message probably did not represent the voice of heaven, but undoubtedly mirrored the sentiments of the people of Medjugorje.

Let me summarize this conceptual model for a second time, but in a slightly different way.

Through years of prayer, hopes, and devotion, I think that mankind has built up a separate reality system somewhere in the cosmos. Within this cosmic realm the Blessed Virgin Mary and other religious personages really exist, but they probably remain moribund until the collective concentration of a parish or community injects them with spiritual power. The community's constant religious preoccupations probably produce some sort of interface between our world and this spiritual realm, the result being 'projections' into our world from this parallel dimension. While real in the sense that they physically exist to a limited degree, these projections, such as Marian figures, might best be pictured as cosmic puppets—puppets with strings pulled by the human race.

This line of speculation might strike the reader as far-fetched, but a remarkably similar suggestion was put forward by Mary Craig in her *Spark from Heaven*. She explains the Medjugorje visitations in terms of an archetypal figure. She draws, in this respect, upon the concepts and psychology of the great Swiss psychiatrist C. G. Jung. This eminent thinker believed that deep within the mind, every member of the human race thinks the same way using common symbols. These shared symbols represent the language of the Collective Unconscious, a substratum of our psyches by which we are communally linked. Ms Craig believes that the Medjugorje messenger is a reactivated archetype—perhaps 'sent' there to reflect the strife that has plagued the region for years.

As I suggested a moment ago, I really don't think that my theory for the Blessed Virgin Mary's visitations to Medjugorje is fundamentally different from Ms Craig's. But I am willing to extend it a step further. When these visitations take place, I think that a portal opens between our world and this other spiritual dimension. Coming into (geographical) contact with the space where this portal is operating could cause people to witness even more miracles—miracles produced when 'energy' from the spiritual realm enters our own consensus reality and interacts with it. Something of this sort may still be taking place in Lourdes, where a celebrated Marian visitation took place in 1858. So before concluding this book, let's turn to some of the cures that have occurred in that famous French place of pilgrimage.

14

Recent Cures at Lourdes

The celebrated healings at Lourdes in France remain both provocative and controversial. Even though the experts estimate that each pilgrim's chances of a cure are remote, thousands of people visit the shrine yearly. Because of its stringent medical standards, the Roman Catholic Church has only proclaimed 64 miracles there in the last 126 years. But even these miracles have not gone unchallenged. In 1957, Dr Donald J. West—a British psychiatrist interested in psychical research—examined 11 of the best Lourdes cures and remained unconvinced by them. His detailed book *Eleven Lourdes Miracles* showed how the evidence for each case was flawed or incomplete. It stood in stark contrast to books such as Ruth Cranston's *The Miracle of Lourdes* (published two years earlier) which supported the evidence.

Lourdes remains today a curious little town. Side by side with the holy Grotto where Bernadette Soubirous first saw the (supposed) Blessed Virgin Mary in 1858, the rankest tourism and commercialization profits from the pilgrim trade. The Lourdes shrine is actually a complex consisting of an underground basilica, the original Grotto, and several baths, where pilgrims can be immersed in spring water. The spring, which gushes forth where the Lourdes apparition bade Bernadette dig, is actually fed from several underground watercourses. Modern technology has also come to Lourdes. Beginning in 1955 the whole Lourdes complex has undergone modernization. More baths have been built near the Pavilion used to treat the sick, while an elaborate circulation system to bring water to the baths has been constructed. It may seem nearly sacrilegious, but the pilgrim bathing in the Lourdes water today is actually taking advantage of an extensive system of pipes, huge reservoirs, electric pumps, and pressure chambers!

Despite the updated plumbing, each year several old-fashioned cures come to the notice of the Lourdes Medical Bureau. The current president of the Bureau is Dr Theodore Mangiapan, who took over the position in 1972 from Dr Alphonse Olivieri, who held it from 1959. Dr Mangiapan is younger than most of his predecessors and studied at the Medical Faculty of Marseilles, from which he graduated in 1952. His speciality is haematology, and his duties with the Bureau entail consulting with 26 other physicians. These physicians constitute the International Medical Committee of Lourdes.

Any cure brought to the attention of the Bureau still receives a long and detailed examination, and very few of them ever receive the sanction of either the Bureau or the Church. For a healing to be proclaimed miraculous, the Bureau still uses the criteria set down by Prospero Lambertini (later Pope Benedict XIV) in his *De Canonizatione*, written in the early eighteenth century. (This impressive work dealt with the procedures by which to study miracles.) The Bureau evaluates whether each cure reversed a serious condition. Each cure should also be instantaneous or sudden, and it must be perfect and complete. The healing must also be permanent. For this reason, each potential cure must be followed for several years before its file is closed. So few healings can meet these criteria, in fact, that only nine cures were proclaimed between 1955 and 1965. (These cases have been summarized on the table opposite.)

The types of cures reported from Lourdes have also changed in recent times. Before the modern use of antibiotics and new discoveries in immunology, the cures focused on patients suffering from tuberculosis, poliomyelitis, and similar life-threatening and/or chronic diseases. Today's pilgrims tend to be victims of traffic accidents, leukaemia patients, and people suffering from heart disease. Since 1971 three pilgrimages have been arranged for the mentally handicapped, even though the Church doesn't evaluate such cases.

Because today's medical standards and technology are so sophisticated it isn't surprising that not many healings receive the endorsement of the International Medical Committee. Nevertheless, five miraculous cures have been proclaimed since 1965, and more may soon be forthcoming.

So who were these lucky patients, and why were their cures so remarkable?

The cure of Elisa Aloi
Elisa Aloi was born in Sicily in 1931 and suffered from tuberculosis by the time she was 17. The infection first struck her right knee and then spread through her joints and spine. Fifty operations were

Miraculous Cures at Lourdes 1955-63

Name and age	Resident	Condition	Date of cure	Certified
Maddalena Carini (31)	San Remo, Italy	Tuberculosis	1948	1960
Alice Couteault (34)	Bouilleé-Loretz, France	Multiple Sclerosis	1952	1956
Thea Angele (29)	Tettnang, Germany	Multiple Sclerosis	1950	1961
Evasio Ganora (37)	Casole, Italy	Hodgkin's Disease	1950	1955
Edeltraut Fulda (34)	Vienna, Austria	Addison's Disease	1950	1955
Henriette Bressolles (30)	Nice, France	Pott's Disease (Tuberculosis) with Paraplegia	1924	1957
Marie Bigot (31)	La Richardais, France	Posterior fossa Arachnoiditis*	1953/4	1957
Yvonne Fournier (22)	Limoges, France	Leriche's Syndrome†	1945	1959
Ginette Nouvel (26)	Carmaux, France	Budd-Chiari Disease** (hepatic vein thrombosis)	1954	1963

* A condition where cranial nerves are embedded in adhesions.
† A form of paralysis, in this case of the left arm.
** Venous obstruction in the liver.

eventually undertaken to drain her abscesses, and treatment with penicillin and streptomycin failed to keep the disease in check. Plaster of Paris casts had to be applied to support her pelvis and feet. She finally made a pilgrimage to Lourdes in 1957, apparently wasting away from the disease. Her first visit to the shrine did little to alleviate her suffering and her condition grew steadily worse.

Despite this setback, the young woman never ceased to hope, so she returned to Lourdes later that same year. She was still suffering from several underlying abscesses, and large tubercular lesions also disfigured her body. While visiting the baths by the Grotto this second time, Elisa asked that the spring water be applied directly to the lesions.

This second visit sparked a sudden change in the patient's condition. Within three days her fistulas ceased discharging pus. She returned to Messina, Sicily, where her casts were removed, and the physician handling her case documented that the lesions were obviously healing. Professor di Cesare, who had examined the patient before her pilgrimage, stated in writing that 'she was completely cured and so well that one could hardly believe it was the same person who had left Lourdes in such a desperate state'. Remember that when this statement was made, the patient had been suffering from tuberculosis for 10 years.

Elisa Aloi returned to Lourdes in 1959 and 1960 to be examined by the Medical Bureau, which unanimously declared her cure extraordinary. Even the healing of her lesions seemed inexplicable since the skin over her knee had not grown into the underlying tissue. The new skin glided over the former deterioration like fine silk. A favourable report on her case was presented to the International Medical Committee of Lourdes, and her healing was declared miraculous by the Church in 1965.

The cure of Juliette Tamburini

Born in Marseilles in 1930, little Juliette first became ill when she was 12. The most serious phase of her illness struck in 1948 when a fistula appeared in her left thigh. The underlying case seemed to be chronic staphylococcal osteitis, a severe bacterial infection of the bone. This initial diagnosis was confirmed by X-rays and by a bacteriological examination of the pus draining from the lesion. The stricken girl was treated regularly in a Marseilles hospital from 1948 to 1959. Several operations were performed to drain the sore, but nothing seemed to help. Juliette also suffered from such severe chronic nosebleeds that her physicians cauterized her septum, but without any positive result.

The patient made the pilgrimage to Lourdes (accompanied by her physician) in July 1959. She was weak and depressed, since her fistula continued to discharge continuously. She attended the Blessing of the Sick when she first arrived, but was hesitant to be immersed in the baths. Instead, her fistula was treated with some of the water taken from the taps near the original Grotto. For some mysterious reason, this treatment stopped the discharge immediately, and the fistula seemed to heal instantaneously. The lesion closed so dramatically that the gauze plug sealing it was forcibly ejected! Juliette was so pleased by this sudden healing that she visited the Piscines the next day. She was eventually immersed in the water twice over the upcoming days.

The fistula that had made her life miserable for 10 years never reappeared, and her nosebleeds ceased. Even the wasting in her legs began to reverse, so Juliette returned to Lourdes in 1960 and the Medical Bureau examined her. She was checked again in 1961 and 1963, and X-rays taken during her second trip showed no evidence of disease. The International Medical Committee looked into the healing in 1964 and issued the following statement:

> On her arrival in Lourdes in July 1959, Juliette Tamburini suffered from a fistula in the left thigh; the fistula was due to chronic osteitis of femur, a disease spanning eleven years and resistant to all therapy.
>
> The disease, up to then without any real and lasting tendency to amelioration, was suddenly modified.
>
> This cure, instantaneous, without convalescence, must be placed amongst the medically inexplicable, extraordinary cures.

The Bishop of Marseilles declared her cure miraculous on 11 May 1965.

Miss Tamburini remained surprised by the healing. During a later television interview she stated, 'I never asked for a cure; I only went to Lourdes to obtain enough faith to sustain me in my illness.'

The cure of Vittorio Micheli

Vittorio Micheli was a soldier in the Italian military when he first fell ill. Originally from the town of Trento in northern Italy, the young man joined the Alpine Corps when he was 22. Shortly after his enlistment, sciatic pain struck his side and resulted in the swelling of his left buttock. In 1962 he was taken to the Verona Military Hospital, where X-rays and a tissue biopsy revealed a pelvic sarcoma. The growth had spread throughout the pelvis, invading the left half of his pelvic bone and destroying the acetabular cup (into which the thighbone fits). The head of the femur had been pushed upwards into the tumour, leaving his left leg limp and useless. No treatment for the condition was possible, so his physicians merely encased his leg and pelvis in a plaster cast.

Vittorio made his pilgrimage to Lourdes in May 1963 and bathed there several times. He felt suddenly better on 1 June, even though the Lourdes physicians were sceptical that his condition was curable—even by a miracle! Yet it soon became obvious that his walking had improved, and when X-rays were taken of his pelvis the following April his physicians couldn't believe what they saw. The X-rays showed that the previously stricken bones had regenerated. They looked perfectly normal, though the acetabular cup was four centimetres too high. The plaster cast was removed, his physicians discharged him from further service despite the cure, and the young man found work. His cure was subsequently examined by Professor M. M. Salmon, a consultant orthopaedic surgeon to the Bureau, who sent a report to the International Medical Committee at Lourdes. The Committee deliberated for two years before declaring the cure inexplicable. Professor Salmon was so impressed by the cure that in 1971 he presented the case to a medical conference meeting in Marseilles. The conference was devoted specifically to bone sarcomata, and physicians from several countries attended. Professor Salmon delivered his report on the unusual case without explaining the Lourdes connection. It was presented merely as a spontaneous healing of sarcoma of the pelvis. Several physicians examined the medical records and remained puzzled by the inexplicable cure.

Only *after* the report was presented did the physicians learn the story behind the healing! The case was later summarized in the *Orthopedic Surgical Review* (Vol. 57, No. 4, June 1971, p. 323).

The cure of Serge Perrin

Early one morning in February 1964, 34-year-old Serge Perrin (of Angers, France) woke up with a severe headache and some speech impairment. More frightening for the accountant was the partial paralysis in his right side. Luckily, he recovered and lived a healthy life until 1968, when the paralysis suddenly returned. This time the condition (caused by a stroke) became progressive, since it was complicated by a bilateral insufficiency of the neck's carotid arteries. This condition significantly impaired M. Perrin's vision, and his condition became untreatable.

Serge Perrin paid his first visit to Lourdes in May 1969, six months after his physicians decided not to try surgery. By this time, the poor man was so disabled he couldn't even look after himself. The pilgrimage did little good, but his family suggested he return in a year. More to please them than really expecting a cure, he returned to the shrine again on 26 April 1970. This time he decided to receive the Anointing of the Sick, so he was taken to the St Pius X Basilica in his wheelchair on 1 May. During the ceremony M. Perrin felt a strange warmth in his toes, which began to spread up into his legs. Within hours his vision returned and his paralysis lifted. It seemed to be an instantaneous cure, and the patient merely walked from his wheelchair and discarded his glasses.

The medical investigation that later documented the cure set new medical standards for the International Medical Committee of Lourdes. The Bureau examined the patient repeatedly in 1970, 1971, and 1972. A total of 174 physicians took part in these proceedings. Two years later, a Diocesan Medical Commission of four doctors was appointed by the Bishop of Angers to examine the case, and they supported the 'unusual and scientifically inexplicable character of the cure'. When this report was supplied to the International Medical Committee, the panel consulted further with both a specialist in nervous diseases and an ophthalmologist. With all these critical evaluations in hand, 15 doctors offered the following statement on 17 October 1976:

> Serge Perrin presented a case of recurring organic hemiplegia, with ocular lesions, due to cerebral circulatory defects, without it being possible to define accurately the nature and the site of the vascular lesions. The cure of this condition, without any effective treatment, by its instantaneous character, absence of convalescence, definitely proved and stable for six years, may be considered as acquired in a completely unusual way, from a medical point of view.

After more deliberations from a formal Canonical Commission, the Bishop of Angers proclaimed the cure miraculous on 17 July 1978.

The cure of Delizia Cirolli

Delizia Cirolli was born and raised in Italy, the eldest of four children. There was little hope that she would lead a normal life. When she was 11 years old, in 1976, she was diagnosed as having a malignant tumour in her right knee, confirmed by both X-rays and bone biopsy. While amputation or radiation could have helped her, Delizia's parents decided against both these options. Since Delizia was a popular girl in Paterno, her schoolteacher soon raised the funds to send her to Lourdes. She stayed in a Lourdes hotel, and frequently visited the shrine, the baths, and the Grotto. When the pilgrimage came to its end, no signs of a miracle were evident. Delizia returned to Italy, where her health declined over the next six months. She was eventually confined to bed, and her parents resigned themselves to her inevitable death. Despite the seriousness of her condition, however, Delizia was treated with Lourdes water every day.

Then suddenly one day in December, the little girl asked for her clothes and explained that she wanted to play outdoors. Her parents were shocked when she jumped out of bed and ran 50 yards down the street! Despite her long stay in bed, there was little weakness in her previously diseased knee, which seemed to be cured.

Since Delizia returned to Lourdes several times, the Medical Bureau examined her frequently and followed her cure closely. The International Medical Committee of Lourdes began their investigation in 1960 and were immediately impressed by the healing. The only problem they found with the case concerned the original diagnosis. Two different medical conditions could have caused Delizia's problem. If the child really suffered from a sympathoblastoma (a nerve tissue tumour) and not from Ewing's sarcoma—the official diagnosis—the cure wouldn't be completely convincing. Sympathoblastomas can suddenly remit, though this had never been known to happen in a 12-year-old child, so the possibility had to be ruled out in this case.

At the present time, enquiries into the cure of Delizia Cirolli have not been completed. Despite the problems with the case, however, the International Medical Committee has stated that the child's healing is 'completely exceptional . . . in the strictest sense of the term, contrary to all known information and expectation in medical experience, and hence inexplicable'. But the Roman Catholic Church has not yet passed its official judgment on the case.

Despite the rampant tourism and commercialism, miracles still seem to take place at Lourdes. While both the Roman Catholic Church and the Lourdes Medical Bureau have become increasingly cautious, now and then healings take place in the city that cannot be explained by modern medicine.

When Dr Donald West examined the Lourdes cures in the 1950s, he pointed to several problems in those healings sanctioned between 1948 and 1956. The psychiatrist emphasized in his book that the patients' original physicians sometimes offered less than reliable medical evaluations. Sometimes they failed to back up their diagnoses with sophisticated medical tests, nor did they look for other possible (and less severe) causes for their patients' conditions. It seems to me, though, that these recent cures reported from Lourdes counter these problems. Rigid diagnostic tests and biopsies usually confirmed the severity of each patient's problems—problems which, in most cases, had never responded to conventional medical treatment. Looking back further to those healings reported between 1955 and 1963, two cases of multiple sclerosis and a case of Hodgkin's disease were cured. These diseases are incurable and permanent remission has never been reported.

Why healings take place at the shrine is probably the greatest mystery of Lourdes though. Nothing peculiar has ever been found in the water, nor is the Lourdes shrine markedly different from many other healing centres in Europe that don't report such frequent cures. So what sometimes takes place at Lourdes remains both a religious and a scientific puzzle.

Do the holy saints of the Church, or the Blessed Virgin herself, really answer prayers at Lourdes? Or could the famous cures be the *result* of faith's special psychic power?

Epilogue

Ending this book poses something of a problem for me. I cannot offer any startling conceptual model to explain the mysteries outlined in the previous chapters. Nor can I offer a scientific way by which my speculations could even be experimentally confirmed or falsified. So perhaps this book should be read in the same way as Marshall McLuhan's books on communications. That famous expert on the role mass communication plays in modern culture urges that his books represent suggestions, not dogmas. Whether these suggestions turn out to be right or wrong is inconsequential, for they are just points of discussion.

I *can* say, however, that writing this book brought me momentarily closer to some unseen dimension. The incident took place while I was working on the first chapter. I was preoccupied with the phenomenon of spontaneously materializing and dematerializing objects and was reading silently in my living room. Nobody else was in the house. Suddenly there was a loud bang behind me. It was so loud that my heart skipped a beat and I jumped from the couch. It sounded as if a metal object had fallen and struck the linoleum entryway at the front door, which is located eight feet from where I was reading. I knew the object struck the linoleum since the rest of the floor surrounding it is heavily carpeted. But when I looked behind me, I could find nothing on the floor, not so much as a pin. I even checked the kitchen (which is adjacent to the entryway) and similarly found nothing. By experimenting with several objects, I eventually imitated the sound by taking a large, three-inch metal bolt, throwing it upwards, thereby letting it strike the floor from a height of five feet. Believe me, that's loud! So whatever caused the din materialized from nowhere and probably disappeared instantly.

But where did it go? Possibly into some other dimension?

I said in the Preface that the possible existence of parallel dimensions to everyday consensus reality is a concept familiar to physicists. While completing this book, I was delighted to discover that Fred Alan Wolf—a celebrated science popularizer who previously wrote *Taking the Quantum Leap*—had recently written an entire book on the subject. *Parallel Universes* is a study of the 'many worlds' interpretation of subatomic physics. This theory posits that the Universe is constantly splitting into more and more parallel worlds. Could this phenomenon, if it really exists, be the basis for some of the phenomena discussed in the previous chapters?

Since I'm not a physicist, I do not have the background to comment on the complexities of the 'many worlds' theory, so I will merely summarize it briefly for the reader. Subatomic (or quantum) physics deals with the principles that govern the way subatomic particles (the particles within the atom) behave. The microscopic world in which these particles exist is completely unlike our own world, which is rigidly governed by the laws of classical physics. Some of the primary laws governing causality and motion break down in curious ways. It is likely, for example, that some particles in this microcosm flow backwards in time, while others move from place to place instantaneously. A curious enigma of subatomic physics is that two particles in a beam of similar particles, even when travelling at the same velocity, can pass consecutively through a pinhole to strike a screen in different places. Even though such a phenomenon seems to make little sense, it takes place commonly in the subatomic realm.

One of the primary rules of subatomic physics is the principle of indeterminacy, which is the field's sacred cow. Because of the difficulties that exist when scientists try to observe or measure a subatomic process, only probabilistic solutions to it really exist. This concept should become clearer if I cite Wolf's definition of the measurement problem. 'Whenever a measurement of a physical system takes place,' he points out, 'the system jumps into one of many possible physical states.' This situation emerges from the simple fact that the process of observing a subatomic process interferes with it. (Some theoretical physicists, however, extend this concept by suggesting that the process of observation is integral to the 'collapse' of the system. In other words, a subatomic tree would *not* cause a noise unless some observer were there to hear it.)

The 'many worlds' interpretation of quantum physics gradually emerged from the seminal work of the Nobel Prize-winner Dr Erwin Schrödinger, who was preoccupied with the measurement problem in physics. An excellent summary of his work was presented in the December 1976 issue of *Analog* by science writers Michael Talbot and

BEYOND REALITY

Lloyd Biggle, Jr. They point out:

> The implications of an unpredictable universe that can be described only in terms of mathematical probabilities have been dramatically illuminated in problems posed by the Austrian physicist, Erwin Schrödinger.
>
> Take, for example, the previous illustration of two equal particles passing through the pinhole. Even though all apparent knowledge concerning the particles is identical, they still strike the screen at different points. Schrödinger developed the differential equations that described the development in time of such a physical system. Schrödinger's final equation, however, predicts two equally probable outcomes for the same particle. In mathematical theory as well as in observation, there is no explanation for the unpredictable behavior of the particles. The system therefore seems to have entered into a schizophrenic state of constantly changing values.

In other words, any specified subatomic process can lead to several outcomes, each of which has an equal likelihood of occurring. The eventual resolution of the process will, by necessity, be both random and unpredictable.

It may seem a strange jump from measuring electrons to positing parallel universes. But this leap was taken in 1957 by Hugh Everett, who was then a graduate student in physics at Princeton University. While studying under the eminent physicist John A. Wheeler, Everett came up with the suggestion. Simply stated, he posited that no single outcome to a subatomic process really occurs. Each of them takes place because the Universe splits into several parallel worlds when the observation takes place, with *each* solution occurring in one of them! I will refrain from discussing the scientific and experimental basis for this interpretation, since it takes Wolf over 300 pages to outline it! Remember, though, that the parallel worlds theory is pure speculation and some physicists completely reject it. But it is an interesting conceptual model which may throw some light on some of parapsychology's problems and/or other scientific borderlands. (The fact that the parallel worlds concept is commonly used in some parapsychological literature is ironic, though, since Dr Wheeler personally loathes the subject!)

Don't be worried, either, if these mind-boggling concepts seem difficult to follow or understand clearly. I'm far from sure that even physicists understand them completely.*

* While writing their book *Frames of Meaning: The Social Construction of Extraordinary Science*, Harry M. Collins and T. J. Pinch (of the University of Bath)

Keeping these caveats in mind, it is interesting to speculate whether the parallel worlds of contemporary physics represent the same multiple realities concept employed in this book. I'm far from sure whether that is the case, but Wolf openly raises a similar issue by suggesting that UFOs and some forms of psychic phenomena could result from the existence of these universes.

So where does this speculation lead us? Perhaps little further than mere speculation. But these science-fiction-style suggestions and constructs at least help us open our eyes to the sheer complexity of the Universe.

Since these concepts do sound like science-fiction, I would like to finish this book by drawing upon it a little further. One of my favourite fantasy creators is Douglas Adams, the writer of such whimsical science-fiction parodies as *The Hitchhiker's Guide to the Galaxy*. In his sequel *The Restaurant at the End of the Universe*, he states, 'In the beginning the Universe was created. This has made a lot of people very angry and been widely regarded as a bad move.' Now personally I don't know if the creation of the Universe was really a bad move, but I can sympathize with the preceding remark in one sense. Trying to understand the nature of reality—with its UFOs, disappearing objects, and Marian visitations—isn't easy. Eventually it could cause science to throw up its collective hands in despair.

For the present, I'm far from reaching that point in my own life and work. I think my fellow psychical researchers feel the same way. If our Universe didn't possess secrets and mysteries it couldn't be a very interesting place. That's the principle that has kept so many of us going for the past several years. I doubt if the situation will change in the foreseeable future.

---

solicited comments from several physicists on the Everett-Wheeler parallel worlds model. Reactions ranged from respectful to downright hostile. Probably the most revealing reaction came from a famous physicist who stated, 'When I taught a course in quantum theory . . . I did it really to understand it by teaching the course and writing [a book on the subject]. Then I finished the book and began to reconsider whether I understood it, and gradually I began to feel that I didn't.'

References

Chapter 1 Spontaneous Dematerialization

Bayless, Raymond, *Experiences of a Psychical Researcher.* New Hyde Park, NY: University Books, 1972.

Carrington, Hereward, 'Mysterious Disappearances', *Psychic Research [Journal of the American Society for Psychical Research]*, 1930, *24*, 554-5.

Gaddis, Vincent, *Invisible Horizons.* Radnor, Pa.: Chilton, 1965.

Hasted, J. B., et al., 'Experiments on Psychokinetic Phenomena', in *The Geller Papers*, ed. Charles Panati. Boston: Houghton Mifflin, 1976.

Loon, L. H. Van, 'Some Unusual Psychokinetic Phenomena associated with the Recovery of Lost Objects' in *Parapsychology in South Africa*, ed. J. C. Poynton. Johannesburg: South African Society for Psychical Research, 1975.

Rogo, D. Scott, *An Experience of Phantoms.* New York: Taplinger, 1974.

—— *The Haunted Universe.* New York: New American Library, 1977.

—— 'Are You a Victim of Psychic Theft?' *Fate*, 1978, *31*, 61-6.

Chapter 2 Psychokinesis: East and West

Braud, William, and Janice Hartgrove, 'Clairvoyance and Psychokinesis in Transcendental Meditation and Matched Control Subjects: A Preliminary Study', *European Journal of Parapsychology*, 1976, *1*, 6-19.

Green, Elmer and Alyce, *Beyond Biofeedback.* New York: Delacorte Press, 1971.

Jacolliot, Louis, *Occult Science in India and Among the Ancients.* New York: Lovell, 1875, 1884.

Keel, John, *Jadoo.* New York: Gilbert Press, 1957.

Koestler, Arthur, *The Lotus and the Robot*. New York: Harper & Row, 1960.

Matas, Francine, and Lee Pantas, 'A PK Experiment Comparing Meditating versus Nonmeditating Subjects', Durham, NC:. *Proceedings of the Parapsychological Association, No. 8, 1971*, 1972.

Ostrander, Sheila, and Lynn Schroeder, *Psychic Discoveries Behind the Iron Curtain*. Englewood Cliffs, NJ: Prentice-Hall, 1970.

Parise, Felicia, Transcript reprinted in *The Power of the Mind* by Susy Smith. Radnor, Pa.: Chilton, 1975.

Radin, Dean, et al., 'Psi Experiments with Random Number Generators: Meta-analysis Part 1', in *Research in Parapsychology 1985*. Metuchen, NJ: Scarecrow Press, 1986.

Richards, Steve, *Levitation*. Wellingborough, Northants: Aquarian Press, 1980.

Wood, Ernest, *Yoga*. New York: Philosophical Library, 1956.

Chapter 3 Living Ghosts

Bates, E. Katherine, *Seen and Unseen*. New York: Dodge, 1907.

Hare, Augustus, *The Story of My Life*. New York: Dodd, Mead, 1896/1901.

Hill, J. Arthur, Review of E. Katherine Bates's *Seen and Unseen*, *Annals of Psychical Science*, 1907, 6, 147–8.

Rogo, D. Scott, *The Poltergeist Experience*. New York: Penguin Books, 1979.

Professor Sidgwick's Committee, 'Report on the Census of Hallucinations', *Proceedings of the Society for Psychical Research*, 1894, 10, 25–422.

Chapter 4 Scientific Evidence for Psychic Self-Defence

Braud, William, 'Blocking/Shielding Psychic Functioning through Psychological and Psychic Techniques: A Report of Three Preliminary Studies', *Research in Parapsychology, 1984*. Metuchen, NJ: Scarecrow Press, 1985.

Fortune, Dion, *Psychic Self-Defence*. London: Rider, n.d.

McHarg, James, 'An Inquiry into the Ostensible Synchronistic Basis of a Paranoid Psychosis'. Paper delivered to the Fifteenth Annual Convention of the Parapsychological Association. 1972.

Mintz, Elizabeth, *The Psychic Thread*. New York: Human Science Press, 1983.

Targ, Russell, and Keith Harary, *The Mind Race*. New York: Villard, 1984.

Chapter 5 Children and the Afterlife

Barrett, William, *Death-bed Visions*. London: Methuen, 1926.

Grad, Gary, and Stephen V. Gullo, 'Education in Thanatology', in *Principles of Thanatology*, ed. A. H. Kutscher, A. C. Carr, and L. B. Kutscher. New York: Columbia University Press, 1987.

Hyslop, James H., *Psychical Research and the Resurrection*. New York: Small, Maynard, 1908.

Kübler-Ross, Elisabeth, *On Death and Dying*. New York: Macmillan, 1969.

— *Questions and Answers on Death and Dying*. New York: Macmillan, 1974.

— *Living with Death and Dying*. New York: Macmillan, 1981.

— *On Children and Death*. New York: Macmillan, 1983.

Osis, Karlis, *Deathbed Observations by Physicians and Nurses*. New York: Parapsychology Foundation, 1961.

Rogo, D. Scott, 'The Spiritual World of Children: An Interview with Keith Harary', *Science of Mind*, 1987, *60*, 10-15/83-8.

— *The Return from Silence*. Wellingborough, Northants: Aquarian Press, 1989.

Tanous, Alex, and Katherine Fair Donnelly, *Is Your Child Psychic?* New York: Macmillan, 1979.

Winkelman, Michael, 'The Effect of Schooling and Formal Education upon Extrasensory Abilities', in *Research in Parapsychology 1980*. Metuchen, NJ: Scarecrow Press, 1981.

Young, Samuel H., *Psychic Children*. Garden City, NY: Doubleday, 1977.

Chapter 6 The Harmonies of Heaven

Barrett, William, *Death-bed Visions*. London: Methuen, 1926.

Bozzano, Ernesto, *Les Phénomènes psychiques au moment de la mort*. Paris: Editions de la B. P. S., 1923.

Crookall, Robert, *More Astral Projections*. London: Aquarian Press, 1964.

Grey, Margot, *Return from Death*. London: Arkana, 1985.

Hill, J. Arthur, *Man Is A Spirit*. London: Doran, 1918.

Johnson, Julian, *The Path of the Masters*. Punjab, India: Radha Soami Satsang Beas, 1939.

Rogo, D. Scott, *Nad, a Study of Some Unusual Other-World Experiences*. New Hyde Park, NY: University Books, 1970.

—— *Nad, Vol. 2: A Psychic Study of 'The Music of the Spheres'*. Secaucus, NJ: University Books, 1972.

Rolle, Richard, *The Fire of Love*. Harmondsworth, Middlesex: Penguin Books, 1972.

Chapter 7 Reincarnation Comes to the West

Brenner, Evelyn, 'The Two Alexandrinas', in *Reincarnation in the Twentieth Century*, ed. Martin Ebon. New York: World, 1969.

Stevenson, Ian, 'American Children Who Claim to Remember Previous Lives', *Journal of Nervous and Mental Disease*, 1983, *171*, 742-8.

—— *Children Who Remember Previous Lives*. Charlottesville, Va.: University Press of Virginia, 1987.

Stewart, Jeannie L., and W. G. Roll, 'Psychotherapeutic Aspects of Rebirth Cases'. Paper delivered to the Twelfth Annual Conference of the Southeastern Regional Parapsychological Association, 15-16 February 1985, Duke University, Durham, North Carolina.

Wilson, Ian, *Mind Out of Time?* London: Gollancz, 1981.

Chapter 8 Janice Leslie's UFO Odyssey

Clark, Jerome, and Loren Coleman, *The Unidentified*. New York: Warner, 1975.

Jung, C. G., *Flying Saucers: A Modern Myth of Things Seen in the Sky*. New York: Harcourt, Brace, 1959.

Mishlove, Jeffrey, *Preliminary Investigation of Events which Suggest the Possible Applied Psi Ability of Ted Owens*. San Francisco, Cal.: Washington Research Center, 1977.

Chapter 9 The Secret Language of UFO Abductions

Barry, Bill, *Ultimate Encounter*. New York: Pocket Books, 1978.

Blum, Ralph and Judy, *Beyond Earth: Man's Contact with UFOs*. New York: Bantam, 1974.

Druffel, Ann, and D. Scott Rogo, *The Tujunga Canyon Contacts*. Reprint. New York: New American Library, 1989.

Fowler, Raymond, *The Andreasson Affair*. Englewood Cliffs, NJ: Prentice-Hall, 1979.

Fuller, John, *The Interrupted Journey*. New York: Dial, 1966.

Hickson, Charles, and William Mendez, *UFO Contact at Pascagoula*. Tucson, Ar.: Wendelle Stevens, 1983.

Lorenzen, Coral and Jim, *Abducted!* New York: Berkley, 1977.

Sprinkle, R. Leo, 'Investigations of the Alleged UFO Experience of Carl Higdon', in *UFO Phenomena and the Behavioral Scientist*, ed. Richard H. Haines. Metuchen, NJ: Scarecrow Press, 1979.

Walton, Travis, *The Walton Experience*. New York: Berkley, 1978.

Chapter 10 Birth Traumas from Outer Space?

Clark, Jerome, 'The Ultimate Alien Encounter', in *UFO Abductions*, ed. D. Scott Rogo. New York: Signet, 1980.

Greenberg, Joel, 'Close Encounters—All in the Mind', *Science News*, 1979, *115*, 106-7.

Hall, Richard, *Uninvited Guests*. Santa Fe, NM: Aurora Press, 1988.

Hopkins, Budd, *Missing Time*. New York: Marek, 1981.

Lawson, Alvin, 'The Hypnosis of Imaginary UFO Abductees', in *Proceedings of the First International UFO Congress*, ed. Curtis Fuller. New York: Warner, 1979.

—— 'UFO Abductees or Birth Memories?' *Fate*, 1985, *38* (3), 68-80.

Randles, Jenny, *UFO Reality: A Critical Look at the Physical Evidence*. London: Robert Hale, 1983.

—— and Paul Whetnall, *UFOs: A British Viewpoint*. London: Robert Hale, 1979.

Rimmer, John, *The Evidence for Alien Abductions*. Wellingborough, Northants: Aquarian Press, 1984.

Rogo, D. Scott, 'Imaginary Facts', *International UFO Reporter*, 1985, *1* (2), 3-5.

—— 'Birth Traumas from Outer Space', *International UFO Reporter*, 1985, *1* (3), 4-5/16.

—— and Budd Hopkins, 'Abduction, Birth Trauma and Tunnel Vision', *Fate*, 1985, *38* (7), 81-6.

Chapter 11 A UFO Abduction in Suburbia

Druffel, Ann, and D. Scott Rogo, *The Tujunga Canyon Contacts*. Revised edition. New York: New American Library, 1989;

Erickson, Milton, and Ernest and Sheila Rossi, *Hypnotic Realities*. New York: Irvington, 1976.

Fuller, John, *The Interrupted Journey*. New York: Berkley, 1966.

Hopkins, Budd, *Intruders*. New York: Random House, 1987.

Rogo, D. Scott, 'The Abduction of Sammy Desmond', *International UFO Reporter*, 1987, *12*, 4-13.

Strieber, Whitley, *Communion*. New York: William Morrow, 1987.

Chapter 12 Psychic Phenomena and the Communion
Cruz, Joan Carroll, *Eucharistic Miracles*. Rockford, Ill.: Tan Books, 1987.

Gerlich, Fritz, *Thérèse Neumann von Konnersreuth*. Munich: Verlag Joseph Kusel und Friedrich Pastet, 1929.

Sanchez-Ventura y Pascual, F., *The Apparitions of Garabandal*. Detroit, Mich.: San Miguel Publishing Co., 1966.

Schimberg, Paul, *The Story of Thérèse Neumann*. Milwaukee, Wis.: Bruce Publishing Co., 1947.

Steiner, Johannes, *Thérèse Neumann*. New York: Alba House, 1967.

Thurston, Herbert, *The Physical Phenomena of Mysticism*. London: Burns Oates, 1952.

Chapter 13 Medjugorje
Craig, Mary, *Spark from Heaven*. Sevenoaks, Kent: Hodder & Stoughton, 1988.

Fox, Thomas C., 'Medjugorje—Miracle or Hoax?', *National Catholic Reporter*, 1988, 24 (12), 3-5.

Kraljević, Svetozar, *The Apparitions of Our Lady at Medjugorje*. Chicago: Franciscan Herald Press, 1984.

Rooney, Lucy, and Robert Faricy, *Mary, Queen of Peace*. Dublin: Veritas Publications, 1984.

Chapter 14 Recent Cures at Lourdes
Cranston, Ruth, *The Miracle of Lourdes*. New York: McGraw Hill, 1955.

—— 'Cures since 1955', in *The Miracles of Lourdes* (updated edition). New York: Doubleday/Image, 1988.

Monahan, Patrick, *Lourdes: A Modern Pilgrimage*. New York: Coward, McCann & Geohegan, 1981.

West, Donald J., *Eleven Lourdes Miracles*. New York: Garrett, 1957.

Epilogue

Collins, H. M., and T. J. Pinch, *Frames of Meaning: The Social Construction of Extraordinary Science.* London: Routledge & Kegan Paul, 1982.

Wolf, Fred Alan, *Parallel Universes.* New York: Simon & Schuster. 1988.

Index

Abducted! (Lorenzen and
  Lorenzen), 147
Abominable Snowman, 47
Adams, Douglas, 229
Aho, Waino, 142–3
aliens, sightings of, 142–3,
  163–4,169–71, 182–3; *see
  also* UFO abductions
Allen, S., 101
allobiofeedback, 75–6
Aloi, Elisa, 218–20
American Psychological
  Association, 150
American Society for
  Psychical Research, 87,
  92
L'Amour aux Colonies
  (Jacolliot), 45
Analog magazine, 227
Anderson, E. W., 211n
Andreasson Affair, The
  (Fowler), 142, 144, 148,
  159
Andreasson, Betty, 142–5,
  156
Angele, Thea, 219
Annals of Psychical Science, 60
Anomalistic Psychology (Zusne
  and Jones), 49
*Apparitions of Our Lady at
  Medjugorje, The*
  (Kraljević), 208
APRO, 146
archetypes, 215–16
Association for the Study of
  Anomalous Phenomena,
  11

Barrett, William F., 86–7, 87n,
  91, 100, 102
Barrington, Mary Rose, 30–32
Bates, Katherine, 60
Bayless, Raymond, 19, 33, 64,
  97–8, 100

bedroom visitors, 163–4
Beyond Biofeedback (Green
  and Green), 50–51
Biggle, Lloyd, 228
Bigot, Marie, 219
Biondi, Vittoria, 196
bio-PK, 75–6
Birkbeck College, 20
birth trauma theory, 149,
  150–61
Boeing Laboratories, 39
Bozzano, Ernesto, 100, 102
Brandon, Ruth, 49n
Braud, William, 53–4, 74–8
Bressolles, Henriette, 219
Britton, John, 101
Butler, Mrs, 58

California State University,
  Long Beach, 150
Campanelli, Carolos, 26–7
Carini, Maddalena, 219
Carrington, Hereward, 17–18
Carter family, 61–2
Castaneda, Carlos, 26–7
Catherine of Siena, St,
  189–90, 196
chakras, 41
children, 83–94
  deathbed visions, 90–2,
    93–4
  ESP tests with, 83
  Marian visitations, 198–216
  previsions of death, 87–90
  reincarnation cases, 107–8,
    108, 108–10, 110–14
  religious experiences, 85–6
  UFOs and, 163–4
*Children Who Remember
  Previous Lives*
  (Stevenson), 110–14, 117
Chinatown (film by Polanski),
  164
Cirolli, Delzia, 223–4

Clark, Jerome, 132, 158
Coleman, Loren, 132
collective hallucinations,
  210–11
Collins, Harry M., 228–29
Cŏlo, Jakov, 203
Columbia University, 86, 89
Communion (Strieber), 175
communism, 187–97
Couteault, Alice, 219
Covindasamy, 45–7
Craig, Mary, 208, 209, 210,
  212, 215–16
Cranston, Ruth, 217
Croglin Grange, 59
Crookall, Robert, 103
Cruz, Joan Carroll, 87

Daily News (Rawlings), 145
death anxiety, 85–6
*Deathbed Observations by
  Physicians and Nurses*
  (Osis), 92
deathbed visions, 86–7,
  90–2, 93–4, 100–2
Death-bed Visions (Barrett),
  86, 100, 101
dematerialization, 17–36
  cases of, 17–18, 19, 26–30,
    34, 35, 174–5
  categories of, 31
  theories for, 31–4
Desmond, Cathy, 182–3
Desmond, Sammy, 29–30, 32,
  162–84
Desmond, Sarah, 182–3
Domians, Alejandro, 195
Donnelly, Katherine, 85
Dragicević, Ivanka, 202, 205
Dragicević, Mirjana, 201–3
dreams, 57–8, 136, 173
Druffel, Ann, 138–41
Dryden, Daisy, 87
Duke University, 83, 84

Dunne, J. W., 11

E. Dr, 59–60
Eastland, Susan, 112–13
Eleven Lourdes Miracles
    (West), 217
embryology, 159
Erickson, Milton, 177
Eucharistic Miracles (Cruz),
    187
Evans, Hilary, 11
Everett, Hugh, 228, 229n
Evidence for Alien Abductions,
    The (Rimmer), 152
Evidence for Visions of the
    Virgin Mary (McClure),
    200
Experience of Phantoms, An
    (Rogo), 22
Experiences of a Psychical
    Researcher (Bayless), 19,
    33
extrasensory perception,
    77–8, 83–4, 133
extraterrestrial hypothesis,
    124, 135, 140, 145

fakirs, 43–9
Faricy, Robert, 208
Fate magazine, 25, 26, 27–8,
    34, 100, 157, 158
Fatima (Portugal), 199–200,
    207, 214
Fire of Love, The (Rolle), 95–6
First South African
    Conference of
    Parapsychology, 34
Firth, Violet (Dion Fortune),
    74
Fournier, Yvonne, 219
Fowler, Raymond, 142
Fox, Thomas C., 213
Frames of Meaning (Collins
    and Pinch), 228n
Franic, France, 213
Fulda, Edeltraut, 219
Fuller, John, 135, 169, 179
Fund for UFO Research, 175

Gaddis, Vincent, 22, 23–4
Ganora, Evasio, 219
Geller, Uri, 20
Gerlich, Fritz, 193
ghosts, 56, 57–8, 59–60, 114
Glamuzina, Darinka, 206
Gonzales, Conchita, 194–5
Gonzales, Mary Cruz, 194
Grad, Gary, 86
Green, Elmer, 49–52, 55
Grenside, Dorothy, 57–8
Grey, Margot, 104
Gullo, Stephen, 86

Haileybury College, 101
Hall, Richard, 158
hallucinations, 70, 159
Hansen, George, 49n
Harary, Keith, 73, 84–5
Hare, Augustus, 58
Hartgrove, Janice, 54
Hasted, John, 20
Hatha Yoga Pradipika, 40, 42
Haunted House Handbook, The
    (Rogo), 20n
haunted houses, 20–3, 56,
    57–8, 59–60
Haunted Universe, The (Rogo),
    24, 123, 124n
Hickson, Charles, 137–8
Higdon, Carl, 145–8
Hill, Betty and Barney, 135–7,
    139, 141, 148, 158n
Hill, J. Arthur, 60, 102–3
Hitchhiker's Guide to the
    Galaxy (Adams), 229
Hopi Indians, 132
Hopkins, Budd, 161, 169,
    175, 182
hypnosis, 15–16, 136, 139,
    143, 149–50, 154, 156,
    162, 173–4, 176–82
Hypnotic Realities (Erickson,
    Rossi and Rossi), 177
Hyslop, James H., 87, 87n, 91

Illustrated London News, 49
imaginary UFO abductions,
    149–55
Imbert-Gourbeyre, A., 188–9
In Search of the Unknown
    (Rogo), 20n
Institute for Advanced
    Psychology, 84
Institute for Parapsychology,
    38
International Medical
    Committee of Lourdes,
    218, 220, 221, 222, 223,
    224
Interrupted Journey, The
    (Fuller), 135–7, 169, 179
Intruders (Hopkins), 169, 175
Intrusions: Society and the
    Paranormal (Evans), 11
Invisible Horizons (Gaddis), 22
Is Your Child Psychic? (Tanous
    and Donnelly), 85
Ivanković, Marinko, 202–3,
    204
Ivanković, Ivan, 202–3
Ivanković, Ivanka, 201
Ivanković, Vicka, 201

Jackson, Erin, 113–14
Jacolliot, Louis, 42–7, 54

Jadoo (Keel), 47–8
'Jenkins, Sarah Jean', 116–17
Johnson, Julian, 96–7
JOTTS, 30–32
Journal of Nervous and Mental
    Disease, 117
Jung, C. G., 123, 215–16

kachinas, 132
Keating, Fred, 18
Keel, John, 47–8
Knock (Ireland), 199
Koestler, Arthur, 41–2, 47
Kraljević, Svetozar, 208
Krudlek, Rudolf, 210
Kübler-Ross, Elisabeth, 87n,
    87–92, 93–4
Kügelin, Konrad, 190
Kulagina, Nina, 37
Kundalini yoga, 40

Labouré, Zoé, 199
Lansing, Stella, 123–34
La Salette (France), 199, 207,
    214
Laviosa, Bernard, 191
Lawson, Alvin, 150–61
Leeds, Mary, 70–2, 73
Leslie, Janice, 123–34
levitation, 41, 46, 48–9, 54,
    188
Levitation (Richards), 54
Life After Life (Moody), 104
lights, 125–33, 164–8
Living with Death and Dying
    (Kübler-Ross), 88
Lončar, Umberto, 209
Lorenzen, Coral and Jim, 147
Lotus and the Robot, The
    (Koestler), 41, 42, 47
Lourdes (France), 209–25
Lourdes Medical Bureau, 28,
    223, 224

M., Betty, 131
Maccabee, Bruce, 175
Magdalena de la Cruz, 196
Maharishi Mahesh Yogi, 54
Maimonides Medical Center,
    37
Mangiapan, Theadore, 218
Man Is A Spirit (Hill), 102–3
'many worlds' theory, 227–8
Marian visitations, 194,
    198–216, 217
    history of, 199–200
    theories for, 214–16
Mary, Queen of Peace (Rooney
    and Faricy), 208
Matarelli, Palma, 188–9
Mata, Francine, 53
McCall, W. C., 150, 153, 158

McClure, Kevin, 200
McHarg, James, 70–2
Meaning of Dreams, The (Grenside), 57–8
Medicine Bow National Forest, 146
meditation, 52–4
Medjugorje (Yugoslavia), 198–216
Menninger Foundation, 49–52
metal bending, 20
Micheli, Vittorio, 221–2
Milford, L. A., 101
Mind Out of Time? (Wilson), 110
Mind Race, The (Targ and Harary), 73
Mind Science Foundation, 53, 74, 77
Miracle of Lourdes, The (Cranston), 217
miracles, 12, 187–97, 197–216, 217–25; see also communion, Marian visitations, miraculous healing
miraculous healing, 208, 217–25
Mintz, Elizabeth, 73
Mishlove, Jeffrey, 124
Moody, Raymond, 104
Morgan, Roberta, 110–12
Moss, Thelma, 172–4, 175, 176
MUFON, 150
music of the spheres, 96; see also psychic music
mystics and mysticism, 95–6, 188–93

Naber, Father, 193
Nad, 96–105
Nad, a Study of Some Unusual Other-World Experiences (Rogo), 104
Nad, Vol. 2: A Psychic Study of the 'Music of the Spheres' (Rogo), 104
National Catholic Reporter, 212–13
near-death experiences, 102–4
negative hallucinations, 31
Nelson, Louis, 103
Neumann, Thérèse, 188, 191–3, 196, 197
New Age, 11, 55
Newsweek magazine, 54
Nouvel, Ginette, 219

Oates, Robert, 54

Occult Science in India and Among the Ancients (Jacolliot), 42–7
Olivieri, Alphonse, 218
On Children and Death (Kübler-Ross), 88–92, 93–4
On Death and Dying (Kübler-Ross), 88
Orthopedic Surgical Review, 222
Osis, Karlis, 92–3
Ostovich, Dave, 63–7
Ostovich, Mike, 65–7
Ostrander, Sheila, 37
out-of-body experiences, 62–8, 102–4
Owens, Ted, 125–6

Pantas, Lee, 53
parallel universes, 226–9
Parallel Universes (Wolf), 227
Parapsychology Foundation, 83, 92
Parise, Felicia, 37–8, 39, 40
Parker, Calvin, 137
past-life recall, see reincarnation
Patanjali, 40
Path of the Masters, The, (Johnson), 96–7
Perrin, Serge, 222–3
Les Phénomènes psychiques au moment de la mort (Bozzano), 100
Physical Phenomena of Mysticism, The (Thurston), 188
Pinch, T. J., 228n
Plunkett, P. T., 48–9
Polanski, Roman, 164
Pollack twins, 108–10
poltergeists, 61–3
Pontmain (France), 199, 214
Powell, Emma, 103, 104
premonitions, 87–90
Prescott Courier, 132
Psychical Research and the Resurrection (Hyslop), 87
Psychic Children (Young), 85
Psychic Discoveries Behind the Iron Curtain (Ostrander and Schroeder), 37
psychic music, 95–105
cases of, 97–8, 99, 101, 102–3, 103, 103–4
doctrines, 96–7
out-of-body reports of, 102–4
related to death, 100–102
theories for, 104–5
psychic self-defence, 69–80

experiments with, 74–8
techniques for, 77–8
theories for, 74
Psychic Self-Defence (Fortune), 74
Psychic Thread, The (Mintz), 73
psychokinesis, 12, 37–55, 188–97
biological experiments, 75–6
demonstrations of, 42–9, 49–52
Holy Communion and, 188–97
meditation and, 52–4
subatomic processes and, 39–40, 53–4
training for, 37–8
Pythagoras, 96

quantum theory, 227–9, 229–30n
Questions and Answers on Death and Dying (Kübler-Ross), 88

R., Mrs, 57–60
Radin, Dean I., 39
Rama, Swami, 49–52, 55
Randles, Jenny, 149, 158
Raymond of Capua, 190
Recollections of Death (Ring), 104
reincarnation, 106–19
cases of, 107–8, 108, 108–10, 110–14, 114–16
criticisms of, 110
research on, 116–19
Restaurant at the End of the Universe, The (Adams), 229
Return from Death (Grey), 104
Return from Silence, The, (Rogo), 84, 76n
Reute, Elisabeth von, 190–1
Revue des Etudes Psychiques, 58
Richards, Steve, 54
Rimmer, John, 152
Ring, Kenneth, 104
Roll, W. G., 114–16
Rolle, Richard, 95–6
Roman Catholic Church, 187–96, 199, 204, 217, 224, 225
Rooney, Mary, 208
Rossi, Ernest, 177
Rossi, Sheila, 177
Royal Naval Medical Service Journal, 211n
Russell, Grace, 99–100

Russian folklore, 26

Sabom, Michael, 104
St Joseph's Medical Center, 28–9
Salmon, S. S., 222
Samona, Alexandrina, 107–8
Samona, Carmelo, 107–8
San Sebastian de Garabandal (Spain), 193–5, 200, 214
Schimberg, Paul, 193
schizophrenia, 69–74
Schlitz, Marilyn, 78
Schmidt, Helmut, 39, 68
Schrödinger, Erwin, 227
Schroeder, Lynn, 37
Schwarz, Berthold, 124n
Science of Mind, 84, 85
Science News, 151
Sealay, Art von, 98, 100
Seen and Unseen (Bates), 60
Sergeyev, Genady, 56
Sharkey, Don, 200
Shaw, Sara, 138–41, 148
Simon, Benjamin, 136
Snowden, Kathleen, 103–4
Society for Psychical Research, 30, 59, 87, 101, 102
solar prodigies, 199–200, 211–12
Solem, Paul, 132–3
Soubirous, Bernadette, 217
Southern Methodist University, 75
Soviet psi research, 37
Spark from Heaven (Craig), 208, 209, 212, 215–16
Spectator, 58
Spiritualists, The, (Brandon), 49n
spontaneous disappearances, 17, 226; see also dematerialization
Sprinkle, Leo, 146, 147
SRI International, 39
Stevenson, Ian, 110–14, 117–19
Stewart, Jennie Lagle, 114–16
stigmata, 188, 192
Les Stigmatisées (Imbert-Gourbeyre), 188

Story of My Life, The (Hare), 58
Story of Thérèse Neumann, The (Schimberg), 193
Strieber, Whitley, 175

Taking the Quantum Leap (wolf), 227
Talbot, Michael, 227
Tales of Power (Castaneda), 26–7
Tamburini, Julietta, 220–1
Tanous, Alex, 75
Tantric Yoga, 40
Targ, Russell, 73
telepathy, 70–4, 109
Thérèse Neumann von Konnersreuth (Gerlich), 193
Thurston, Herbert, 188
Transcendental Meditation, 53, 54
transcendental music, see psychic music
Tujunga Canyon cases, 138, 41
Tujunga Canyon Contacts, The (Druffel and Rogo), 179
tunnel imagery, 151

UFO abductions, 135–49, 149–61, 162
 birth trauma theory, 156–61
 cases, 135–7, 137–8, 138–41, 142–5, 145–8,162–84
 criticisms of imaginary cases, 152–61
 imaginary cases, 149–55
 theories for, 141–4, 148, 155–6
UFO Abductions (Rogo), 158
UFO Dynamics (Schwarz), 124n
UFO Reality: A Critical Look at the Physical Evidence (Randles), 158
UFOs, 11, 12, 29, 12–34, 135–48, 149–62, 162–84
UFOs: A British Viewpoint (Randles and Whetnall), 149

Unidentified, The (Clark and Coleman), 132
Uninvited Guests (Hall), 158
United Church of Religious Science, 84
University of California, Berkeley, 124
University of California, Irvine, 83
University of California, Los Angeles, 103
Untrodden Fields of Anthropology (Jacolliot), 45

Van Loon, Louis, H., 34, 35
Vasiliev, L. L., 49
visions, 208–12; see also Marian visitations
Vita di S. Maria Francesca della Cinque Piaghe (Laviosa), 191
Vuyević, Ante, 204–5

Waldorf, Ginger, 114–16
Walton, Travis, 138
Watertown, S.S., 22
West, Donald J., 217, 224
Wheeler, John A., 228, 229n
Whetnall, Paul, 149
Whitley, Jan, 138–41
Wilson, Ian, 110
Winfrey, Oprah, 182
Winkelman, Michael, 83, 85
Wolf, Fred, 227
Woman Shall Conquer, The (Sharkey), 200
Wood, Ernest, 48

X., Mrs (Betty Andreasson), 155–6

Yoga, 40–2, 53
Yoga Sutras (Patanjali), 40
Young, Samuel, 85
Z., Miss (Sara Shaw), 155–6
Zanic Pavao, 207
Zeitoun (Egypt), 200, 214
Zen, 53
Zovko, Jozo, 205–6, 206–7, 209